$1

TOUGH CHOICES

TOUGH
CHOICES

JEWISH PERSPECTIVES
ON SOCIAL JUSTICE

≡

ALBERT VORSPAN
·AND·
DAVID SAPERSTEIN

UAHC PRESS   ·   NEW YORK, NEW YORK

Library of Congress Cataloging-in-Publication Data
Vorspan, Albert.
    Tough choices : Jewish perspectives on social justice / Albert
Vorspan and David Saperstein.
        p. cm.
    Includes bibliographical references and index.
    ISBN 0-8074-0482-9 : $11.00
    1. Jews—United States—Politics and government. 2. Judaism and
social problems. 3. Judaism and politics. 4. Social justice.
5. Afro-Americans—Relations with Jews. 6. Antisemitism—United
States. 7. Jews—United States—Attitudes toward Israel. 8. United
States—Ethnic relations. I. Saperstein, David. II. Title.
E184.J5V69   1992
323.1'1924073—dc20   92-31747
                                                            CIP

To the grandchildren—Emily, Zachary, Ben, Sammy Ray, and Jonah—May they confront the tough choices of life with grace, courage, and commitment to a better world.

Albert Vorspan

To my parents, whose lives have instilled in me the passion for *tikkun olam.*

David Saperstein

This book is also dedicated to Paul Kodimer, good friend and coworker, a rare and courageous spirit, who has dedicated himself to nurturing the dream of social justice in his own life, in Reform Judaism, and in his beloved community of Los Angeles.

CONTENTS

Contents

Contents

Contents

Contents

Contents

Contents

Contents

PREFACE

Not long ago, one of the coauthors of this volume was privileged to meet the Dalai Lama of Tibet at a Buddhist retreat center in New Jersey. He was part of a small Jewish delegation that wanted to convey its deep empathy with this great leader, living in exile since 1959, when China occupied his homeland. The recipient of the 1989 Nobel Peace Prize thanked the delegation for Jewish support of his efforts to place the tragedy of Tibet before the conscience of the world.

The Dalai Lama himself is colorful and engaging. Wearing brown and purple robes, perching comfortably on a couch with his legs crossed under him, with a warm smile lighting up his face despite the grimness of his situation, and displaying a puckish sense of humor, the Dalai Lama told us in a soft voice about the thirty-year campaign of genocide his Tibetan people have endured at the hands of the Chinese invaders and about the ongoing destruction of Tibetan religious, ethnic, and national identity. As Jews, we found it easy to commiserate. But the Tibetan leader had something on his mind. "Tell me," he said, *"what is your secret?* How can a people that has been persecuted and exiled and villified throughout the centuries maintain its religion and its sense of national identity? No other people has done this except you. *I want to know your secret so that I might better help preserve my people."*

We gave a variety of responses to the Dalai Lama. One told the story of Yochanan ben Zakkai and how his small school at Yavneh preserved Jewish values—values that outlasted the Roman conquest of Judea. Another explained the story of modern Israel itself, of how the Jewish people, exiled for centuries, achieved national liberation out of the ashes of the Holocaust. The miracle of Israel was a product of faith, memory, and peoplehood. Some of us said that the Dalai Lama had already learned our secret in his championship of the values of nonviolent resistance to evil, the quality for which he was honored by the entire civilized world. The power of the spirit, which he helps to symbolize in the world today, is ultimately more powerful than all the armies and weapons of repression. In that, both his people and our Jewish people share a common vision of peace, justice, and cooperative relations among all the brothers and sisters of the world.

One of our group said that persecution keeps a people alive. Another said that Judaism, as a way of life, was the key to Jewish survival and that the synagogue is the fount of Jewish immortality. Several added that the Jewish passion for social justice had made a difference not only to Jews but to all the world. The refusal to yield to despair, fatigue, or cynicism; the stubborn belief in *tikkun olam,* "repairing the shattered world"; the *chutzpadik* notion that we are copartners with God in refashioning a humane and civilized world—these Jewish compulsions, we said, have helped preserve the Jewish spirit.

This book is about that yearning for *tikkun olam.* It confronts the most compelling issues of social justice for our era—issues that will dominate the American political agenda well into the third century of American life. These issues involve complex dilemmas and require delicate choices. In this volume, we seek to place those tough choices into a context of Jewish tradition and ethics, to analyze the factual setting, and to lay out some real dilemmas for the reader to examine and resolve.

This book's "tough choices" are those confronting American Jewry generally and, more particularly, the Commission on Social Action of Reform Judaism, which represents the Union of American Hebrew Congregations, the Central Conference of American Rabbis, and all the affiliated bodies of the Reform movement. The commission in 1962 created its Religious Action Center in Washington, D.C., to apply Jewish ethics to issues of legislation and public policy in the nation's capital. The Religious Action Center has become a dynamic center of Jewish moral and political energy, immersed in issues of particular Jewish concern—Israel, Soviet Jewry, Ethiopian Jewry, anti-Semitism—as well as such issues of universal concern as the environment, church-state relations, civil rights, civil liberties, and world peace. Augmenting its dedicated staff with brilliant and energetic young legislative assistants, the RAC represents a unique Jewish enterprise: the only Jewish building in the world devoted exclusively to the pursuit of social justice.

The "real dilemmas" in this book, for the most part, were actually faced by the UAHC, the CCAR, the Commission on Social Action and/or its Religious Action Center, and by the synagogues of America. We do not pretend that our responses stem from Sinai or from a dramatic epiphany, only that the questions arise from real experience and that the answers are guided by Jewish historical experience and informed by long-held Jewish values. We acknowledge at the outset that our answers are fallible and that some dilemmas may not even be resolvable.

Do Jews still have a passion for social justice? A young Jewish woman, a social activist in California, put it this way: "Most people in the world live heroic lives merely trying to survive for one more day. They are powerless to evoke change, let alone help others. That is why I feel so strongly that those of us who *can* make things better *must* do so. And, if we don't, we are depriving ourselves of perhaps the greatest opportunity life can offer: to help change the world and, in turn, give true meaning to our lives."

ACKNOWLEDGMENTS

It is the particular nature of the social justice movement within Reform Jewry that this book is the combined effort of scores of people. In synagogues throughout the United States and Canada, social action committees have created programs of social justice that touch every aspect of the domestic and international agenda of the Jewish community. Individual rabbis and lay leaders have taken positions of conscience—sometimes against the grain of popular opinion—that have made a real difference in the Jewish community and in America. At the local and national levels, lay people and professionals are bound by the common thread and belief that to be a Jew is inexorably bound up with being a "light to the nations," a partner with God in shaping a better world. In their totality, the voices and actions of these people have brought the Reform Jewish movement to the forefront of America's social justice agenda.

The work of many of those people is reflected throughout the book. The stories of synagogues and individuals who grappled with moral dilemmas are retold in our "Real Dilemma" sections. Speeches, sermons, and articles by social justice leaders, lay and rabbinic, are cited in many chapters. Prominent among these leaders is Rabbi Alexander M. Schindler, president of the UAHC, who has significantly strengthened the social action work of the Reform Jewish movement.

Scattered throughout the book are the writings of several generations of Maurice N. Eisendrath LAs (legislative assistants, a.k.a.

interns) who serve at the Religious Action Center of Reform Judaism (RAC) in the nation's capital. These young people keep alive the memory of Rabbi Eisendrath, the UAHC president from 1946 to 1973, who presided over the creation of the Commission on Social Action and the Religious Action Center.

While the number of people to whom we are indebted is too large for individual acknowledgment, there are several whose contributions simply cannot go unrecognized. Among those who drafted text or provided writings from which we have quoted at some length are

- Rabbi Richard Hirsch, founding director, Religious Action Center of Reform Judaism; executive director, World Union for Progressive Judaism—Economic Justice

- Leonard Fein, senior scholar, Religious Action Center—Multiculturalism

- Robert Greenstein, director, Center for Budget and Policy Priorities—Economic Justice

- Marc Saperstein, Goldstein Professor of Jewish History and Thought, Washington University, St. Louis—Gun Control; Bioethics; Anti-Semitism

- Rabbi Robert Kirschner, former rabbi, Congregation Emanu-El, San Francisco—AIDS

- Rabbi Sharon Kleinbaum, former director of congregational relations, RAC; rabbi, Congregation Bet Simchat Torah, New York—AIDS; Gay and Lesbian Rights

- Ed Rehfeld, former Eisendrath LA; development coordinator and writer, RAC—Censorship; Religious Liberty

- Steve Derringer, former Eisendrath LA—Religious Liberty; Economic Justice

- Brad Ortman, former Eisendrath LA—Environment

Acknowledgments

- William S. Meyers—*Cruzan* Case
- Aimee Zeltzer—Fetal Tissue Transplants

We are equally grateful to Rabbi Lynne Landsberg, associate director, Religious Action Center of Reform Judaism; Dr. Leonard Fein, senior scholar at the Religious Action Center, founder of *Moment* magazine and Mazon, whose contribution to the book is appreciated but whose larger contributions to Jewish ideals in this generation have been monumental; Temma Schaller, RAC administrator; Eisendrath legislative assistants: Julie Youdovin, Mickey Meyers, Adam Spilker, Rachel Stock, Jennifer Marx, Rebecca Laibson, Michael Wigotsky, Jeff Danziger, Jamie Fleckner, Beth Wiener, Tamara Cofman, Jessica Roth, David Rosen, Ryan Lilienthal, Debbie Banks, Mitch Malkus, and Eric Putnoi—all of whom drafted, edited, and checked facts in the policy areas for which they were responsible while working at the RAC and have already transformed many of these chapters into educational and programmatic activities for synagogues; Julie Ridberg, who was unflappable in compiling draft after draft of the book, editing and advising the whole way; Dorothy Albelo, at 838 Fifth Avenue, New York City, who deciphered Vorspan's hieroglyphics when nobody else had a clue; Roz Morrow, who typed the first draft of the book; Carole Specktor and Jonathan Polish, who helped with the finishing touches on the book; and Bonnie Dunninger, former assistant to the director, RAC, whose talents and intelligence enriched the book in many ways.

We also thank Randi Locke, who helped mind the store at the UAHC Social Action department in New York City while this book gestated; Rabbi Dan Syme, vice-president of the UAHC, whose suggestions for the structure and form of the book were invaluable; Rabbi Harold Saperstein and Marcia Saperstein for their advice on substance and style; Annette Abramson, who copyedited with unfailing care and professionalism, as she does all the books at the UAHC; Stuart Benick, director of publications at the UAHC, who skillfully oversaw the production of the publication itself; and

Acknowledgments

Aron Hirt-Manheimer, editor, who also reviewed and edited the book and whose wise suggestions are reflected on every page of this text.

And, finally, we thank our wives, Shirley Vorspan and Ellen Weiss, whose wise observations about life and politics we steal incessantly and whose humor and patience help save us from each other.

If we have as many readers as contributors, fasten your seat belt, this book will be a best-seller.

TOUGH CHOICES

1

GRAPPLING WITH THE DILEMMAS OF SOCIAL JUSTICE: A JEWISH PERSPECTIVE FOR 2000

In the days of the historic civil rights struggle, it seemed so easy to make a clear moral judgment on the big issues in American society. It seemed so easy to tell the good guys from the bad, to stand up and be counted. It did not require great ethical sophistication to distinguish right from wrong when witnessing black children in Birmingham being killed in church bombings and assaulted by police equipped with attack dogs, fire hoses, and electric cattle prods. It was not difficult to salute those fighting to win the elementary right to vote and to condemn those who sought to frustrate that right.

On the international scene, it was easy to shout "Let My People Go" on behalf of Soviet Jewry. And, although making an initial judgment on the Vietnam War was less clear-cut than the civil rights issue, most Americans came to see the war as morally wrong.

The clear-cut issues of yesteryear have faded into the complex dilemmas of today. While racial justice is still a high moral goal, through what methods is it to be achieved: affirmative action, busing, quotas? Censorship and limitation of freedom of speech are contrary to American principles. Do American Nazis, however, have

1

the right to march through a community consisting largely of Holocaust survivors? Do people have the right to place ads denying the truth of the Holocaust? And what limits, if any, do we set upon a woman's right to abortion? All tough questions.

The certainties of yesterday have become the uncertainties and conflicts of today, especially when one right collides with another right. This is true for all Americans; for Jews *only more so.*

A snapshot of this dilemma: When the Romanian dictator Nicolae Ceausescu was overthrown in 1989, all lovers of freedom rejoiced. But Jews confronted a nagging dilemma: Ceausescu had been a murderous despot, but he had also protected Romanian Jews, allowing many to emigrate to Israel, albeit for his own personal profit. As Jews, we continually face such dilemmas. How do we reconcile our desire to redirect our resources to meet domestic needs with our commitment to a defense capability strong enough to support Israel and other democracies; the rights of homosexuals and the importance of the traditional Jewish family; our commitment to close Black-Jewish relations and our opposition to quotas; our efforts to find peaceful ways for nations to resolve differences and our support for the Persian Gulf War as SCUDs landed in Tel Aviv? How should we balance our Jewish universal ethics and the ethics of our communal self-interest when they collide? That is the subject of this book.

What is the Jewish dimension in each of these issues? What is the Jewish stake? And what do Jewish values teach us about these issues? If Jewish tradition speaks to these conflicts, it does not always do so clearly. No "You shalls" and "You shall nots" provide specific answers to our thorny political issues. There are no easy answers as we approach the twenty-first century.

But the complexity of these issues does not exempt us Jews from facing their moral challenges. We may have to walk a moral tightrope, but we cannot escape our Jewish mission. With greater modesty and less certainty than in the past, with more tentativeness and greater tolerance for dissenting views, we still bear our historic Jewish burden: to face this world and its pain head on; to engage in endless study and moral debate; to cherish human life

and to pursue justice; to enhance the life of the mind and to struggle; to be God's partner in repairing this broken and incomplete
world. It was never easy, even in the old days; it is more difficult
today and will be even harder tomorrow. But, if the agenda is
more complex today, our duty to do the right thing is as compelling as ever. The year 2000 can be not only a new millenium but
a fresh beginning, provided the years that make up the balance of
the 1990s are used for *tikkun olam,* the "repair of our broken
world."

Using the Jewish Tradition in Political Debate

Can the Jewish moral tradition contribute to a better America and
a more peaceful world? A new world is being fashioned before our
eyes. That new world has within it the seeds of great possibilities
and also of great dangers. The choices made in this decade of decision will shape the next century and beyond. In these decisions,
the historic insights and the moral intensity of a Jewish value system can make a vital contribution.

Will we find specific answers to current political debates in the
Bible or the Talmud? Rarely, if ever. Not even the rabbis of old
could be sure of the political answers they fashioned, constantly
revisiting them, testing them in debate with other rabbis, ever striving
to refashion more ethical and compassionate solutions to problems.

In more recent times, Reform Judaism, especially, felt the answers had to be constantly adapted to the fresh challenges of modern life. The answer that Hillel may have given to the problem of
poverty in his time will not necessarily be the answer we choose
for ours. But, in understanding the halachic system that he applied, as well as the moral God-inspired values that impelled him,
we can certainly find guidance for our own moral explorations.

While Jewish law, *halachah,* was not envisioned as applicable to
a non-Jewish society (Jewish law is a contract between God and
the Jewish people), there are values found in the *aggadah,* the non-

legal component of the tradition, that are applicable to all people for all time.

What are these values? We list nine:

1. The inherent dignity and value of all human beings, derived from the belief that we are all made in the image of God.
2. The equality of all people, rooted in the tradition of our common descent from Eve and Adam.
3. The capacity of all people, given the will and the right educational opportunities, to improve themselves.
4. The concept of wealth ("The earth is *Adonai*'s, and the fullness thereof." Psalms 24:1) as lent by God in a trust relationship that requires sharing with the less fortunate. Hence, the special concern that God has mandated for the poor, the widowed, the hungry, and the orphaned.
5. The belief that out of that same trust relationship we have a responsibility of "stewardship" over the earth and must protect it.
6. The existence of certain laws (the seven Noachide Laws) that are regarded as basic to any civilized society, including prohibitions against murder, robbery, blasphemy, idolatry, sexual crimes, and the eating of living flesh, as well as requiring that every community establish courts of justice.
7. The rule of law to which even the highest human ruler is accountable.
8. Freedom of choice and the responsibility of each person for his or her own actions.
9. The paramount obligation of individuals and societies to pursue justice, righteousness, and *darchei shalom,* the "ways of peace" (i.e., to be involved in the work of social justice).

Our tradition, therefore, has not dictated specific answers but rather provided values to be applied to life. Judaism does not mandate for the nations of the world either monarchies or democracies, socialism or capitalism; nor has it endorsed food stamp programs or supply-side economics. These are human inventions. Our role as Jews is to test these human theories and policies by the standards of our tradition to see if they advance or impede the universal moral values of Judaism.

And, while good people—good moral Jews—can and do debate the answers to these questions, a good person can never avoid the questions themselves. Indifference to the problems that confront society is the unforgivable Jewish sin. "Do not separate yourself from the community." (*Pirke Avot* 2:5) The Talmud teaches us: "Whoever has the ability to prevent his household [from committing a sin] and does not is accountable for the sins of his household; if he could do so with his fellow citizens [and does not], he is accountable for his fellow citizens; if the whole world, he is accountable for the whole world." (*Shabbat* 54b) We are Jews and thus we are mandated to dirty our hands in the gritty task of building a better world.

The 1990s: A Unique Decade

Such a mandate could not be renewed at a more exciting or challenging time. The exploding technologies of the twenty-first century mean that, for the first time, we have the technological capability to cure disease, to feed the hungry, to restore the environment, to enhance the freedoms of all peoples, to eliminate illiteracy, and to build a peaceful world. But, if misused, the same technologies can also visit horrible destruction.

Will technology be used to find peaceful ways for nations to resolve their differences or to blow up the world in a nuclear war or accident? All of us together will decide. Will technology be used to clean up the environment or to destroy our ozone layer and permanently alter the climate of the earth? We will decide. Will technology be used to enhance our freedoms or to make Orwell's nightmare of *1984* the reality of 2000? Will technology be used to make the rich richer at the expense of the poor or to distribute God's wealth fairly? Will the technology of genetics be used to engineer a cure for birth defects or to create a new "master race"? That, too, we will decide. As we are commanded in the Bible: "Choose life and live." (Deuteronomy 30:19)

In each case, decisions *will* be made. Somebody will decide. The only choice is whether we will participate in shaping those decisions or allow ourselves to be passive spectators or victims of those decisions. If we remain silent, the outcome may wreck our values and poison our dreams. A handful of passionate people can change any community, for good or ill, because *most* people are too self-absorbed to get involved in public affairs.

Jewish theology teaches us that, when God created the universe, one small part of creation was intentionally left undone. That part was social justice! God gave to human beings alone the ability to understand the difference between right and wrong, to choose between good and evil, to love, to empathize, and to dream. Then God challenged us to use those tools to complete creation. By allowing us to be partners in completing the world, God has given to our lives destiny and purpose.

To be involved in the work of social justice is to do God's work. Those who wrestle with the dilemmas of life and struggle for ethical solutions link their lives to the Jewish mission, which was set out so simply 3,000 years ago in the words of the prophet Micah (6:8): What does *Adonai* require of you? "Only to do justly, to love mercy, and to walk humbly with your God."

≡ **2** ≡

CIVIL RIGHTS
AND RACIAL JUSTICE

Civil Rights and the Jewish Tradition

The fiery cataclysm in Los Angeles in 1992 sent moral shock waves through America, vividly illuminating the state of race relations, the condition of the inner cities, and the priorities of the nation.

Of all the great issues of our times, perhaps none evokes a stronger resonance from Jewish teaching than the search for human rights. Judaism gave to the world the concept of the sanctity and dignity of the individual. Respect for the fundamental rights of others is each person's duty to God. "What is hateful to you, do not do to your neighbor." (B. Talmud, *Shabbat* 31a)

Equality in the Jewish tradition is based on the concept that all of God's children are "created in the image of God." (Genesis 1:27) From that flows the biblical injunction: "You shall have one law for the stranger and the citizen alike: for I *Adonai* am your God." (Leviticus 24:22)

This is not to say that the Jewish tradition is free from racist attitudes. There are, of course, some powerful ethnocentric strands in the Bible (i.e., the idea that somehow the surrounding nations are inherently not as good as Israel). These ideas have persisted through the centuries: the writings of the medieval poet Yehudah Halevi, many medieval kabbalists, some nineteenth-century chasidic writers, and some modern Israeli champions of the Greater

7

Israel—all of whom believed that somehow the Jewish soul is distinct and superior to that of others.

But this ethnocentricity was never allowed to run unchecked. Permeating the tradition is the understanding that God is the God of all people. The radical message of Jonah's prophecy to Nineveh (coincidentally Nineveh was located in what is today modern Iraq) is the belief that God's concern extends equally to all people, not only to the children of Israel. It is also one message of the prophet Malachi's query: "Have we not all one parent? Has not one God created us? Why do we deal treacherously everyone against their siblings, profaning the covenant of our ancestors?" (Malachi 2:10) It is likewise the vision of Amos: " 'Are you not as the children of the Ethiopians to Me, O children of Israel?' asks God. 'Have I not brought up Israel from the land of Egypt and the Philistines from Caphtor and the Arameans [Syrians] from Kir?' " (Amos 9:7) If God could equate the Israelites with the most exotic peoples known to the Jews, even Israel's hated enemies, then truly all of God's children must be equal.

In the Talmud (*Mishnah Sanhedrin* 4:5) it is asked: "Why did God create only one person, Adam?" The answer is illuminating. "All people are descended from a single human being, Adam, so that no one can say, 'My ancestor is greater than yours.' " Even more applicable to the issue of race is the version found in *Yalkut Shimoni* 1:13: God formed Adam from the dust of all the corners of the earth—yellow [clay] and white [sand], black [loam] and red [soil]. Therefore, the earth can declare to no race or color of humankind that it does not belong here, that this soil is not its home.

These ideas were not abstract moralisms of people who, as the quintessential victims of history, set forth standards they hoped others would follow for the protection of the Jews. These ideas were translated into laws when Jews had power. Thus, throughout the Torah, the Jews are reminded that they should treat equally and with compassion the stranger (i.e., the resident alien who is willing to accept their laws and values) in their midst.

And, in the Jerusalem Talmud, the *halachah* sets a standard by which Jewish communities should treat the minorities within them, a standard called *mipnei darhei shalom,* "for the sake of peace."

When Jews and non-Jews live together in a community, they collect *tzedakah* together, they administer it together, and they give to Jew and non-Jew alike, for the sake of peace in their community. (J. Talmud, *Demai* 24a) Those Jews knew that, without sharing the social and economic benefits that Jewish social law provided, they would generate the bitterness and anger that would undermine the good communal relations indispensible to Jewish values and Jewish self-interest.

For decades, a priority concern of synagogue social action and of Jewish community relations has been the protection and enhancement of equal rights and equal opportunities for all persons and the creation of conditions that contribute to vital Jewish living. The security of the Jewish group, as of all groups, rests on the foundation of full equality, individual rights, and personal liberties for all, without regard to race or religion.

The Jewish Role in the Civil Rights Struggle

Jews have been in the forefront of the struggle to achieve equality of opportunity for African Americans [Blacks], Hispanics, Asians, and members of all groups suffering from discrimination. Jews recognize that discrimination against any racial or religious group in American life threatens the ultimate security of the Jew. More important for our purposes is the view that Judaism, to fulfill itself, must exert the full weight of its moral prestige towards the achievement of equal rights and opportunities for all persons, regardless of race or national origin. For this principle is the essence of our religious faith, as it is the essence of democracy itself.

The term "civil rights," as used in this book, refers to the inherent right of *every* citizen to equality of opportunity. The term "civil liberties," used to designate freedoms of speech, assembly, press, religion, and others, will be taken up in a later chapter. While these two areas are related, each has had in recent years a markedly different development.

It is not surprising that Jews responded powerfully to the fight against racial segregation and discrimination in America. After all, no group in history has been so frequently the victim of racial hatred.

Jews, more than any other segment of the white population, played an active role in the dramatic civil rights struggles of the fifties and sixties when the Black-Jewish alliance was at the heart of the civil rights movement.

- When the Mississippi Summer of 1964 was organized to break the back of legal segregation in the then most stubbornly resistant state of the Union, more than half of the young people who volunteered from all parts of the United States were Jews. In that struggle, two of the three martyrs killed by white extremists in Philadelphia, Mississippi, Andrew Goodman and Michael Schwerner, were Jewish; the third, James Earl Chaney, was black.

- Jews contributed substantially to the funds raised by such organizations as the National Association for the Advancement of Colored People, the Southern Christian Leadership Conference, and the Student Non-Violent Coordinating Committee.

- For many years, Kivie Kaplan (a vice-chair of the Reform Jewish movement) was the national president of the NAACP; Arnie Aronson and Joe Rauh, Jr., served as secretary and general counsel, respectively, to the Leadership Conference on Civil Rights (LCCR); Jack Greenberg was a key leader of the NAACP Legal Defense Fund—all of them Jews.

- Rabbis marched with Martin Luther King, Jr., throughout the South; many were jailed, some were beaten. Prominent among these was Rabbi Abraham Joshua Heschel, who was a spiritual partner to King in the struggle against racism.

- Jewish political leverage contributed to passage of landmark civil rights laws, nationally and locally.

Indeed, the Civil Rights Act of 1964 and the Voting Rights Act of 1965 were drafted in the conference room of Reform Judaism's Emily and Kivie Kaplan Religious Action Center building in Washington, under the aegis of the Leadership Conference on Civil Rights, which for decades was housed in the center.

Affirmative Action

In the last three decades of the twentieth century, on one major issue in the realm of race relations, affirmative action, the Jewish and black communities diverged and clashed in an intense debate. As major civil rights laws were passed in the sixties, it became clear that it was not enough to prohibit discrimination against Blacks. Society had to do something positive to make amends for centuries of past injury to racial minorities. Federal courts, executive branch agencies, and Congress mandated "affirmative action," requiring colleges, employers, and government agencies to reach out in positive steps to bring long-deprived members of minority groups into the mainstream of American life.

Implicit in this effort was the idea that it is not enough for a professional school, for example, to say that *from now on* we will accept anybody without discrimination when millions of black Americans are *already* handicapped by generations of poor schooling, unfair treatment, and blatant inequality. Moreover, racist attitudes can find ever more subtle ways to prevent qualified members of minority groups from breaking through the barriers of job and education discrimination. Affirmative steps were seen as necessary to break the cycle of discrimination.

Thus, affirmative action programs mushroomed in all phases of life. And, inevitably, conflicts about them simmered and exploded.

At first glance, it would seem that reconciling affirmative action with Jewish tradition might prove difficult, as suggested by the following statement that says the rich and poor should not be treated differently by judges: "You shall do no unrighteousness in judgment; you shall not respect the person of the poor nor favor the person of the mighty, but in righteousness shall you judge your neighbor." (Leviticus 19:15) Yet, even this clear position was bent to the realities of creating justice. In a well-known talmudic story about a dispute between brothers, the rules of evidence were changed to put an excessive burden on the rich and powerful brother when witnesses for the weaker brother were fearful of testifying. "Thus do we do for all who are powerful," says the text. (B. Talmud, *Baba Metzia* 39b) The *promise* of equality is not sufficient if there are obstacles that make the *reality* of equality impossible.

Affirmative Action and Israel

Modern Israel, when faced with an imbalance between Sephardic Jews (many of them having been educationally and economically deprived) and Ashkenazic Jews, took forceful steps in mandating affirmative action programs for the Sephardim in education and employment. Special remedial programs were set up to assist them to become competitive. On basic high school standardized examinations, all Sephardic Jews were given an extra point over Ashkenazic Jews—a process similar to "race norming" (which in the United States has been so harshly criticized) in which minority students are measured against others in the same minority group rather than against all those who take the standardized exams.

Qualified Sephardim received a number of guaranteed university placements. As a result, the back of anti-Sephardic discrimination was broken faster than even the most optimistic sociologists and politicians of the 1960s and 1970s had predicted. In Israel today, affirmative action programs are also being utilized to bring Soviet and Ethiopian Jews into the mainstream.

The words of the Israeli statesman Yitzhak Rabin illuminate the moral questions that affirmative action raise for the American Jew in the 1990s:

> . . . years ago we thought that an equal opportunity would solve the problem of the gap between the various . . . communities. If we have learned anything in these last . . . years, it is that equal opportunity is not sufficient. Preferential treatment is necessary if we are to bridge the gap and catch up with the 50 percent of our population who . . . through no fault of their own, but because of centuries of cultural and educational discrimination, could not compete.

Reverse Discrimination?

Many white Americans feel that special treatment for qualified minorities amounts to *reverse discrimination* against themselves and their children. During the 1970s, eighties, and nineties, protest and anger swelled into legal challenges, tilting public opinion against affirmative action. Blacks felt betrayed and cheated by an America that seemed to be turning its back on the goal of full equality. When unemployment reached depression-era levels within the black community, particularly among young Blacks (40 percent of whom were jobless in some cities), fuel was added to the storm of resentment.

Yet the concept of affirmative action contains an inherent moral contradiction. On the one hand, equality promises that every person will be judged on the basis of merit without regard to race, sex, creed, age, handicap, sexual orientation, or national origin. On the other hand, when society systematically discriminates for generations against a segment of that society, society has a responsibility to lessen the impact of that discrimination for specific minorities. How can these two valid principles be reconciled?

To insist that abstract equality be used as the only standard of allocating job opportunities is to keep millions of minorities and women from having a fair chance to shape their destinies. On the other hand, if we assign opportunity on the basis of group identity only, we destroy the principle of individual merit.

And where is it written that a person is automatically deprived merely because he or she is black? The child of a prosperous black lawyer or surgeon may be no more deprived than is the white next-door neighbor. This scenario has led opponents of traditional affirmative action to argue that the measure be applied to *individuals*—regardless of color, religion, or ancestry—who have suffered actual deprivation and who are, therefore, entitled to a special hand. But the state and the school and the employer must be *"color-blind";* otherwise, racial injustice will be replaced by reverse discrimination. Moreover, if we rely too heavily on proportional representation, what does this mean for Jews who comprise only 2.2 percent of the United States population?

Affirmative action advocates respond that Blacks *as a race* were enslaved, mistreated, and cheated by society; women *as a class* were disadvantaged. Blacks, women, and other disadvantaged *groups* suffered deprivation, and the society must redress these past grievances by introducing genuine affirmative action using *group* remedies. It is in the public interest to overcome the ugly heritage of the past and to bring the disadvantaged into the mainstream of American life.

Racism against Blacks is a particularly invidious, deeply entrenched aspect of Western civilization, and no one can measure how three hundred years of slavery, segregation, and deprivation have damaged each individual. Without a special effort to guarantee qualified Blacks entrance to higher education and corporate opportunities, there would never be adequate minority representation in the nation's colleges, graduate schools, and corporations. Even with affirmative action programs, the percentage of black students at professional schools actually has fallen in the past fifteen years. Equality is not served by bringing everyone to the starting gate to compete in a race in which minority youngsters have been crippled by a history of inferior schooling, bad housing, and demoralizing treatment.

The controversy surrounding affirmative action reached its peak during a series of landmark legal cases in the 1970s and 1980s. In the *DeFunis, Bakke, Webster,* and *Fullivove* cases, the policy arguments over affirmative action were sharpened in legal briefs. In the early 1990s, a bitter battle over the Civil Rights Act of 1991 brought the issue into even sharper focus.

*A Real Dilemma: The DeFunis Case—
Should We Oppose a Fellow Jew Who Claims
to Be Harmed by Affirmative Action?*

In 1973, the Commission on Social Action faced one of its thorniest dilemmas: whether to join with a coalition of civil rights organizations in supporting an affirmative action program at the University of Washington Law School. Through affirmative action, the university was attempting to diversify its essentially white male student body by reaching out to qualified women and members of racial minorities, bringing them into the school.

Several Jewish organizations publicly opposed the University of Washington program, saying it was basically a quota. They supported the plaintiff, Marco DeFunis, a Jewish student who alleged he was the victim of reverse discrimination. The Commission on Social Action (CSA), after examining the facts in depth, concluded that the university's affirmative action program did not resort to a fixed percentage—a quota—but relied only on good-faith general goals and timetables. Should the fact that DeFunis was a Jew have affected the CSA's decision on whether to support the university's position against Marco DeFunis's legal challenge?

Response

The Commission on Social Action joined an amicus ("friend of the court") brief in support of the university, believing its affirmative action program was a flexible, good-faith effort to bring into the mainstream of the law school members of groups long discriminated against. They made this judgment even in the face of the information that DeFunis's parents were members of a Reform synagogue in Seattle, Washington.

As this and other affirmative action cases worked their way to the Supreme Court, they gradually caused the breakup of the old Black-Jewish civil rights coalition that had helped forge the landmark civil rights legislation of the 1960s.

Goals and Timetables vs. Quotas

Almost all Jewish organizations supported affirmative action programs that used goals and timetables to measure whether progress was being made in eliminating discrimination. Only the Orthodox

Jewish agencies and the Anti-Defamation League of B'nai B'rith (ADL) opposed the use of goals and timetables, arguing they would inevitably lead to quotas. Two other agencies, the American Jewish Congress and the Women's American ORT, support the use of temporary quotas after court findings of discrimination. Today, most Jewish groups support goals and timetables but oppose quotas under any circumstances.

But the nuances and splits in the Jewish community were lost on much of the black community when, during the major affirmative action cases of the seventies and eighties, some of the most high-profile opponents turned out to be those few Jewish groups who rejected affirmative action. In the minds of many Blacks, these groups spoke for all Jews, despite repeated public opinion polls showing that Jews support affirmative action with goals and even quotas at higher percentages than any other segment of the white community of America.

While the courts were upholding affirmative action programs well into the 1980s, the Reagan administration was vigorously trying to destroy these programs and to stop other civil rights legislation. In the late eighties, the Supreme Court began to join in efforts to limit the scope of civil rights laws generally. In response, at the very height of President Reagan's popularity, a regalvanized civil rights coalition, including Blacks and Jews, achieved a series of legislative victories that continued into the Bush presidency, expanding the scope of civil rights coverage. Among them: the extension of the Voting Rights Act, the Fair Housing Act of 1990, the Japanese Reparations Act (compensating Japanese Americans for having been unfairly incarcerated during World War II), the Americans with Disabilities Act, and the Civil Rights Act of 1991 overturning the effect of six Supreme Court decisions that sharply narrowed the protection against discrimination in the workplace.

A Real Dilemma: Richmond v. Croson

In 1989, the Supreme Court heard a number of cases dealing with employment discrimination. In most of those cases, the Jewish community stood with the rest of the civil rights community. But one case posed a particularly difficult question. In the *City of Richmond* v. *J. A. Croson*, Richmond had attempted to guarantee minority business involvement in city contracts by requiring that prime contractors on city projects subcontract at least 30 percent of the job to minority business enterprises. The black community strongly endorsed this approach and requested that the UAHC and other Jewish groups join in a "friend of the court" brief supporting this so-called set-aside program. What should the Jewish community have done?

Response

The UAHC and all other Jewish organizations declined to join the civil rights groups in the case. This program provided an effective means of guaranteeing that minority firms had a fair share of contracts by relying on fixed, inflexible numbers based only on race, with no regard to any other characteristics or qualifications. The program thereby legitimized a quota system in which race became the sole determinant. In the view of the UAHC, the harm of such an approach outweighed the benefit.

The Supreme Court rejected the *Richmond* "set-aside." When the Civil Rights Bill of 1991 was introduced to undo the damage of the other Supreme Court decisions, the civil rights coalition decided not to include provisions undoing the *Richmond* decision in order to keep the Jewish community and other antiquota groups as part of the coalition.

The use of quotas poses a major problem for Jews, who historically have been excluded from schools and professions in Europe and in the United States because of anti-Semitic quota systems.

A small but vociferous group of black conservatives also has challenged affirmative action, saying that, if most Blacks achieved their advancement as a result of affirmative action, how could one be sure that they were truly qualified? Even the most qualified Blacks will be shadowed by suspicions engendered by programs to help less able people. Furthermore, what incentive will Blacks have to stand on their own feet if society is willing to give them special benefits? Supreme Court Justice Clarence Thomas is among those Blacks who have opposed racial preferences as harmful to the self-reliance, independence, and pride of Blacks. This view is rejected by the substantial majority of black and Jewish organizations.

The Current Status of Blacks in America

Discussions about affirmative action should not blind us to the dire condition of American Blacks today. Among black adults, the rate of unemployment is 2.5 times higher than among white workers; for black teenagers the rate is 2.6 times higher than for white young men and women. Blacks are approximately 12.3 percent of our total population, but they comprise only 2.3 percent of lawyers and judges, 3.3 percent of physicians, 1.9 percent of dentists, 3.8 percent of engineers, and 4.0 percent of college and university professors. As former Justice Marshall said in his angry dissent in the *Bakke* case, "At every point, from birth to death, the impact of the past is reflected in the still disfavored position of the Negro [Blacks]." In a shrinking job market, the chances of the average black person working his or her way out of poverty and despair are very bleak indeed.

Even the most far-reaching affirmative action programs would barely scratch the surface of our most serious racial problems. Forty years ago, Gunnar Myrdal, in his classic *An American Dilemma,* put the challenge squarely: "You are cutting off an underclass that is not needed, not employable. . . . You must create out of this underclass, or their children at least, human beings who fit into modern America, who are needed, who are productive, who have a value." The riots of Los Angeles demonstrated that we have not yet heeded Myrdal's warning.

This "underclass" remains essentially cut off. Many black youths find little or no future in America. They are trapped in decaying slums and failing schools, permanently unemployed. To survive, they are dependent on an inhumane welfare system and/or street crime. Many end up hustling on the street, the training ground for serious crime and the dead end of the drug world.

This waste of a generation is not only a human disaster, but it creates a society where no one is safe. History shows that Jews have most to fear in an angry and polarized society. Recent events prove again that, in an atmosphere of tension and hopelessness, Blacks, like many other groups, seek easy scapegoats to blame for their misfortunes (Koreans in the Los Angeles riots), and Jews are often the target.

Black America is mired in a crisis marked by the disintegration of the family; the dominance of single-parent, female-headed families; children bearing children; the catastrophic drug epidemic; AIDS; and the startling reality that a black male in Harlem has the same life expectancy as a peasant in Bangladesh. The United States Supreme Court, once the champion of minority rights, seems to have abandoned its defense of the vulnerable in our society. Reinforced by the appointments made by Presidents Reagan and Bush, the Supreme Court has embraced a right-wing interpretation of the Constitution, whittling away the right of women to have an abortion and making it significantly more difficult for a victim of discrimination to get redress from the courts.

Integration: Successes and Failures; the Breakdown of Public Education

In the 1950s and 1960s, racial integration in public education was not only a national goal but a moral imperative. Protestants, Catholics, and Jews played prominent roles in the massive effort to end segregated schooling in America, recognizing the truth of the Supreme Court's seminal school desegregation decision, *Brown* v. *Board of Education,* that "separate but equal is inherently unequal."

Today, new questions arise. Do minority students learn better in desegregated schools? Does desegregation cause "white flight" (whites who move out of integrated school districts)? Does integration lessen or increase racial conflict? Can integration really be achieved without combining city and suburb? Have Blacks begun to give up on integration?

These questions must be seen in the context of the declining quality of public education generally. For three generations, the public school system was the great leavener of American life. Rich and poor, immigrants and longtime residents, Christians and Jews, Blacks and whites met for what was the only close interaction of their lives. For three generations, the public schools educated America's youths, raising the level of literacy, resulting in a more technically proficient and competitive, as well as a more humane and tolerant, society.

In the past generation that pattern has reversed itself. White flight left urban schools the squalid province of minorities and poor whites. In the face of declining tax revenues, facilities deteriorated, the general quality of education fell, and rates of literacy sank alarmingly. In this context, hopes of breaking the cycle of deprivation and victimization appear bleaker than ever.

Jewish attitudes toward public education often reflect the same dilemmas. That system helped convert a poor immigrant community into one of the most upwardly mobile and successful minority groups in the history of America. But, increasingly, Jews who remain in the city feel compelled to put their children in private schools. Indeed, the rising Jewish interest in Jewish day schools stems, in part, from a desire to escape the impact of busing and integration on the quality and safety of public schools.

The overwhelming majority of Jewish youngsters still attend public schools. But, where public schools have declined in quality and are swept by violence or tension, can Jewish parents be expected to sacrifice their child's education on the altar of high principle?

What then is the future of public education? Perhaps public education is to become a dumping ground for poor nonwhites—a school for children left behind in the mass exodus to suburbia or to the sanctuaries of private schools. In the long run, is such a prospect good for America? Is it good for Jews? Is it good for anybody?

For Jews, the breakdown of the public school system poses other particular concerns. Studies indicate that those with higher levels of education are less likely to hold racist and anti-Semitic attitudes. But, over the past two decades, educational levels have fallen sharply. Will this result in increased anti-Semitism? Quite likely. The despair that those confined to the worst schools feel as they are increasingly locked out of the better jobs in a technological world requiring good education can only breed the kind of anger that helped fuel the violent conflicts between Chasidim and Blacks in Crown Heights, Brooklyn, in 1991.

Jewish Day Schools, Integration, and the Public Schools

Some Jews have argued that the breakdown of public schools has been exacerbated by the expansion of Jewish day schools. A growing number of Jewishly motivated parents, increasingly frustrated by the obvious limitations of the usual "weekend/after-school" Jewish education programs offered by most Reform and Conservative synagogues, enrolled their children in a full-time education program providing the best of both worlds: a first-rate Jewish education and a first-rate general education.

How should the Jewish community, which has so benefited from the public school system in America and which recognizes that the future strength of this nation depends on the quality of public education, balance these concerns against its commitment to strengthening Jewish education?

A Real Dilemma: UAHC and Jewish Day Schools

At its biennial convention in 1985, the UAHC considered a resolution on whether to encourage full-time Reform Jewish day schools. Some delegates argued that to do so was an abandonment of the public school system; others that it was a necessary affirmation of an intensive Jewish educational option. If you had been a delegate, how would you have voted?

Response

The UAHC held that its commitment to public schools should not preclude its support for legitimate efforts to strengthen Jewish education through the option of day school. Such support, however, was predicated on two conditions: first, that synagogues undertake efforts to strengthen the public schools in their communities, and second, that the movement reaffirm its commitment to separation of church and state, including opposition to federal aid to full-time religious education.

The result: By 1991 the Reform Jewish day-school movement had grown to fourteen schools. The UAHC has maintained its opposition to parochiaid (although some pressure to reevaluate this position has come from some day schools), but most congregations have been able to do little to assist the public schools in their communities.

The many questions that arise from the desegregation process require constant and candid examination. All this should not obscure the fundamental truth that America is the only nation that, despite a history of racial arrogance and slavery, has broken the back of legal segregation and paved the way for a truly open, free, and multiracial society. We still have much to do to achieve this goal, but we have already come a long way.

≡ 3 ≡

JEWS, BLACKS,
AND OTHER MINORITIES

A Real Dilemma: Confronting Extremist Statements

In the 1980s, Ed Koch, New York City's flamboyant Jewish mayor, repeatedly antagonized minority groups in the city by using insensitive language such as welfare "queens" and poverty "pimps." While few Jews thought that Mr. Koch was a bigot, many were concerned by the cumulative, divisive impact of his occasional inflammatory comments. A black leader in New York City called the UAHC and urged that a Jewish voice be raised against the mayor's "insensitivity" to minority groups. Other Jewish leaders were hesitant to speak out, asserting that we as Jews should avoid criticizing a Jewish mayor except in the most extreme situations.

Response

After studying the matter, the UAHC did issue a critical statement. As expected, it drew an angry rebuke from the mayor, but it heartened elements of black and Hispanic leadership.

A few years later, in 1991, Leonard Jeffries, a black professor at the City College of New York, claimed publicly that Jews were responsible for the slave trade, that Jews and Italians in Hollywood conspired to denigrate Blacks, that

Jews run the Mafia, etc. The UAHC wrote to the same black leader, asking him to speak out in the same spirit he had once elicited from Jews in denouncing Koch's remarks. He refused, saying that Blacks are sick of being paraded out, on Jewish demand, to attack "brothers," that they are being judged as a group for the mouthings of an individual, and that they are not responsible for every offender who happens to be black.

Another New York black leader, on the other hand, stated he was appalled not only at Jeffries's statements but at the eloquent silence of civic, political, and minority leaders in the face of such vicious and stupid bigotry.

So what is the dilemma? Do we have a right to demand reciprocity from Blacks and others? Can we understand the restraints they might have about criticizing their own group? Are Jews any more willing to criticize their own extremists than are other groups? Can we deal effectively with the anti-Jewish extremists when "responsible" leaders of the extremists' own communities remain silent?

As a religious tradition, Judaism rejects racism; but, as individuals, Jews are as prone to racial bigotry as other people. Many Jews are sensitive to the impact of discrimination through their own history; but Jews can also be found among the slum landlords and merchants who exploit the poor. Jews rarely resort to violence when Blacks or Hispanics move into the neighborhood; instead, Jews leave the cities. Indeed, in pursuit of a better life for their families, Jews joined the massive post-World War II exodus, moving from the cities to the all-white suburbs, one effect of which was to abandon poor Blacks to virtual urban ghettos.

A Real Dilemma: When Synagogues Join White Flight

Until the 1950s, the vast majority of Jews belonged to synagogues in urban centers, enriching the lives of all who lived in the community through cultural, educational, and communal activity.

In the past two generations, a radical shift in living patterns sent most Jews to the suburbs. Those Jews who were mobile enough to flee the problems of the cities and live out the "American dream" literally moved their synagogues with them to the suburbs.

But what happened to those left behind: the older and poorer Jews who could not leave or those who preferred urban life? Without the synagogue, the Jewish support system that sustained them eroded. The public schools and other communal institutions in the area deteriorated as Jews withdrew from the political and civic leadership they had long provided.

Was it wrong for congregations to have moved? How would you have voted if you were a board member of an urban synagogue considering relocation to the suburbs?

Response

Scores, if not hundreds of congregations, had to deal with this problem. For many, the feasibility of staying downtown simply did not exist. The distance between the old facility and the new center of Jewish population was too great. Moreover, the deterioration of the quality of life in the old neighborhood was so severe that many members were afraid or unwilling to attend Friday evening Shabbat services. To have remained behind would have ill-served the members of the congregation and, as new synagogues were founded in the suburbs, might have spelled the death-knell of those that failed to adapt.

Nevertheless, a surprising number of congregations made a conscientious effort to remain downtown or, at least, to maintain a presence in the city. In a few communities, where the distances were not great, congregations decided to stay, drawing suburban members downtown. Some congregants had always remained downtown, enriching the community and now benefiting from urban renewal as a new generation of families returned to the city from the suburbs. In many other communities, the congregation kept the old facility and then built a suburban annex and/or religious school to meet the needs of both the urban and suburban segments of the Jewish community.

Crown Heights

Tragically, one of the few inner-city communities where Jews chose to stay erupted into violence in 1991. On the evening of August 19, 1991, seven-year-old Gavin Cato was riding his bicycle on the sidewalk in front of his home at the corner of Utica Avenue and President Street in Crown Heights, Brooklyn. He was with his cousin, Angela.

At 8:20 that evening, Lubavitcher Grand Rebbe Menachem Schneerson was being driven home in a three-car motorcade, following his weekly visit to the cemetery where his wife is buried. The motorcade was escorted by police. Twenty-two-year-old Joseph Lifsh, one of the motorcade drivers, reportedly ran a red light, collided with another car, and veered onto the sidewalk. His car struck Gavin and his cousin. Gavin was dragged underneath the car. Twelve of Gavin's neighbors lifted the car off the dying child. Angela, seriously injured, was pinned against the wall of the apartment house.

Rumors spread through the community that a private Jewish ambulance had arrived at the scene first and attended to Joseph Lifsh rather than to the young black victims. In fact, the private ambulance and the city ambulance arrived at the same time, and the police ordered the private ambulance to rescue the injured Lifsh, who was being beaten by the crowd. Gavin Cato died at the hospital.

The grand jury testimony later revealed that Lifsh had tried desperately to avoid hitting the children. He was not indicted, thus generating a firestorm of controversy in the community, which is 85 percent black and 15 percent Jewish, mostly chasidic.

With wild rumors sweeping the community, violence erupted throughout Crown Heights. Three hours after the incident, Yankel Rosenbaum, an Australian chasidic scholar visiting Brooklyn, was stopped in his car by a gang of twenty young hoodlums, assaulted, stabbed, and left bleeding on the hood of his car. He subsequently died in the hospital, a victim of what black Mayor David Dinkins later called "a lynching." This was the first physical confrontation between Blacks and Jews in the twentieth century that resulted in fatalities or casualties.

Several days of anti-Jewish rioting and rampaging ensued. Jews were attacked at random by black youths, shouting "Heil Hitler" and "Kill All the Jews." The violence was triggered by the incendiary statements made at the Cato funeral and elsewhere by such community leaders as Sonny Carson, Al Sharpton, and Vernon Mason. The Chasidim and other Jews likened the attacks to a pogrom and denounced them as a modern reenactment of Kristallnacht.

More than 65 civilians and 158 police officers were wounded over three days of rioting. Al Sharpton equated the accidental death of Cato with the slaying of Rosenbaum, demanding that Lifsh be arrested for murder, thus inflaming group relations and inciting violence.

Despite the close cooperation between Blacks and Jews in the civil rights movement, it is probably correct to say that Black-Jewish relations were never as good, even in the old days, as we romanticize them to have been. They were inherently unequal, not peer to peer. Jews once provided much of the expertise, the legal resources, and the leadership in the civil rights coalitions, creating a subordinate role for those we sought to help. The black community, determined to take control of its own destiny, has rejected the former relationship as patronizing. Many Jews felt betrayed. While the revolt against condescension was healthy and overdue, it often led to excesses of black separatism, further estranging Blacks from Jews.

Many Jews who abandoned or were pushed out of the civil rights movement became more conscious of their own ethnic identity and the particular agenda of the Jewish people. These activists plunged into the battle for Soviet Jewry and Israel. Ethnic assertiveness became the new battle cry in America, and the sense of national cohesiveness began to sputter. After the traumas of civil rights, the

Vietnam War, and Watergate, no single issue united all groups. With each group going its own way, fighting its own battles, civil rights lost its sense of coherence as a definable movement.

In this new mood of group separatism, Jews and Blacks have largely drifted apart. Given the suburban middle-class character of Jewish life, most Jews do not know other minorities on a personal basis. Employing a black or Hispanic domestic does not contribute to relationships of equality. Increasingly, Jews and Blacks have little human contact, resulting in negative stereotyping. Too often, Blacks think of Jews as rich, powerful, and racist; Jews regard Blacks as living on welfare, violent, anti-Semitic, and pro-Palestinian.

The reality is that most Blacks and even higher percentages of black political and organizational leaders have been stalwart supporters of Israel. To the average black person, however, Israel is as remote as Nigeria is to the average Jew. Blacks are preoccupied with their own situation, particularly the depressed economic conditions in which so many languish.

The Reverend Jesse Jackson: A Bone in the Throat?

For years, Jesse Jackson embodied a more potent impediment to Black-Jewish amity than did affirmative action or any other issue. To Blacks, Jesse Jackson symbolized the highest achievement of any black American in the nation's political arena. No black person had ever before commanded the serious attention of the American people as did this presidential candidate. No black person, not even Martin Luther King, Jr., had risen to such a dizzying position on the national political ladder reaching for the presidency. No black person had earned so many votes, commanded so much respect, so surpassed his opponents in wit and charisma, so inspired young Blacks and many whites as well, nor so captivated the media.

Jews, however, generally saw Jesse Jackson as a threat because Jackson had called New York City "Hymietown" and, even worse, he embraced two of our most implacable enemies: Black Muslim leader Louis Farrakhan and PLO chief Yasir Arafat. Although he apologized for the insulting remarks, Jackson failed to persuade most Jews of his sincerity. And, although he had distanced himself from the notoriously anti-Semitic Farrakhan, he did not repudiate him.

In fairness, Jesse Jackson has frequently reached out to Jews and supported Jewish causes. He confronted Gorbachev on behalf of Soviet Jews. He not only denounced President Reagan for honoring Nazi S.S. soldiers at Bitburg but visited a former German concentration camp in protest. He lobbied President al-Assad of Syria to ameliorate the plight of Syrian Jews. He moderated his positions on Israel and the Middle East.

Repeatedly, Jackson sought opportunities for Black-Jewish cooperation, participating in such events as a special interracial Kristallnacht commemoration. Speaking to the World Jewish Congress in Brussels in 1992, Jackson affirmed that Zionism is the liberation movement of the Jewish people. But, while he has reached out to the Jewish community on many occasions, most Jews continue to be troubled by his views on Isreal and his relationship with Farrakhan.

A Real Dilemma: Should Jews Meet with Farrakhan?

In 1991, several Jewish leaders in the Chicago area were surprised to receive a telephone invitation to Louis Farrakhan's home for dinner to help "clear the air" between Jews and Farrakhan. Some of the people who received the invitation refused to attend, arguing that their presence would only help make an anti-Semite respectable. Others said they wanted the chance to try to help Farrakhan understand what damage his words (e.g., "Judaism is a gutter religion") had caused and how he could make amends to ease relations with the Jewish community. If you were invited, would you go?

Response

Those who accepted the invitation reported that Farrakhan was personally hospitable. He denied he was an anti-Semite and pleaded for an understanding of his words. But he also repeated some of the very canards about "Jewish power" and "control" of the media that caused the conflict in the first place. Anti-Semites sometimes do redeem themselves by overcoming their prejudices and apologizing for their malice; Louis Farrakhan has yet to do so.

Looking Ahead

Can Black-Jewish relations be salvaged? The bloody Crown Heights confrontation certainly brought the two groups to a historical low point. But there are also still substantial grounds for hope. Many Blacks and Jews still share a vision of a just, generous, and open society. Despite our dramatic economic differences, public opinion polls show that our attitudes and values are remarkably alike: we both recoil against bigotry and advocate a primary role for government in solving social inequity; and we are essential partners in virtually every successful coalition for social justice.

In presidential, congressional, and local elections, Jews and Blacks vote more alike than any other identifiable groups. Approximately 70 percent of Jews and 90 percent of Blacks opposed the 1984 Reagan and the 1988 Bush candidacies. No other groups gave the Democratic candidates a majority. An even higher percentage of Jews supported Bill Clinton in 1992.

In fact, in communities across America, Blacks and Jews are working together daily to address their common concerns. In 1991, the Religious Action Center of Reform Judaism, through its Marjorie Kovler Institute for Black-Jewish Relations, published a manual on cooperative programming in black churches and Jewish synagogues, based on existing successful programs from across the country. Over 250 such programs are described at length. Consider the following:

- In Los Angeles, black and Jewish doctors, nurses, and congregants sponsor an annual health fair that serves over three hundred people with basic checkups, bloodwork, referrals to city agencies, and follow-ups with local clinics.

- In Hamden, Connecticut, a black church and Jewish synagogue have founded an interfaith AIDS network that provides financial and emotional support for people living with AIDS.

- In Plainfield, New Jersey, a black Episcopal church and a Reform synagogue jointly bought a dilapidated building and, with their own hands, rehabilitated it to house low-income families.

- In Manhasset and Great Neck, Long Island, the black and Jewish communities created a summer employment workshop to teach teens job-hunting skills. The same coalition also closed down a crack house that threatened the safety of a local housing project.

Such mutual efforts promote better Black-Jewish relations. But lasting improvement will require Blacks and Jews to change their perceptions of each other. This generation of Blacks—especially young people—has little awareness of past Jewish contributions to human equality. And even those who are aware want to know "What have you done for me lately?" This attitude often infuriates Jews who want to feel some appreciation for sacrifices they have made to achieve equal rights for Blacks and other minorities.

Black youths will have to understand recent history, including the Holocaust and its profound impact on the Jewish psyche, if any new relationship is to be forged.

And Jews, too, will have to modulate injured feelings and stop expecting constant gratitude. Jews must understand that Blacks see us as more often blocking their hopes for progress than advancing them—in affirmative action, in minority housing, as well as in Jewish support for the death penalty, which many Blacks see as code words for "get tough with Blacks."

Can this drift be arrested? It is difficult to look ahead with confidence at this time, but we must try because both Jews and Blacks have a common stake in an open and compassionate society.

When Jews and Blacks square off against each other, we elate our common enemies—Nazis, the KKK, and other foes of equality in America. Whether we like it or not, Blacks and Jews are joined together in a common destiny. It is time to join together to renew that special relationship and to unite in the struggle against poverty, ignorance, bigotry, crime, and an ineffective welfare system.

Hispanics and Asians: Two Emerging Powers in American Society

By the year 2015, Hispanics are expected to exceed Blacks as the largest ethnic minority in America. In the Twin Cities of St. Paul and Minneapolis, for example, Mexican Americans already have replaced Blacks as the largest minority group. In Los Angeles, some 35 percent of public school students are now of Hispanic origin, but the percentage in kindergarten rises to almost 50 percent. In Seattle, the Hispanic population is growing almost twice as fast as that of non-Hispanic whites. High levels of immigration, larger than any since the turn of the century, together with a high birthrate, have made Hispanics the fastest growing minority group in American life.

Hispanic power can grow significantly if Spanish-speaking communities think of themselves more as a coherent and unified group rather than as Puerto Ricans, Cubans, Hondurans, or Mexican Americans. The tide of Hispanics who come, legally or illegally, to escape poverty and unpopular regimes in Latin America has become a flood. The Hispanic population is markedly young, urban, and widespread across the entire United States continent. There are profound differences among various Hispanic groups, including their relative assimilation to American life and their readiness to reach out to other ethnic and minority groups in common cause.

There is a broad range of issues in which the Jewish and Hispanic communities have common concerns, including issues of civil rights, social justice, health, welfare, and education. Jews and Hispanics have been allied in the past, most notably in support of union leader Cesar Chavez defending the rights of American farm workers. And Jews remain concerned about the high rate of job-lessness among Hispanics, which cuts off avenues of hope and improvement—a problem compounded by the fact that 54 percent have had less than high school education as compared with 33 percent of Blacks and 14 percent of whites.

But there are serious limitations to our relationship. The recent arrival of many Hispanics to the United States means that we have little shared history. They know little of Jewish concerns, of Israel, Soviet Jewry, and church-state separation. We are often limited in communication because of language differences.

The Jewish community has even less contact with the various Asian communities. Many of them, particularly from Southeast Asia, are also recent arrivals. We do not share a common history, common language, or even the common religious roots we share with Hispanics and Blacks.

Yet, we have much in common with Asians: strong family and community structures, ancient historical and cultural traditions, a tendency to do well academically. All of these offer opportunities for coalitional activity that we need to explore.

As both Hispanics and Asians become more potent political forces in America, Jewish self-interest will mandate that we make a conscientious effort to reach out to these communities and strengthen our coalitional activities with them.

A Real Dilemma:
Hispanic-Jewish Relations in New York City

In New York City's Washington Heights section, a community of politically powerful Orthodox Jews lives side by side with a politically underrepresented Dominican majority. Having lived in that part of the city since the 1930s, Jews have formed their own schools and cultivated a strong internal sense of community. The Dominicans, by and large recent immigrants, are working to establish themselves, as have many other immigrant groups before them.

In recognition of serious overcrowding, the New York City School Board decided to build a number of schools in the surrounding area. One of the schools was to be located directly behind a yeshivah. The Orthodox community opposed the location, claiming that traffic patterns and construction obstacles made it an inappropriate site. Despite Orthodox protests, the school board maintained that this location was the best choice to serve the needs of the community.

For the area's Reform Jews, the situation was also problematic. As the children and grandchildren of immigrants whose families achieved success through public education, they understood and empathized with the Dominican community's desire to improve public education. But, as Jews, they felt themselves a part of *Klal Yisrael* and, though they disagreed with the Orthodox position, did not want to take issue openly with them. Ultimately, the Reform Jews accepted the school board's assessment that the site was appropriate. In fact, many were convinced that the Orthodox concerns shielded an underlying fear that the new school would bring minority crime to the neighborhood, endangering Orthodox youths attending the yeshivah.

Nevertheless, many Reform Jews worried about creating a rift in the Jewish community, believing that the damage to intra-Jewish relations might outweigh the benefits of taking a public stand on the underlying ethical issue.

Should the Reform synagogue in the area have taken a public stand on this important community issue?

Response

Temple Beth Am in Washington Heights decided that the most constructive approach for the entire community required their public support for the construction of the new school.

In addition to supporting the school's construction, Temple Beth Am initiated several programs that would build bridges between local Jews and Dominicans. The congregation stimulated efforts in both communities to increase enrollment in the public schools and to develop a multicultural curriculum. In addition, such interfaith activities as joint worship services provided an opportunity for the two communities to work to increase understanding.

Native Americans

While Blacks and Hispanics suffer conditions of great deprivation, arguably their status is better than that of Native Americans.

> As we near the end of the twentieth century, American Indians [Native Americans] remain largely trapped by nineteenth-century poverty: 16 percent of reservation homes lack electricity, 21 percent an indoor toilet, and 56 percent a telephone. And, for the most part, federal policymakers and administrators are still held captive by the ghosts of paternalism and dependency. . . . This has created a federal bureaucracy ensnared in red tape and riddled with fraud, mismanagement, and waste.

The above comes from a 1990 congressional report—the forty-third such study since 1792—on the disastrous consequences of United States policies on Native American affairs. In 1990, 45 percent of all reservation-based Native Americans lived below the poverty line. Roughly half of all adult Native Americans are unemployed; of those working, a majority make less than $7,000 a year. By law, Native American-owned businesses are entitled to preferential treatment where federal contracts are concerned. In practice, however, the Bureau of Indian Affairs, much despised by Native Americans, has virtually ignored enforcement, often offering such contracts to phony front companies run by non-Native Americans.

The 1990 report also found widespread child abuse by teachers at bureau schools and charged the B.I.A. with failure to protect the health of Native Americans. On reservations, three out of eight people die before they reach the age of forty-five (in contrast with one out of eight in the general population). Housing is mostly sub-standard and much is uninhabitable. It will take more than a momentary spasm of national sympathy, such as Kevin Costner evoked with his award-winning movie, *Dances with Wolves,* for America to come to grips with the tragic plight of its indigenous people.

While some effort has been made to build relations between Native Americans and Jews, these two communities rarely cross paths. Jews live mostly in urban or suburban, middle-class neighborhoods. Native Americans, the poorest single group in America, live mostly in isolated rural areas. Yet, Jews and Native Americans have much in common.

Both Jews and Native Americans share the legacy of oral traditions and historical memories of exile from their homelands. Many of their religious rituals are grounded in the cycles of life, in agriculture, and in connection to the land. We have both suffered at the hands of majority communities frightened by our "strangeness," eager to force "outsiders" to fit *their* perception of the world. Unable to fit, Jews and Native Americans have undergone the trials of ghettoization and persecution. Ironically, Native Americans and Jews both consider 1492 a turning point in their history of persecution.

Contemporary Native Americans and Jews share certain common concerns as well. In the face of powerful assimilating cultural forces, both seek many ways to preserve their heritage.

Native Americans face the additional burdens of widespread poverty, unemployment, and illiteracy in their heroic efforts to recapture and reinvigorate nearly extinguished cultures.

In the summer of 1991, the youth group from Central Synagogue in New York, led by Rabbi Tom Weiner, journeyed to the Rosebud Reservation in South Dakota. During their three-week visit, the students participated in various Lakota ceremonies and experienced a number of customs: most memorably, preparation for the summer Sun Dance.

The Native Americans found inspiration in the Hebrew songs sung every night and in the Shabbat services conducted by the group. Recalling the experience, Rabbi Weiner stated, "We, in the end, helped them in the practice of their newly rediscovered tradition, just as our students became more knowledgeable and proud of being Jews."

All this points to the possibility for a rich Jewish-Native American dialogue if we can create opportunities for such encounters. Visits to reservations are but one example. Some Jews live near reservations, providing greater chance for common activity. Native Americans face the task of developing their own agriculture and small industry. Several exchanges have taken place between kibbutzim and reservations. Israeli drip irrigation technology, for example, has greatly increased the agricultural yields among the Navajo. This type of creative approach to Jewish-Native American relations holds open the hope for additional constructive exchanges in the future.

Multiculturalism

In the 1990s, a new debate facing the civil rights movement pitted group identity on one side and the problematic ideal of America as a "melting pot" on the other. The debate has focused on what is known as "multiculturalism": programs and curricula to promote racial and ethnic diversity and respect for differing backgrounds.

The issues raised in this debate go to the heart of America's understanding of itself. This nation has, traditionally, been uncommonly hospitable to people of diverse backgrounds. But, for most of our history, the working assumption has been that the diversity would, in time, diminish, that each new cohort of immigrants would, in a generation or two, adapt to the American environment and become "American."

But what does "American" mean? By the year 2020, most Americans will be of non-European background. Is diversity really something to overcome or is it actually a source of strength? And how can we ask or expect that people will assimilate so long as bigotry and discrimination remain so biting a part of the American way?

On the other hand, if we choose to celebrate America's diversity, do we not run the risk that we will fragment, that we will end up with a mosaic with no grout to hold the stones together or connect them to one another?

The arena where these issues are most frequently and contentiously played out today is the college campus. It is one thing to move beyond Western tradition by insisting that the curriculum be opened up to include the history and literature of diverse groups. It is another to claim that only members of particular groups are competent to teach the history and literature of their group or that the Western tradition be regarded as "just another" tradition rather than as the tradition that has most powerfully shaped this country, its institutions and its patterns. How, in fact, can we ensure that a mature recognition and acceptance of America's diversity will become a source of strength rather than of fragmentation? And where, in all this, do the Jews—with their own history and their own literature—fit?

The Jewish community recognizes that the goal of multicultural education is fully compatible, in theory, with the diversity and pluralism it advocates. We are mindful of the benefits that we, and others, will derive from the exposure to the range of human experience and to the range of the Jewish experience. But we are concerned when, under the banner of diversity, inept and even fraudulent scholarship is endorsed, racialism is encouraged, and walls rather than bridges are erected.

≡ 4 ≡

CIVIL LIBERTIES

A Real Dilemma: Anti-Semitic Rock Lyrics

In 1990, the rap group Public Enemy—already embroiled in a controversy ignited by the anti-Semitic statements of one of its members—released a song titled "Welcome to the Terrordome," which included the following lyrics:

> Crucifixion ain't no fiction
> So-called chosen, frozen
> Apology made to whoever pleases
> till they got me like Jesus.

These words smack of anti-Semitism. They revisit the repulsive and discredited charge that the Jews killed Jesus Christ. Most Jews would agree that these offensive and inciting lyrics do not belong on the airwaves or in music stores. The wide circulation that the recording industry affords its products would seem to justify such concern.

But would banning these lyrics violate the First Amendment to the Constitution? Are Public Enemy's lyrics a form of free speech, protected by the very same Constitution that allows every citizen to speak his or her conscience free from the censorship of government and of society? Anti-Semitic or not, does not the rap group have a legal right to sing its lyrics, just as other groups or individuals have every legal right to criticize them? Or does the right of free speech end when incitement to bigotry begins? What about the lyrics of the 1991 album by rap artist Ice Cube, *Death Certificate*, calling for the assassination of a Jewish music group manager and threatening Koreans with death? Do such threats make a difference?

This dilemma is particularly acute for the Jewish community. We are, of course, committed to the fight against anti-Semitism. At the same time, we have remained vociferous critics of any attempt to curtail free speech. In the Public Enemy dilemma, these two agendas are pitted against each other. Danny Goldberg, former chair of the ACLU Foundation of Southern California and president of Gold Mountain Entertainment, a personal management agency, summed up the conflict when he wrote that "the real issue here lies in the conflict between the need for free expression and the desire to fight bigotry."

Should Jewish organizations have supported efforts to ban such expressions of hate?

Response

The debate involving Public Enemy's lyrics illustrates that Jews are found on both sides. Jewish groups denounced the lyrics as an overt and offensive anti-Semitic attack on the Jewish community. Some militant Jews demanded that the song be removed from the airways.

Others, including the UAHC, feared that censorship would only hurt minorities, especially Jews, arguing that the best way to deal with offensive speech is to condemn it, not cut it off.

If American Jews have attained an unprecedented measure of security and success in America, one major reason is the majestic sweep of the Constitution and its Bill of Rights. Indeed, the Constitution protects every American but especially those who are, by definition, different (i.e., minorities). For Jews, the Bill of Rights is the very sanctuary of our liberties. It keeps us from being what we

have been virtually everywhere else in all the centuries of our wan-
derings: strangers at the gates, subject to the vagaries of popular
opinion and prejudice.

Here, in America, as nowhere else in our long history, Jews as
individual citizens enjoy equal justice. Here, too, we are free to
live Jewish lives and to speak out as a community on great public
issues in accordance with the ethical insights of our tradition.

If the Bill of Rights is our primary protection, it is nonetheless
true that tension sometimes exists between the rights of free
expression and our sense of dignity and security. Every year seems
to generate new examples of such dilemmas:

- A university invites Reverend Louis Farrakhan, considered a blatant anti-Semite by most Jews, to address the student body.

- A gang of neofascist skinheads seeks to recruit students at a local junior high school.

- A former high official of the KKK runs for the United States
  Senate.

- A racist organization runs newspaper ads inviting open debate
  on whether the Holocaust really happened.

America's Revolutionary
Contribution to the Concept of Rights

In the 1980s, the attack on our fundamental liberties arose primarily from a new and particularly pernicious source: the Religious Right. It vigorously backed right-wing candidates who supported prayer in schools, scientific creationism (teaching the Bible
instead of evolution), eliminating school busing, and rescinding
abortion rights.

The danger posed by the political vision of the Religious Right
offers dramatic insight into the unique concept of fundamental rights
as it developed in America. To understand the nature of America's

freedoms, we need to take a brief journey through the history of "rights" in Western civilization.

Prior to the creation of our Constitution, the rights one enjoyed were "derivative" or "subsidiary" rights (i.e., they came by dint of one's membership in some *group* or *class*). Wherever Jews lived, the leaders of their community negotiated the rights their members were accorded. No country supported the concept of *individual* citizenship with inherent *individual* rights, the very foundation of American life.

The true revolutionary genius of America was to reverse the relationship between the group and the individual, declaring that our "inalienable," God-given rights were not granted from without but came from *within*. Among these rights were life, liberty, freedom of speech, press, worship, assembly, and the right to petition the government for redress of grievances. The role of government was not to ladle out those rights but to protect them. Failure to do so, argued Thomas Jefferson, was grounds to change the government, even by revolution if necessary.

Thus, America became the first country in the world in which one's basic rights were not subject to arbitrary limitation by the government or the whims of the majority.

In America, it does not matter whether all 250 million Americans believe that what you say is absurd; it does not matter whether the 535 members of the Congress, the nine members of the Supreme Court, and the president of the United States agree that the way you worship is incorrect. So long as your exercise of your rights does not interfere with the exercise of the rights of anyone else or does not endanger the nation, you have the inalienable right to say what you want and to worship the way you want.

In America, as in any genuine democracy, we celebrate these rights not just for their own sake but because only through the exercise of these rights in a free marketplace of ideas can we find out what is best for society. This ability to test ideas allows us to discover truth.

The Religious Right asserted a contrary vision of America: the vision of a nation based on certain fundamental and unalterable *Christian* values. And, if the use of coercive muscle of government was necessary to control what we read in libraries and schools (censorship), how we pray (school prayer), what we learn in biology (scientific creationism), and what we see in our art galleries or on our televisions, then so be it.

Two radically different visions of America fought it out on the political battleground of the 1980s. As with Senator McCarthy in the 1950s, the Jerry Falwells and Pat Robertsons of the Religious Right represented those who were afraid of the great American experiment of democracy, afraid to test their beliefs and policies in the robust clash of ideas. That they are willing to jeopardize the First Amendment and our basic rights to impose their goals on our society alarmed all who cherish freedom.

In fact, the American people repudiated the Religious Right, just as they had the late Senator Joe McCarthy. Not a single agenda item of the Religious Right was implemented into law on the national level. And where these items were enacted on the state level, state and federal courts generally struck them down as unconstitutional, albeit by decreasing margins on the High Court as Presidents Reagan and Bush appointed more and more judges.

Compelling State Interest and Fundamental Rights

We know that the Constitution and the Declaration of Independence hold that fundamental rights are ours by dint of our humanity. But what happens when a fundamental right comes face to face with a conflicting societal interest? How do we decide when the societal interest must give way, and when the fundamental right? How do we avoid creating an anarchic society in which murder may be defended as ritual sacrifice without creating a fascist society where every individual is subservient to the state? The Court had previously answered this question by ruling that fundamental rights could be abridged by the state only when the state could prove a compelling interest in doing so and only if the state then abridged that right as narrowly as possible.

The most famous illustration of this is the restriction against yelling "fire" in a crowded theater when there is no fire. An individual's right to free speech must give way to the state's "compelling interest" in public safety. And, while the state can narrowly prevent one from saying something that endangers public safety (e.g., falsely crying "fire"), the state (as opposed to the theater) cannot prevent a person from otherwise talking in theaters.

In 1990, in the *Employment Division of Oregon* v. *Smith* decision, the Supreme Court entirely discarded the "compelling state interest" test in favor of a more general interest. Now, to prevent religious rituals from being impacted by general state laws, we must lobby state legislatures for religious exemptions rather than having these rights protected by the courts. This turns the two-centuries-old American understanding of fundamental rights on its head, suggesting now that these rights no longer proceed from our own humanity but must be granted by elected legislatures and subjected to the whims of the majority. If the Court applies the same analysis to our other fundamental rights, then we will be saying *Kaddish* for our basic liberties in this decade of the 200th anniversary of the Bill of Rights.

When Free Speech and Jewish Security Collide

In the American experience, Jews have tended to be strong supporters of civil liberties. It is no accident that Jews constitute a significant proportion of the membership of the American Civil Liberties Union (ACLU), the principal nongovernmental agency in America dedicated to safeguarding the First Amendment of the Constitution. To the ACLU, the right to a free press and free expression is virtually absolute for everyone including Nazis and Communist party members. To begin to make exceptions, even in a good cause, is to begin to whittle away the force of the American Constitution. To its critics, the ACLU is rigid, unrealistic, and extremist.

For the past fifty years, American Jews have tended to identify Jewish security with the maintenance of the very constitutional freedoms the ACLU seeks to defend against all threats.

Nothing dramatized these tensions more vividly than the gut-wrenching conflict over the right of Nazis to march in Skokie, Illinois.

A Real Dilemma: Should Nazis March in Skokie?

Skokie, Illinois, is a suburb of Chicago that in 1978 had a population of approximately sixty thousand persons, including some forty thousand Jews of whom seven thousand were survivors of Nazi concentration camps. To America—and perhaps to much of the world—Skokie is remembered as the place where American Nazis sought to organize a protest march in 1978 "to combat Jewish control of America." City officials refused to grant a license for such a demonstration. The Nazis went to court, asserting that their First Amendment right to march publicly in Nazi uniform and to express their ideas had been violated.

The American Civil Liberties Union went to court in *support* of the right of the Nazis to march. Opponents argued that, just as one cannot yell "fire" falsely in a crowded theater because of the harm it would do, American Nazis displaying swastikas and yelling anti-Jewish obscenities should not be allowed to inflict emotional harm on concentration camp survivors. Leaders of the Jewish Defense League (JDL), a militant right-wing Jewish group that advocated using force to protect Jewish interests, announced that, whatever the courts held, that group would forcibly prevent the Nazis from marching. Mainstream Jewish organizations had to respond both to the Nazis and to the JDL. What should they have done?

Response

While most Jewish organizations agreed that Nazis have freedom of speech, even for their repellent message, the Jewish community split on the substantive issue: Do the Nazis have the right to bring that noxious message to a specific neighborhood where it would cause pain to a particular group: the Holocaust survivors of Skokie? In the end, the UAHC, while continuing efforts to have the locale switched, decided not to express formal opposition to the march for substantive and tactical reasons. First, in our view, the effort to block them had given this tiny crew of misfits millions of dollars worth of publicity. Second, all decent Americans oppose Nazi kooks, and this should not be Jews vs. Nazis but Americans vs. Nazis. Finally, we were doomed to lose in the courts, and it would be better to get the march over with and off the network news so that the Nazi termites would return to the woodwork.

In the end, as the danger of violent confrontation reached a fever pitch, the Nazis relocated their planned march from Skokie to Marquette Park in Chicago, where it passed with only minor disturbances.

The Skokie dilemma raised many disturbing questions among America's Jews. How secure are we really? Can we rely for our safety on the abstractions of constitutional safeguards? Should we support the approach of Canada, where speech advocating group hatred is a crime? Have we become so liberal that we have bartered away our particular Jewish interests for a vague universalism? Or, on the other hand, have we become so intimidated by extremists that we would sacrifice long-term protections (preservation of the First Amendment) for short-term gains (banning anti-Semitic displays)? Has the Jewish community abandoned its faith in civil liberties now that the issue has come home to roost for us, just as some Jews gave up on racial integration when it came to *our* schools and *our* neighborhoods?

A Real Dilemma: Jews for Jesus

A branch of Jews for Jesus reserved space for a conference in a local hotel. The town's rabbi criticized the hotel for allowing its premises to be used by an organization that pretends to be a movement of Judaism but is condemned by all branches of Judaism. The area ACLU defended the hotel's right to rent to Jews for Jesus, however repugnant the group may have been to other Jews. What would you have advised? Should the Jewish community have sought to persuade the hotel to cancel the meeting? Should other, less restrictive options have been employed, such as organizing a countermeeting to educate the public about the "false advertising of Jews for Jesus"? Does the right of free speech extend to those who advertise falsely?

Response

Many Jewish groups did try to get the meeting canceled, and they succeeded, arguing this was not a free speech issue but one of false advertising. The Supreme Court has held that there is a "compelling state interest" in preventing false advertising, even if it means limiting free speech. In this situation, the Jewish community pressured the hotel into canceling the meeting. Jews for Jesus went to court, claiming invasion of its First Amendment rights. The court did not sustain their claim.

Censorship

Censorship can be defined as any action by an individual, a group of individuals, and/or by the government that results in the removal, alteration, or repression of a particular item because that item is deemed objectionable, preventing other individuals, or groups of individuals, from gaining access to that item. The "item" may be a book, a piece of art, a theater performance, a school curriculum, or anything else that can be defined as a form of expression.

Since censorship can be both direct (through governmental sanction) and indirect (through the withdrawing of otherwise approved funding), the consequences are more important than the motivations. For example, an attempt to prevent the American Nazi party from distributing its literature, however well-intentioned, is still censorship because it results in preventing those who wish to be exposed to the Nazis' message from doing so. Attempts to restrict public funding of the arts on the grounds that tax dollars should not be used to support what many might consider obscene is another manifestation of censorship. Which art will be funded and which will not should be determined on the basis of artistic merit, not on the *message* of the art.

Both nationally and locally, Jews have been outspoken opponents of censorship, believing that the First Amendment becomes an empty, meaningless promise when applied selectively. When Jews have held ideologies or have been members of political groups considered to be offensive by mainstream American society (a few as members of the Communist party in the 1930s; more as members of civil rights organizations and as anti-Vietnam War protesters in the sixties and seventies), we have been quick to condemn the selective application of the First Amendment. We have asserted that even those who advocate the overthrow of the United States government should not be prosecuted as long as their words are not translated into illegal acts. The Jewish commitment to free speech, both as Jews and as members of a democratic society, must not falter simply when it is now *our* ox that is being gored.

Censorship and the Jewish Tradition

Judaism was, arguably, the first legal tradition in history to enshrine the concept of majority and minority views. If one reads the classic texts of the talmudic/rabbinic era, the *Mishnah* and the *Gemara,* every page brims with the arguments both of the majority and of those who dissented against them, recognizing that each reflected aspects of God's truth. Implicit in such an approach was the realization that today's minority could become tomorrow's majority.

Our almost automatic opposition to censorship, wherever it occurs, reflects a long Jewish history in which learning and the cultivation of the mind have been seen as deeply pious acts. In medieval Europe, when most of their Christian neighbors were illiterate, Jews undertook to teach every child how to read. That tradition lives on. The population of Israel reads more books per capita than any other nation in the world. And that tradition drives our defense of academic freedom in America.

Jewish tradition cherishes free speech. "When a person refrains from speech, the ideas die, the soul stops, and the senses deteriorate," said Moses ibn Ezra, insisting on respect for honest differences of opinion. (*Shirat Yisrael* 12c) The assertion of unpopular opinions permeates the Bible: the prophet Nathan denouncing King David for having stolen Bathsheba from her husband; Elijah excoriating King Ahab for his evil doings; prophets chastising neighbors and ruling powers alike; Job asserting his innocence; Abraham arguing with God—these are but a few of the many examples of fiercely unpopular opinions freely and openly expressed.

This tradition continued over the centuries. The schools of Hillel and Shammai differed sharply in most of their interpretations of the law; so the Talmud included both positions and an ocean of opinions, majority and minority. Studies of the *shtetl*, small Jewish towns in Eastern Europe, confirm the long tradition of respect for differing views that animated these tightly-knit Jewish communities. This regard for free expression and this sensitive respect for differences have left their mark upon modern Jews.

This is not to pretend that Jewish history was 100 percent libertarian. Often it was marred by efforts at censorship: Jeremiah was sentenced to die as a traitor; Amos was denounced; Elisha ben Abuyah was thrown out of the Sanhedrin for heresy; the writings of Maimonides were put under a ban by some scholars; Spinoza was excommunicated for his views; Orthodox rabbis have excommunicated chasidic and Reform Jewish leaders at different times in history; and, certainly, the Orthodox rabbinate in Israel is no friend of civil liberties. But these failures to implement the ideal have not destroyed the ideal itself.

Yet, because Jews had an almost universal capacity to read, these censorship efforts failed. In the end, the Jews' love of learning proved to be irreconcilable with efforts to control the mind.

Seven Incidents of Censorship in the 1980s

What do the following books have in common: *The Adventures of Huckleberry Finn; Anne Frank: Diary of a Young Girl; The Grapes of Wrath; Nineteen Eighty-Four; To Kill a Mockingbird; The Scarlet Letter; Of Mice and Men;* and *One Day in the Life of Ivan Denisovic?* In 1990, they were the targets of censorship by local communities across America. Below are examples of other censorship campaigns conducted by right-wing groups in the 1980s, as documented by People for the American Way:

1. 1982: Phyllis Schlafly's Eagle Forum objected to the teaching of certain classics in the high schools of St. David, Arizona. School administrators responded by eliminating all required reading lists and by refusing to renew the contracts of teachers who had protested the censorship.

2. 1983: In Folsom, California, a teacher labeled thirteen words in *The American Heritage Dictionary* as "inappropriate." Offended by the inclusion of such words as "French kiss" and "queer," the teacher and the principal quarantined 146 copies of this "subversive" text in a storage closet.

3. 1983–1984: Despite recommendations from a review committee that the book be retained, school district officials in Greenwood, South Carolina, removed the sex-education book *Finding My Way* from their curriculum and libraries. The Pro-Family Forum had denounced the book for allegedly advocating "secular humanism."

4. 1985: A Hanover, Massachusetts, school superintendent removed the book *Go Ask Alice* from the library of the South Shore Vocational and Technical High School because of its "profanity" and "explicit descriptions of experiences of a prostitute."

5. 1986: A group of parents in Lolo, Montana, succeeded in removing highly successful innovative teaching programs from the schools. They objected to team teaching as "fostering communism" and charged that a journal writing exercise promoted

pornography because one student included "lewd" and "sex" in his poem.

6. 1987: Bowing to objections that the book encouraged rebellion against society and parents, school officials banned the book *Early Disorders* from the library of a middle school in Sequim, Washington, because of its "portrayal of anorexia nervosa . . . and 'pornographic' language."

7. 1989–1990: In Beaufort County, South Carolina, community pressure prompted the local school board to drop a state-approved high school sex education course in favor of an abstinence-only curriculum aimed at sixth graders.

People for the American Way (PFAW) documented 244 cases of censorship nationwide between 1989–1990—up from 172 one year earlier. For every censorship case it documents, PFAW estimates another ten are not documented. If correct, in 1989–1990 alone, thousands of books and other materials were removed from school libraries and curricula. As a result, tens of thousands of public school students were denied access to certain ideas and materials because somebody else thought these ideas "inappropriate." Is this the way a democratic society, interested in equipping its citizens to deal comfortably with complex and controversial issues, should educate its citizens?

Censorship from the Left

Recent attempts at censorship have come from left-wing and liberal groups as well. Motivated by genuine concerns about the rise of racist and anti-Semitic incidents over the past decade, and the alarming rise in violence against women and children, certain liberal groups have called for the censorship of art and literature they regard as racist, anti-Semitic, misogynist (antiwomen), or pornographic.

While one may certainly question the ways in which publications like *Playboy* and *Penthouse* depict women, censorship is not the answer. Preventing the local newsstand from selling pornographic magazines will do little to defeat sexism. Nor will their removal from the marketplace encourage men who view women solely as sex objects to regard them differently. It will, however, erode valuable freedoms.

Similarly, preventing the American Nazi party or the Ku Klux Klan from distributing their literature will not wipe out anti-Semitism, racism, homophobia, intolerance, or bigotry. Permitting only "politically correct" language on college campuses would stifle expression in precisely the place where free thought and discourse ought to be nurtured. Nor will banning *The Adventures of Huckleberry Finn* (as some Blacks urge because of what they see as a negative depiction of Jim) or *The Merchant of Venice* (as some Jews urge because they believe Shakespeare's depiction of Shylock feeds anti-Semitic stereotyping). Indeed, both of these works can be seen as eloquent commentaries on the evils of racism and anti-Semitism in their immediate societies.

Censorship in the Schools

> I hope I live to see the day when, as in the early days of our country, we won't have any public schools. The churches will have taken them over again and Christians will be running them.
>
> (Reverend Jerry Falwell)

The following scenario has become increasingly familiar: a small band of parents, disturbed that their children are being taught what they consider "secular humanism" and/or "situation ethics," protests the inclusion of a book in the school curriculum. One school system, while refusing to strike the book from the curriculum, did eliminate several offending passages. What was the book? *Composition and Applied Grammar: The Writing Process,* a widely used grammar textbook.

While opposition to a grammar book may seem comical, those who ban books take themselves very seriously and approach their mission with a religious fervor. Often, they seek to impose a strict fundamentalist interpretation of the Bible on every subject from science to English, denouncing opposing views as "godless" and "valueless."

The object of their wrath is so-called secular humanism, which they say pervades the educational establishment, impairs traditional Christian values, and undermines parental authority.

Groups such as Citizens for Excellence in Education (CEE), Concerned Women for America (CWA), Eagle Forum, National Legal Foundation (NLF), and Education Research Analysts (ERA) all have one goal in mind: to destroy secular education and bring public schools under fundamentalist Christian control. To achieve this goal, they carefully set up parents' committees in local communities to harass public school officials; elect like-minded individuals to local school boards; and create an atmosphere of intimidation and fear, intimidating textbook publishers from covering controversial subjects.

Dr. Robert Simmonds, founder of CEE, the activist component of the National Association of Christian Educators, has stated: "There are 15,700 school districts in America. When we can get an active Christian parents' committee (CEE) in operation in all districts, we can take complete control of all local school boards. This would allow us to determine all local policy: *select good textbooks, good curriculum programs, superintendents, and principals. Our time has come!*"

The Gablers: Establishing a Link between Mathematics and Drug Abuse

Mel and Norma Gabler have a mission as they see it: a mission from God. In the worldview of the Gablers, nothing is as it seems. Every topic of discussion in the classroom reflects the struggle between the forces of good and evil, between the forces of the Christian God and the "secular humanist" anti-Christ. The Gablers have targeted a variety of standard textbooks as the demonic instruments by which atheists and secular humanists are converting impressionable young minds to their faith. "Until textbooks are changed," they have declared, "there is no possibility that crime, violence, venereal disease, and abortion rates will decrease." Their views on countless academic topics reveal this paranoid view of academic inquiry and exploration. Consider the following example concerning the teaching of math:

> When a student reads in a math book that there are no absolutes, suddenly every value he's been taught has been destroyed. And, the next thing you know, the student turns to crime and drugs.
> (Donna Hulsizer, *Protecting the Freedom to Learn* [Washington: People for the American Way, 1989], p. 15)

If the Gablers were merely a kooky couple who spent their time complaining about the state of the world, their primitive views would be nothing more than a curious amusement. But they are not, and it is not. They are, in fact, founders of Educational Research Analysts (ERA), a Texas-based group that appoints itself to "monitor" textbooks for offensive material. If the examples of the Gablers' wisdom (or lack thereof) quoted above left you chuckling, don't laugh too loud: chances are that some, if not all, of your textbooks have been modified to mollify the Gablers.

Since founding Educational Research Analysts in 1973, the Gablers have had a powerful influence on which textbooks are approved for use in Texas public schools and which are not. As Texas and California are the largest textbook markets in the country, publishers have traditionally geared their textbooks to sell well in these two states. In 1991, the two states announced their intention to begin purchasing the same textbooks—a decision that could give them extraordinary control over which textbooks survive financially in America.

With the Gablers' impressive influence in Texas, this means that for the past nineteen years textbook publishers have been reluctant to include anything in their textbooks that the Gablers—and others of their ilk—would find offensive. The results have been devastating. If your biology textbook made little or no mention of evolution, thank the Gablers. If your American history textbook skipped over the Vietnam War, the problems faced by Native Americans, or slavery, thank the Gablers. If your European history textbook ignored the Crusades, the Spanish Inquisition, or the Holocaust, the Gablers may be responsible.

Censorship in the Arts

A Real Dilemma: NEA Funding

Jewish organizations have a long history of opposing censorship. Recently, however, a new and difficult issue emerged that stretched the definition of censorship almost beyond recognition.

In 1989, two United States senators, Jesse Helms from North Carolina and Alfonse D'Amato from New York, pressed legislation to withdraw funding for the National Endowment of the Arts (NEA) because of its sponsorship of such controversial, "homoerotic" art as the photographic exhibit of Robert Mapelthorpe.

A retrospective of that artist's work was to be exhibited at the Corcoran Gallery of Art in Washington, D.C., an institution that receives funding from the NEA. The Corcoran had selected this exhibit based on its artistic merit. Objecting especially to works they deemed child pornography and homoerotic (neither senator had actually seen the show), the senators made slightly veiled threats regarding the Corcoran's continued funding if it did not immediately cancel the upcoming show. They argued that taxpayer money should not be used to support art that offends the sensibility of the public.

They argued that what they were doing was not censorship since the museum could display the art as long as the display was not financed through government funding.

This pressure against the NEA succeeded in canceling the

show at the Corcoran just weeks before it was to have opened. The National Endowment for the Arts then began to withhold funding from avant garde artists whose paintings, writings, and poetry were judged to be offensive to community standards. Further, the NEA tried to require artists who seek individual grants to sign a kind of "loyalty oath": a statement that they will not use NEA funds to produce "offensive" or "pornographic" art.

Is this censorship? Should Jewish organizations take a stand on this issue?

Response

Many Jewish organizations saw this as too close to call. The UAHC, however, took a strong stand against the proposed restrictions on NEA funding. We saw this as a clear affront to our First Amendment right to freedom of expression.

For the government to sponsor or not sponsor art on the basis of a political consideration is to say, *"This* particular idea or mode of expression is correct, but *this* one is not." Such a statement, even though not accompanied by legal sanctions of any kind, clearly is at odds with the spirit of the First Amendment.

If the government is going to remain neutral, it should allocate its money on the basis of artistic merit, not content. Such, in fact, has long been the formal mandate of the NEA.

Privacy and the Jewish Tradition

The right to privacy has ancient Jewish antecedents. In commenting on the story of Balaam's refusal to curse the children of Israel, the Talmud tells us that "he saw that the entrances to their tents were not directly opposite each other, so that one family did not visually intrude on the privacy of the other." (B. Talmud, *Baba Batra* 60a) This legend presaged the ruling that houses in Jewish communities had to be built so that residents of one house could not look into the homes of neighbors. If the builder failed to abide by this rule, he was required to erect at his own expense a wall that protected the privacy of the neighbors. (*Baba Batra* 6b)

Today, perhaps more than ever before, personal privacy is at risk. Wiretaps, electronic bugging, and computerized filing systems can yield vast amounts of information to secret intelligence agencies and credit rating corporations, among others.

The late Supreme Court Justice William O. Douglas warned that personal privacy "has almost vanished in the United States." He added that Americans "may, in time, rebel against its loss."

The Fourth Amendment to the Constitution reads:

> The rights of the people to be secure in their persons, houses, papers, and effects against unreasonable searches and seizures shall not be violated and no warrants shall issue but upon probable cause, supported by oath or affirmation, and particularly describing the place to be searched, and the person or things to be seized.

Jewish law went even beyond the modern Fourth Amendment in securing a person's right to privacy, as illustrated in Exodus 22:25–26 and quoted in Deuteronomy 24:10–11: "When you lend your neighbor any manner of loan, you shall not go into his house to fetch your pledge. You shall stand outside, and the person to whom you made the loan shall bring the pledge to you."

Eavesdropping, gossipmongering, and slander are strongly condemned in Jewish teaching. Unauthorized disclosure of information was strictly prohibited. In the Talmud, we read that Rabbi Ami expelled a scholar from the academy because he disclosed a report he had received confidentially *twenty-two* years earlier. By the eleventh century, the privacy of mail was absolutely safeguarded by Rabbenu Gershom.

In Judaism, privacy was seen as an aspect of one's sanctity as a child of God and as a shield to human personality. Without this protection, one is stripped of individuality and selfhood—dehumanized. Jewish sensitivity to civil liberties—and to the precious right to be left alone—has much relevance to our current struggle to resist the onslaught of brainwashing, subliminal advertising, bugging, wiretapping, and other technological intrusions.

A Real Dilemma: A Friend Contemplates Suicide

Josh is a camper at a UAHC camp. His father taught him about the growing plague of youth suicide and gave him a copy of Sol Gordon's book *When Living Hurts* (New York: UAHC Press, 1985), which lists some of the danger signals of youngsters contemplating suicide. The book urges intervention if one sees a friend or a classmate showing these telltale signs. Josh became painfully aware that one of his bunkmates, Sam, was acting strangely and saying things that fit the description of a person at risk. Sam confided in Josh: "Nobody loves me. . . . Nobody will care if I die. . . . What's the use of going on like this?" Josh went to his counselor and told him about Sam. Sam was called in and, later, lashed out at Josh for invading his privacy. Did Josh do the right thing? What would you have done?

Response

Josh felt terrible at first, but he may have saved Sam's life. In the Jewish tradition, the principle of *pikuach nefesh* requires that to save a life almost any Jewish law can and should be broken—including the obligation to keep secrets. Sam was crying out for help; Josh heard him and took responsibility. He did the right thing.

Privacy and Testing for Drugs and AIDS

In the United States, the right to privacy has faced a particular widespread challenge in the recent trend towards drug testing in the workplace. Many companies and some federal agencies have instituted random urine tests for drug use for all employees. While employers and the public have a clear interest in maintaining a drug-free workplace, the right of a person to "be left alone" is flagrantly violated by a urine test, which is degrading, sometimes inaccurate, and unrestricted by the rule of law.

Only when there is a "compelling state interest" in limiting our privacy, such as when there is "probable cause" to suspect a crime or when the workers are responsible for public safety (e.g., pilots, nuclear plant operators, and school bus drivers), should such testing be mandated. The basic concept of "innocent until proven guilty" embodies the idea that, unless there is probable cause to suspect someone of a crime, the government cannot invade that person's privacy. While this standard applies in theory to the government and not to private employers, our basic freedoms will be sharply curtailed if private parties feel free to use modern technology to invade our privacy and find out information about us we wish to keep secret. Workplace drug testing opens a Pandora's box.

Furthermore, such invasions of the privacy of employees can reveal extensive information unrelated to the drug issue. Urinalysis can disclose not only drug use but also if an employee or job applicant is being treated for a heart condition, depression, epilepsy, or diabetes; it can reveal if a woman is pregnant. To allow employers, in the public or private sector, to have indiscriminate access to such information is to rip away the right to privacy, which Supreme Court Justice Louis Brandeis called "the most comprehensive of rights and the right most valued by civilized men."

In 1989, the Supreme Court upheld the right of federal agencies to test employees for drug use without reasonable suspicion. The Court ruled that the employees' right to privacy was outweighed by the government's interest in insuring a drug-free workplace. Lower courts and state legislation have been more restrictive in the use of drug testing, allowing it only in individual cases where there is sufficient suspicion of criminal use of drugs or in jobs involving public safety. Usually such legislation also requires confirmatory tests and confidential handling of the results.

The urgency of AIDS raises a host of issues surrounding privacy and civil liberties. (For an in-depth discussion, see Chapter 12, "Life-and-Death Issues.")

A Jewish Seat on the Court?

The larger question of Jewish vigilance on matters of civil liberties issues may be seen through the prism of the question of a "Jewish seat" on the Supreme Court. Recently, one federal judge raised a surprising question about the religious composition of the Supreme Court. Judge Stephen Rheinhart of California, in a speech in 1990, asked: "Why no Jews on the Supreme Court?" Answering his own question, the judge, himself Jewish, blamed the Jewish community for "a conspiracy of silence" in failing to demand the perpetuation of a "Jewish seat" on the Court. This argument was forcefully echoed in the 1991 book, *Chutzpah,* by Alan Dershowitz, a Harvard law professor.

Once, Rheinhart recalled, there was a "Jewish seat," and it was occupied with great distinction by Louis Brandeis (1916–1939), Felix Frankfurter (1939–1962), Arthur Goldberg (1962–1965), and Abe Fortas (1965–1969). To Rheinhart (a liberal judge appointed by President Jimmy Carter), these judges reflected a wisdom and integrity that owed much to the sensitivity derived from their Jewish heritage.

Why had Jews not pushed President Nixon and succeeding presidents to continue the "Jewish seat"? The judge believes it was a fear of stirring up anti-Semitism as well as the "mistaken belief" that, in a new era of equality, Jews would be appointed on merit alone.

Should Jews fight for a "Jewish seat" on the Supreme Court as a way of helping to ensure that our civil liberties are protected?

Almost all Jewish organizations have resisted calls for a "Jewish seat" although they strongly hope that there will be the appointment of a Jew with excellent legal credentials in the near future. It is true that ethnic and racial considerations have played a role in Court nominations: Thurgood Marshall and Clarence Thomas, the first Blacks, and Sandra Day O'Connor, the first woman, were obviously selected not merely for their judicial excellence. It is another thing, however, to designate seats specifically as black, female, Jewish, disabled. Many feel this would introduce an obnoxious quota system into a court system in which justice is better served if the admirable goal of diversity is not permitted to compromise the principle of merit.

A Real Dilemma: The Thomas Nomination

The question of a "Jewish seat" is today rather academic. For the black community, however, the right to a "black seat" on the Supreme Court became very real indeed. Justice Thurgood Marshall served on the Court with great distinction for seventeen years. When he retired in 1991, President George Bush named Clarence Thomas as Marshall's successor. While Thomas's lack of experience and deeply conservative philosophy, including his opposition to affirmative action, made him suspect to black leadership, there was deep ambivalence about opposing him. A majority of grass-roots Blacks rallied to his support. Even those who disliked his views felt racial pride in his remarkable rise from poverty. And, if he were defeated, with the help of the NAACP and other black organizations, would the president send up another black nominee? Not likely.

Moreover, was not the presence of a black man on the Supreme Court more important, actually and symbolically, than the divergent and perhaps controversial nature of his opinions on some issues? Appointed to the Court for life, was it not likely he would surprise his ideological supporters with his own independent views?

If you were a black person, would you have agreed with this argument and supported Thomas? If the candidate were Jewish, would you support him solely out of group solidarity and pride? If you were a member of the Commission on Social Action, a joint instrumentality of the UAHC and the Central Conference of American Rabbis (CCAR), responsible for debating and developing policy on issues of social justice, how would you have voted on the question whether the Reform movement should oppose or support the nomination of Clarence Thomas for the United States Supreme Court?

Response

Both black and Jewish organizations were divided on the Thomas nomination. The NAACP opposed him; so did the Leadership Conference on Civil Rights. The Urban League and the Southern Christian Leadership Conference were neutral. In the Jewish world, the Jewish Labor Committee, the National Council of Jewish Women, and the Union of American Hebrew Congregations opposed; the American Jewish Committee and the Anti-Defamation League were neutral; and the Orthodox community endorsed Thomas. All these decisions were made *before* the tumultuous controversy over sexual harassment charges leveled by Professor Anita Hill against the nominee.

You Can Make a Difference

As the Supreme Court withdraws from its historic role as the primary guarantor of our fundamental rights, and as it turns decisions regarding those rights back to the states and localities, the role of individual activists takes on greater significance.

An individual, by taking a stand, can make a difference in the ongoing battle for freedom and civil liberties. We saw this dramatically on the world stage when Boris Yeltsin and a few other heroic leaders inspired the Russian people to defy the tanks in opposing the 1991 coup that would have reversed the Soviet Union's drive toward democracy. They made a historic difference.

Sometimes that difference can make itself felt right in your own community. The Gablers, for example, appointed themselves arbiters of what you read and learn in public schools. If this Texas couple can make a difference, so can you. Students and parents must let teachers, administrators, and school board members know that the vast majority of Americans support academic freedom as the surest road to educational excellence. Parents need to be very careful when electing school board members: look very carefully at the views of candidates, ask for definitions of vague references to "traditional" and "family" values, and demand that candidates for the school board are committed to academic freedom.

Lastly, where necessary, create a local coalition of concerned groups to monitor censorship efforts in your schools and local libraries, and be ready to take a stand against attempts at censorship.

A Real Dilemma: Standing Up for Free Speech

In the winter of 1975, when the Jewish world was reeling from the shock of a United Nations resolution equating Zionism with racism, protests and demonstrations were mounted everywhere. In Dallas, 2,000 delegates to the General Assembly of the UAHC, led by the youth delegation of the North American Federation of Temple Youth (NFTY), joined in passionate song and prayer against this international anti-Semitic outrage. Similarly, in thousands of local communities, Jews called upon their Christian neighbors to rally with them to protest the United Nations resolution.

In one California city—San Jose—Jewish youngsters from the Reform Temple Emanu-El gathered at a nearby shopping center to collect signatures on a petition opposing the United Nations resolution. Leading the temple youths were Michael Robins and David Marcus. The managers of the shopping center (Pruneyard) came out and accused the petitioners of "trespassing on private property" and demanded they leave the shopping center. Michael and David refused, contending that they had a right to reach the public and that a petition is a fundamental expression of free speech. The boys were outraged by what they regarded as a denial of their civil rights. They shared their concern with their families and others in the congregation. What should they and the Jewish community have done about it?

Response

An attorney, who was past president of the temple (Philip Hammer), agreed to take their case without charge. In court, they asserted the right of free speech at privately owned shopping centers, arguing that such premises are public forums. Viewing this case as a threat to their property rights, the shopping center owners spent more than $250,000 before the United States Supreme Court finally resolved the case.

Step by step, Michael and David pushed their case through the legal system, losing in the superior court, appealing to the next higher court. Finally, after five years, the Supreme Court, in June of 1980, handed down its landmark decision *(Pruneyard Shopping Center* v. *Robins et al.)* unanimously upholding the right of Michael and David—and, therefore, all citizens—to freedom of speech and assembly on the premises of a privately owned shopping center that is open to the public. Michael and David had struck a blow not only for their own rights; they had enlarged the definition of civil liberties for all Americans.

"Some people thought it was an absurd attempt," said Michael after the victory. "They didn't think we could take on big business and win. But, in this case, the democratic process worked—financial resources were not an issue." Added David: "It proves that the individual can still make a difference. Two people can still make their mark on society." David celebrated by having lunch with his father, a Jewish educator who had come to America to escape Nazi persecution. He had taught David that free speech is always worth fighting for.

≡ 5 ≡

RELIGIOUS LIBERTY

Double Jeopardy: The Twin Threats to Freedom of and Freedom from Religion

The religious freedom provisions in the First Amendment of the Constitution are embodied in two key clauses: the establishment clause and the free exercise clause. These two clauses that begin the Bill of Rights read: "Congress shall make no law respecting an establishment of religion, or prohibiting the free exercise thereof. . . ." Using the Fourteenth Amendment, the Court has extended these prohibitions to state and local governments. Now, as we enter the third century of the Constitution and its Bill of Rights, these twin pillars of religious liberty are under severe attack from a conservative Supreme Court anxious to limit the Court's role as guarantor of rights and insensitive to the concerns of religious minorities.

In 1990, the Supreme Court issued a decision that, although comparatively little noted, was perhaps the most revolutionary decision on religious rights in this century. The damage done to the free exercise clause—that part of the First Amendment that guarantees freedom of religion—was staggering.

The case was *Employment Division of Oregon* v. *Smith*. Dealing with the right of Native Americans to use peyote in religious ceremonies as they have done for centuries, the Court virtually ignored this specific issue. Instead, the Supreme Court greatly

65

weakened the protection of freedom of religion, casting a pall over a two hundred-year-old tradition of religious liberty in America.

Until this case, the Court had always held that our First Amendment rights were "fundamental" or "inalienable" rights that came from being a God-created human being. No Congress or legislature could arbitrarily take such rights away; they had to be given special protection. As discussed in Chapter 4, "Civil Liberties," over the past several decades, the Court translated this idea into a "compelling state interest" test; in the realm of religious liberty, this meant that the state had to exempt religious groups from general laws unless it could prove a compelling reason not to.

Two examples: While the Court had ruled, in *Wisconsin* v. *Yoder,* that the state of Wisconsin could not prove a compelling state interest in forcing Amish children to attend school beyond the eighth grade (violating their religious beliefs), the Court later ruled, in *United States* v. *Lee,* that the federal government had a compelling interest in requiring an Amish employer to withhold social security taxes from his predominantly Amish employees' wages.

Although the "compelling state interest" standard had allowed the court to strike a balance in difficult cases in which the needs of government conflicted with religious liberty, in *Employment Division of Oregon* v. *Smith,* the Supreme Court threw the "compelling state interest" criterion into the dustbin.

In the aftermath of *Smith,* when facing laws restricting free exercise, religious constituents must now appeal to their state legislature for protection of religious practices that had previously been considered constitutionally protected. Justice Antonin Scalia, writing for the majority, sent an ominous message to all religious groups when he stated that the traditional protection of religious freedom—the "compelling state interest" test—is a "luxury" that America can no longer afford.

The implications of this ruling are staggering. Armed with *Smith*-shaped jurisprudence, courts could conceivably ban the use of sacramental wine by Christian and Jewish minors, deny the right of students to wear religious garments like yarmulkes (head coverings), and forbid public school students from taking time off for religious holidays. Through the doorway opened by the *Smith* decision, government-sponsored restrictions on religion have already found their way into American life.

Indeed, lower courts, responding to *Smith*, have already handed down rulings in favor of the state and against minority religious practices in several cases:

- *Minnesota* v. *Hershberger*, where the Amish objection to putting large orange reflecting triangles on the back of their buggies was rejected.

- *Montgomery* v. *County of Clinton*, where a Jewish woman's objection to an autopsy on her son (because it violated Jewish law) was spurned.

- *Hunafa* v. *Murphy*, where a Muslim prisoner's objection to being served pork in violation of his religious practices was brushed aside.

In these and scores of similar decisions, courts indicated the result would have been different before *Smith*.

This incursion into the most fundamental of our civil liberties—freedom of religion—is disconcerting evidence that the cornerstone of the great American experiment must be given determined protection, lest it be dismantled brick by brick. So long as the Court does not function as the guarantor of our basic rights, it will fall to Congress to preserve these rights. Thus, in the early 1990s, Congress considered the Religious Freedom Restoration Act (RFRA), which would restore the "compelling state interest" test.

Unfortunately, freedom *of* religion is not the only religious freedom currently in peril.

A Real Dilemma: Prayer at Graduation Ceremonies

In 1989, Daniel Weisman's daughter, Deborah, graduated from the Nathan Bishop Middle School in Providence, Rhode Island. Like many across the country, this graduation ceremony began with an opening prayer, delivered in this instance by a Reform rabbi. Believing that this religious presence at a public, federally funded school violated the separation of church and state provisions of the First Amendment, Daniel Weisman brought the case, known as *Lee* v. *Weisman,* to court.

Lower federal courts ruled in favor of the Weismans, stating that graduation prayers amounted to an official endorsement of religion in violation of the establishment clause of the First Amendment. At the urging of the Bush administration, which supports school prayer, the United States Supreme Court agreed to review the case.

Actually, the case began the previous year when a Christian clergyman gave the prayer at the graduation ceremony in the name of "the Father, the Son, and the Holy Ghost." When school officials were challenged on this, Rabbi Leslie Gutterman was asked to deliver the prayer the following year. Even though this constituted a "religious" prayer in a state instrumentality (a school), the intent was to provide a prayer that would be universal instead of sectarian and divisive. If you were the rabbi, would you have accepted the invitation or not? Why? If you were the CCAR and the UAHC, would you have supported or opposed the Weisman's position in the Supreme Court?

Response

Rabbi Gutterman agreed to do the opening prayer. The rabbi, who believes strongly in church-state separation, felt that a general and universal mention of God in such a ceremonial setting was not itself a violation of church-state separation. In addition, he believed it would avoid the discomfort that a Christian sectarian prayer had caused for Jewish youngsters in the past.

Rabbi Gutterman was startled to find that his words were being used by forces hostile to church-state separation and the case was going to the Supreme Court as a landmark test of religious liberty. When the Department of Justice asked the Supreme Court to use the case to redefine the traditional separation of church and state, both Rabbi Gutterman and the Reform movement became deeply concerned that his invocation might be used to redefine the First Amendment through a Supreme Court *endorsement* of prayer in the public school classroom. The UAHC and CCAR supported the Weismans, arguing that even a nondenominational prayer is a violation of the First Amendment. In the end, the Supreme Court, by a narrow five to four vote, rejected the government's attempt to mandate prayer as contrary to the First Amendment.

There are many students of American Jewish life who believe that the commitment to the separation of church and state is one of the greatest contributions Jews have rendered to the enlargement of American freedom.

Bear in mind that the United States is the first country in the history of the world to build its society on the foundation of the separation between church and state. This is one of America's unique gifts to civilization and the chief guarantor of our religious liberty. The First Amendment is the cornerstone of American freedom when it states: "Congress shall make no law respecting an establishment of religion, or prohibiting the free exercise thereof. . . ."

But have we been too strict, too absolute in our defense of the First Amendment? Has our position run counter to our own Jewish interests, undermining our effort to maintain Jewish day schools through public funding? If public education is failing to maintain the quality of education that Jews cherish, should we not reassess our long-held stand? Or does strict separation of church and state remain the best policy for Jews because it is best for America?

To answer these questions, a brief history of the Jewish community's role in the struggle for church-state separation is instructive. In the twentieth century, when Jews became secure and organized as a community, they fought openly to eliminate government support for religious activity in the public schools, remove religious symbols from public property, and stop federal aid to parochial schools. We have taken this position not out of prejudice against other religious groups but as a consequence of our own long historical experience, which demonstrates that, whenever the state was controlled by any church, or vice versa, Jews—and freedom—suffer.

Only in America have we Jews been free to pursue our faith and to organize our communal lives, equal under law and in practice, without government interference. Jews also have learned, through history, that both religion and the state flourish best when they are separate. Thus, America—through its Constitution—created a system of religious liberty that has proved to be generally fair and effective, one that Jews wish to preserve. Jewish organizations frequently have gone to court to challenge violations of the First Amendment, playing a crucial role in supporting the *McCollum* case in 1947, in which an atheist non-Jew challenged a program that required children to be released for an hour of religious instruction inside the public school building

The Supreme Court upheld *McCollum* and declared released time on public school premises unconstitutional. Later, Jewish groups joined in legal challenges against such practices as Bible reading and reciting the Lord's Prayer in the public schools, arguing that religion belongs in the church, synagogue, and home, not in the public school where every child is entitled to be free from any religious compulsion or coercion, however subtle. The Supreme Court, until recently, has sustained these challenges, eliminating these practices from the public schools. The essential doctrine of the Supreme Court was articulated in *Everson* v. *Board of Education* (1947):

> The establishment of religion clause of the First Amendment means at least this: neither a state nor the federal government can set up a church. Neither can pass laws that aid one religion, aid all religions, or prefer one religion over another. Neither can force nor influence a person to go to or to remain away from church against his will or force him to profess a belief or disbelief in any religion. No person can be punished for entertaining or professing religious beliefs or disbeliefs, for church attendance or nonattendance.

> No tax in any amount, large or small, can be levied to sup-
> port any religious activities or institutions, whatever they
> may be called, or whatever form they may adopt to teach
> or practice religion. Neither a state nor the federal govern-
> ment can, openly or secretly, participate in the affairs of any
> religious organization or groups and vice versa. In the words
> of Jefferson, the clause against establishment of religion by
> law was intended to erect a wall of separation between church
> and state.

Supreme Court decisions such as this have not been universally
popular with the American public. Propaganda campaigns by right-
wing and fundamentalist groups have sought to depict these decisions as "antireligious" and as "eliminating God from the public
schools." Senators and congresspersons repeatedly sought to over-
ride the Supreme Court by introducing a constitutional amendment that would permit religious practices in the public schools.
The Republican National Convention of 1992 was heavily influ-
enced by Religious Right leaders, demanding prayer in public education.

In the past, such attempts have failed; the good sense of the
American people has recognized the folly of tampering with the
Bill of Rights.

But, as the Supreme Court tilts to the right, many of the battles
won in the past will have to be refought, this time against a judiciary less committed to strict separation and religious freedom, as
evidenced by the Oregon peyote case discussed earlier.

The Supreme Court vs. the Founders: Changing Views of the Establishment Clause

What made the *Lee* v. *Weisman* case so important was that the
Bush administration has played an aggressive role in urging the
High Court to use the case to reinterpret the Court's existing understanding of the establishment clause. For years, the courts have
decided cases involving governmental establishment of religion ac-

cording to the strict guidelines of the *"Lemon* test," named for the Supreme Court's 1971 decision in *Lemon* v. *Kurtzman.* Under the *Lemon* test, to be constitutional a law or other act of government must have: (1) a secular purpose; (2) must not have a primary effect that either advances or inhibits religion; and (3) must not foster "excessive entanglement" between religion and government.

In *Lee* v. *Weisman,* the Bush administration asked the Court to adopt a more lenient standard that would weaken the wall separating church and state. By a narrow 5 to 4 vote, the Court refused to change the existing law, thus providing a reprieve to the wall. In his decision, Justice Kennedy argued that graduation prayers endorse religion and coerce the attending graduates into religious activity. Nevertheless, it seemed clear from his decision that, in a case dealing with adults or in a setting other than a school, Justice Kennedy would have joined the four dissenters in abandoning *Lemon.* If Kennedy's "coercion" test ever becomes the new standard, it will likely end prohibitions against religious displays on public property, state support for religious schools, and state regulation of religious institutions. None of these involve actually coercing anyone into any particular religious activity—but all have long been held to be a clear violation of separation of chuch and state.

These issues must be viewed as part of the wider war over the First Amendment's establishment clause. What do the words of the First Amendment really mean? What do they allow; what don't they allow? And what purpose did the Founding Fathers intend for them? Was the establishment clause meant to prevent the state from expressing a preference for one religion over another (as Chief Justice Rehnquist argues) or was it really meant to build a "wall of separation" between church—including all religions—and state?

As contrasted with many other controversies regarding the meaning of the Bill of Rights, at least part of the specific intent of the Framers on this question is clear—and it directly repudiates the "nonpreferential" school of thought. The Founders did indeed mean to construct a wall of separation.

During the course of the original debates over the wording of the relevant section of the First Amendment—"Congress shall make no law respecting an establishment of religion, or prohibiting the free exercise thereof"—several alternative formulations were proposed:

1. One motion would have deleted the words "religion, or prohibiting the free exercise thereof," inserting in their stead, "one religious sect or society in preference to others." This is exactly the position asserted by the chief justice. Yet this motion was defeated.
2. A second motion would have stricken the entire amendment. It too was defeated.
3. A third would have substituted for the language that was ultimately approved the following: "Congress shall not make any law infringing the rights of conscience, or establishing any religious sect or society." It too was defeated.
4. Finally, a fourth effort that proposed to amend the amendment to read, "Congress shall make no law establishing any particular denomination of religion in preference to another, or prohibiting the free exercise thereof, nor shall the rights of conscience be infringed," was likewise defeated.

Four substitutes, each designed to insure that there would be no governmental discrimination in favor of (or against) a particular religion, were each defeated. In their stead, language was used that flatly prohibits the establishment of religion—not of this religion or that religion but of religion in general.

It is precisely because of this important distinction, between "preference" on the one hand and "establishment" on the other, that the Framers drafted their language this explicitly. This language speaks across the gulf of two hundred years to affirm the establishment clause as a wall separating church and state. This nation has nurtured a religious and spiritual vitality unparalleled in human history precisely because it has protected religion from government interference with it in any form, including the governmental establishment of any and all religion.

Far from being hostile to religion—as some would suggest—this policy of neutrality has allowed religion to flourish and grow with a strength and diversity unmatched anywhere in the world. Indeed, polls indicate both church/synagogue attendance and the importance of religious beliefs in the lives of its citizens are substantially higher in the United States than in any other Western country— including those with established religions.

How tragic that Chief Justice Rehnquist and others have lost sight of this fundamental connection between church-state separation and religious vitality. When religious activities—any religious activities—carry the overtones of coercive government sponsorship, these symbols of faith that lift the spirit and enliven the mind become rote rituals of uniformity that dull the spirit and stifle the mind.

Federal Aid to Education

Federal aid to religion has always been a fundamental issue in the sphere of church-state relations. Until the 1960s, the United States had never given massive public funds to private and parochial schools. From 1965 to 1985, the Elementary and Secondary Education Act opened the doors to significant funding, which was reduced but not eliminated in the 1985 *Aguilar* v. *Felton* decision of the Supreme Court.

Most Jewish groups oppose federal aid to nonpublic schools for two reasons: First, because they believe government support for religious education undermines the separation of church and state; second, because Jewish agencies are committed to the preservation of the public school as perhaps the most important training ground for democratic values in our society. Public aid to nonpublic schools diverts resources from, and thereby weakens, public education. It inevitably leads to the growth of separate networks of parochial schools, which reduces interaction of children from varied backgrounds and leads to conflict among religious groups to secure public funds. In the Netherlands, for example, state aid to church schools in the fifties and the sixties resulted in an 80 percent decline in public education.

Because private schools can select among applicants while public schools are open to all, publicly aided private schools would likely become the schools of the white middle class, abandoning poor nonwhites to public schools. The fundamental question concerns equal justice and religious freedom: Does the government have a right to give my tax money to a church whose religious teachings may violate my deepest religious conscience?

In recent years, the Jewish community has been split on the key issue of federal aid to parochial schools. The Orthodox community, which maintains a large and growing system of day schools, believes that federal aid to religious schools is not a violation of separation of church and state. Orthodox leaders have argued that the United States government must take responsibility for the education of every American child, no matter what kind of school he or she may attend. Most Jewish groups—including the Conservative and Reform movements, each of which has in the past several decades begun its own day-school systems—continue to believe that, while a person has every right to send a child to a nonpublic school that teaches religious dogma, he or she has no right to ask the government to pay for it. (See the discussion "Jewish Day Schools, Integration, and the Public Schools" in Chapter 2, "Civil Rights and Racial Justice.")

Vouchers and Educational Choice

In recent years, a new attempt at government support for parochial schools has arisen under the guise of "educational choice." President Bush has forcefully projected this proposal. Essentially, "educational choice" allows parents to choose among the public schools in a district and, in most proposals, between public and private schools. Government funds for education are given to parents in the form of tax credits or vouchers, which are then applied to tuition. Proponents argue that this approach treats all Americans equally: it gives tax credits or vouchers to the parents, and they can then choose at whichever school they want to use the money. Because the benefits go to people and not directly to the schools, proponents (including President Bush) argue that these benefits do not violate church-state separation requirements. Furthermore, they argue that the plan would create healthy competition for students (and thereby for money) among schools, giving better schools rewards for performance and encouraging poor schools to measure up.

Critics of "educational choice," including most in the Jewish community (except the Orthodox), argue that such "voucher" proposals are grave violations of the church-state separation enshrined in the Constitution's establishment clause. Both the intent of the proposal and its end result are to provide federal funds to parochial schools. Critics also point out that public schools would be severely crippled by the loss of funding that a choice plan including parochial schools would entail, as taxes are diverted from public school expenditures. Public school programs for disadvantaged children would suffer enormously, and those children, whose parents lack the resources to send their children across town or to pay private school tuition, would be left behind without the means to make a true choice for better education.

The Child Care Debate: Making Tough Choices

A Real Dilemma: Child Care

In 1990, the United States Congress, after years of delay and posturing, finally began to move on comprehensive child care legislation. Designed to help the millions of families with working parents, the bill would have put $2.5 billion into child care programs, would have greatly expanded child care slots, and would have set safety and quality standards nationwide. The Reform Jewish movement, long a supporter of some sort of national child care program, supported the bill from the start, as did most of the Jewish community.

Yet changes on church-state provisions in the bill, made just weeks before a final vote, forced the Reform movement and civil liberties groups to question their support of the bill. The original version of the bill would have allowed federal funds to go to churches and synagogues conducting child care programs, as long as those programs were nonsectarian and did not discriminate against pupils and employees on the basis of religion. Some civil libertarians felt that even this support of religious institutions violated the First Amendment; most religious groups, however, including mainstream Jewish organizations, supported this compromise.

At the last minute, however, an amendment was added to strike the limitation, allowing for federal support for overtly sectarian child care programs.

Some of the bill's supporters said that the child care bill was too important to let die over such an issue: Pass the bill, then fight these particular provisions in court. Others said that to support such a flagrant church-state violation, particularly when we could no longer count on the courts, would set a precedent that would lead to widespread destruction of First Amendment guarantees and increased governmental regulation of the religious institutions that accept these funds.

What should the Reform movement have done?

Response

As desperately as this country needs child care, the Union of American Hebrew Congregations and other Jewish groups felt that to allow the child care bill to blast a hole in the wall separating church and state would ultimately do more harm than good and to accept it would betray our own integrity.

As with many national groups, we remain passionately committed to increasing the quality and quantity of child care. But we knew that no one else would care about a Jewish couple in a small midwestern town, who, although armed with federal child care vouchers, would not be able to find a program in which their three-year-old daughter would not be expected to say the Lord's Prayer or be taught that Jesus was the son of God.

Despite the Jewish community's opposition, the bill passed. The UAHC is looking for an opportunity to contest the church-state provisions of the bill by bringing our case to the courts, but, considering the changing complexion of the judiciary, we are not optimistic.

The Survival of Public Education

A key consideration in evolving Jewish opinion about the importance of church-state separation concerns the deteriorating condition of public education in America. (See the discussion in Chapter 2, "Civil Rights and Racial Justice.")

Between 1963 and 1990, national average scores on Standard Achievement Tests (SAT) fell forty-eight points in verbal aptitude and twenty-two points in mathematical aptitude. [Source: United States Department of Education] Clearly our public schools graduate many students who are functional illiterates. For instance, each year, 40 to 60 percent of the students at the University of California are required to complete a course in remedial English. A Carnegie Foundation report concluded that "general education is now a disaster area, which instead of being shaped by a coherent educational philosophy is often determined by a number of internal and external forces—faculty interests, student concerns with the job market, 'relevance,' social fads, and the like."

These failures are particularly acute in some urban centers, where the average SAT scores of mostly minority students are as much as 200 points below the national average. In New York City, only 50.3 percent of ninth graders are able to read at their grade level. To graduate, students must pass an exam that requires only eighth-grade knowledge. This shocking decline in academic achievement is accompanied in many urban schools by mounting violence and substance abuse, further impairing education.

The Carnegie Foundation's report found that SAT scores are directly proportional to family income: Students from families with income under $10,000 score an average of 768 (combined verbal and math scores) out of a possible 1,600. The average for students with family incomes in the $30,000 to $40,000 range was 884, compared to the 997 average of students from families with incomes over $70,000.

This deterioration of public education can be fatal to democracy. Illiterates are not likely to know or care about their rights. Some 47 percent of a sample of seventeen-year-olds did not know that every state elects two senators. One out of two of these youngsters believed that the president appoints members of Congress. What does this mean for the great hope of universal public education that was to cultivate a community of informed and civilized citizens as the very bedrock of democracy? How can democracy survive the intellectual wasteland of a television age, a "Me Decade," and a collapsing school system? Can public education be rescued from swift decline? How? Jews—along with all other concerned persons—must confront such questions and help find answers.

As the historic Jewish honeymoon with the public schools began to fade, Jews, like others, began to examine alternative educational systems, including private Jewish day schools.

Such schools are booming within Conservative Judaism, and the Reform movement—which had once bitterly opposed day schools as a threat to public education—now has fourteen day schools in the United States and Canada. The zealous opposition has melted away. A strong determination to give our children an excellent Jewish education—something beyond the brief hours a Sunday school education affords—has made the Jewish day school more attractive. That positive impulse, plus the negative response to the problematic aspects in many public schools, has fostered a major and continuing change within the Jewish community of America.

If these trends accelerate, will America resemble an apartheid state—a separate and unequal society? What would be lost if we allowed the public school system to collapse?

Is support for full-time Jewish education a betrayal of public education? Do we lessen the chance to correct the deficiencies of public education when we put our own children in private schools? Perhaps to some extent, but, on the other hand, are we not obliged to send our children to safe and effective schools?

Today we remain largely committed to public education, but

increasingly disquieting doubts disturb our traditional support for the institution that equipped our immigrant forebears with the tools to live in a pluralistic and free society.

Religious Symbols: Public Lands and Public Funds

Every December a host of church-state controversies make headlines: most notably, the intrusion of religious symbols on public lands and in government buildings. The debate over the Chanukah menorah or the nativity scene (crèche) displayed on public property has become so common that Marc Stern, an attorney for the American Jewish Congress, has called Chanukah the "Festival of Litigation."

By displaying a religious symbol in a public place and/or by using government funds to pay for such symbols, the government would seem to be offering sponsorship to beliefs that, the Constitution tells us, belong to the private sector of the church and not to the public arena of the state. The menorah on the steps of city hall or the Christian nativity scene in its lobby appear to violate the First Amendment's prohibition against establishing religion. And, while many argue that these displays are merely a recognition by the government of holidays celebrated by its citizenry, the fact remains that, when they are allowed on public land or paid for with public funds, the state appears to accept and endorse their religious content.

As convincing as this argument might seem, two Supreme Court decisions in the 1980s permitted such displays under certain circumstances. In its 1985 decision, *Lynch* v. *Donnelly,* the Court ruled by a 5 to 4 majority that Pawtucket, Rhode Island, could use state funds to pay for its nativity scene even on private property. The Court arrived at this decision by rationalizing that, if secular objects such as Santa Claus and his reindeer, a wishing well, and a dancing bear were closely and inseparably linked with the nativity scene, the religious content of the scene would be adequately subsumed by the larger display of secular items. Thus, the whole scene, including the crèche, would become a secular seasonal display of American culture. But do secular items effectively cancel out the religious symbolism of a crèche or a menorah? Has the Supreme Court the authority to divest Christian (and Jewish) symbols of their religious significance? Furthermore, even if secular items could negate religious symbols, how many secular items are needed to neutralize the display?

The Supreme Court affirmed its puzzling interpretation of the religious symbol issue in a 1989 decision, *County of Allegheny* v. *American Civil Liberties Union*. In this case, the Court decided that a crèche standing in a courthouse lobby was a religious symbol inappropriate for display on public property. At the same time, however, the Court upheld the constitutionality of a menorah on display on the plaza outside of the county courthouse.

Why the menorah and not the crèche? The Court reasoned that the menorah was a religiously neutral symbol because it stood next to a Christmas tree and a sign proclaiming the blessings of freedom. In contrast, the crèche stood alone inside the courthouse, fully maintaining its religious symbolism. How curious! Does a menorah lose its religious significance when in proximity to a Christmas tree? On the outcomes of such tortured logic rests the fragile future of church-state separation.

A Real Dilemma: Menorahs on Public Property

The Lubavitch chasidic group in your community announces that it will place a ten-foot menorah in a public park to balance the nativity scene annually displayed there. The local Jewish Community Relations Council calls an emergency meeting to consider whether or not to oppose in court the chasidic display. You are a member of the committee. How would you vote?

Response

In several Jewish communities, local Jewish Community Relations Councils, joined by organizations like the American Jewish Congress and the UAHC and CCAR, have taken legal action to stop the Lubavitch project, arguing that, on public property, *Jewish* religious symbols are just as inappropriate as are *Christian* symbols. These Jewish groups believe that the Lubavitchers are undermining the Jewish community's church-state position.

In Burlington, Vermont, Rabbi James Glazer opposed the Lubavitchers and won an important federal appeals court case, relying on the Pawtucket case *(Lynch* v. *Donnelly)*, ruling that menorahs cannot stand alone on public property.

A Question of Priorities

In past decades, the maintenance of separation of church and state has been one of the highest priorities of the American Jewish community. Today we are divided, neutralizing Jewish influence and impact. The Orthodox community stands with the Roman Catholic community and the more fundamentalist segments of Protestantism on the key issue of public funds for parochial schools. And some Jewish observers now feel that American society is so sufficiently tolerant that local violations of church-state separation are not worth opposing for fear of antagonizing our Christian neighbors.

They say the Jewish leadership has been too rigid, too absolute, unwisely challenging seemingly innocuous programs. They say we have risked serious community and interfaith conflicts in many cities and suburbs by challenging such insignificant Christian practices as silent prayer. And they say we have eroded our position as a faith group by lining up with atheist and secular groups in court tests and public controversy. What do you think?

The Religious Right: What Does It Want?

In the past two decades, two major factors caused religious fundamentalists to move more aggressively into the political arena. The first was unhappiness with the decisions of the Supreme Court and other federal courts that asserted the rights of women and minorities (Blacks, Hispanics, the handicapped, Jews, Catholics, and atheists among them) against the views and control of the majority. The fundamentalists became increasingly alarmed as these court decisions radically affected the communal institutions they saw as theirs, particularly in taking religion out of the public schools that trained their children. They found themselves held to a standard that in their view weakened the religious underpinnings of the value system that had long anchored the public school curriculum.

The second factor making for the politicization of the Religious Right was the intrusion of radio, movies, television, and rock and roll records that flooded their children's world with abhorrent images and values. All efforts to persuade their children to shun those intrusions were futile. In justifying his call for kids to destroy their rock records, TV evangelist Jimmy Swaggert told one of the authors of this book, "You know, if only Norman Lear had not put 'All in the Family' into our homes, we would not be facing the problems our nation faces today."

Gradually, the reality began to sink in: if fundamentalists could not protect their children from the negative political, social, and cultural environment out there, then it was time for them to go out and change that environment.

Interestingly, one of the techniques adopted by the Religious Right to achieve their goal was to co-opt the very same technologies and public tactics they had so vehemently opposed. It remains to be seen whether in the long run such tactics as televangelism, Christian rock music, fellowships of athletes, beauty queens, and moral majorities will empower or subvert the fundamentalists. The moral and legal scandals that have disgraced TV figures like Jim Bakker and Jimmy Swaggart have weakened the credibility of the Religious Right, no doubt reducing their threat to church-state separation. But, at the 1992 Republican convention, the likes of Pat Robertson and Pat Buchanan were alive, well, and brimming with calls for a "religious war" to control the culture of America.

Pressure on the States and Local Communities

Although the Religious Right was not successful in having its agenda implemented in Congress in the 1980s, the far right has begun to shift its efforts to the local and state level. Many far-right organizations now have grass-roots affiliates in local communities throughout the United States, mobilizing to demand of city and state governments concessions to religious groups, which openly breach the wall of separation between church and state.

This tactical shift is very important, especially in light of the recent decisions of the Supreme Court. As the Court increasingly abdicates its role of protecting the inalienable rights of citizens, church-state decisions will be made more frequently at the state and local levels. This will require a significant shift in the tactics of liberal activism—from the national to the local, with less emphasis on court victories and more on state and local electoral and legislative victories—if we are to preserve what we can of religious freedom.

Such a shift has already occurred in the pro-choice movement as pro-choice activists, once secure in the knowledge that *Roe* v. *Wade* protected a woman's right to terminate her pregnancy, mobilize to ensure that the right to choose is not restricted at the local level and to replace anti-choice state and local officials with pro-choice challengers. In some states, these efforts have been enormously successful (California, Florida, and Virginia). In other states and territories, the right to choose is being dramatically destroyed (Pennsylvania, Louisiana, Guam).

If the current geography of the abortion debate is an indication of things to come in other areas where the Court is relinquishing its role, the nature of religious liberty in the United States will soon be determined state by state, locality by locality.

In states where we, as Jews, constitute a formidable political force (New York, for example), we can be fairly sure that our rights will be protected and respected. But what about midwestern and southern states in which Jews do not constitute a significant force?

To succeed in such states, we must rejuvenate the traditional Christian-Jewish coalition for decency. Whenever possible, it is important that non-Jewish leaders be involved in these efforts. Allowing such disputes to be perceived as Jewish-Christian conflict can only distract people from the important issues involved and can spell harsh intergroup conflict. And what of other religious minorities—Muslims, Hindus, Native American church members, and many others—whose rights are also threatened by the Religious Right? If we are to protect their rights and ours, we must be prepared to fight as fiercely on the local level as we have on the national level.

≡ 6 ≡

ISRAEL, ZIONISM, AND THE JEWISH PEOPLE

We Jews may differ about God and religion, politics and education, but on the existence of Israel we are solidly united. So why include Israel in a book on Jewish dilemmas?

The answer is that Israel is the paramount Jewish achievement of modern Jewish history, but deep beneath the surface are embedded the heaviest of dilemmas, the most elusive to grasp and the most painful to confront.

Centrality of Israel for the Jewish People

It is often puzzling to Christians, and even to some Jews, to speak of Jews as a people, a culture, or a nation. "Isn't Judaism a religion?" they ask. In doing so, they envision Judaism as a religious tradition akin to Methodism, Unitarianism, or Catholicism. But the civilization of Judaism long predated most of the religious traditions practiced today.

Judaism arose as one of the world's early civilizations. Were the other ancient civilizations—Babylonia, Persia, Greece, Rome, and Egypt—religions? Yes. Each civilization had its own religion. Were they cultures with their own language and literature? Yes, that too. Were they nation states with a national consciousness? Each possessed a powerful nationalist identity. Were they peoples with

86

a distinct sense of unity that remained with them when they traveled beyond the borders of their own country? That as well.

The main difference between Judaism and these other ancient cultures is that most of them died out long ago while Judaism and the Jewish people endure. Jews today still reflect all the characteristics that marked the Jewish people from their beginnings: a culture, a religion, a people, a nation.

Some Jews express their identity in nonreligious cultural terms (hence the existence of so-called secular Jewish organizations—another paradoxical idea for many Christians). Other Jews express their identity in Judaism's religious beliefs and synagogue observance. Still others do so by embracing the nationalistic Zionist aspirations of our people. Indeed, for some, that is the *only* component of their Jewishness. The majority of Israelis equate their Jewishness simply with their living in the historic homeland rather than with the Jewish content of their lives.

All but a tiny minority of Jews affirm the central role of Israel. We are a proud people, and our peoplehood transcends our religious and racial differences. In moments of peril for Israel, as well as in moments of exaltation, we are not Reform, Conservative, Reconstructionist, Yiddishist, Zionist, Orthodox, or atheist. We are *Jews,* a united people sharing a common destiny, knowing in our bones that what happens to Israel will shape much of our future as Jews. Jewish commitment to Israel is a powerful force, a fact recognized by the American people, our government, and the international community.

What is meant by the centrality of Israel for the Jewish people? Does it mean that American Jewry should subordinate its own needs to the overriding needs of the center, the State of Israel? As a practical matter, we have done this gladly since 1948 in response to the series of crises in Israel. But, should we do it as a matter of *principle,* even if full peace, for example, came to Israel? Are we saying by "centrality" that the basic future of the Jewish people will be forged in Israel while in America and elsewhere Jews are doomed to assimilate and to live on the margins?

These are not just idle questions. There is a haunting dilemma here. For what is the meaning of Israel's centrality if more Israelis go "down" *(yeridah)* to America than American Jews go "up" *(aliyah)* to Israel?

Some Jews regard Israel as primarily the *spiritual* and *religious* center of the Jewish world and Jerusalem as the focus of our historic faith and spiritual ideals. Others view Israel as the ultimate champion of the Jewish people, providing a haven for Jews in harm's way.

Still others argue that "centrality" is a mere slogan. They contend that the Jews of the Diaspora are *equal* partners with the Jews of Israel, not senior or junior, central or marginal. Each of the great Jewries—and especially in America and in Israel—has a crucial role to play and a future to safeguard. It can even be argued that Judaism as a *living religious civilization* has a better chance of creative fulfillment in America than in Israel. After all, the Jewish community in America is large, affluent, powerful, enjoying the blessings of church-state separation and pluralism in the freest and wealthiest nation on earth.

In America, the synagogue community plays a large role, and American Jewry is free to build as vital, powerful, and affirming a Jewish life as we have the will to achieve. Here, as opposed to Israel, a wide spectrum of Jewish religious forms and ideas is encouraged and thrives. We are not hostage to external threats to our existence or limited by the meager resources of a small country. So, why talk of "central"? Israel is part of the Jewish people, not the other way around.

This view is one of "affirmation of the Diaspora." In an influential paper, the late Dr. Gerson D. Cohen, former chancellor of the Jewish Theological Seminary of America (Conservative), challenged the concept of the centrality of Israel, countering with the theme of the *"centrality of the Jewish people."* He wrote that "Israel will have to send some of its best youths to the Diaspora . . . to study . . . how to be Jews in the modern world."

A Normal State for a Normal People?

What *kind* of state do we want Israel to be? There are those who say that, since Zionism set out to cure the abnormal condition under which the Jewish people had previously lived, the Jewish state needs to aspire to be no more than a normal state, like any other state in the world. It is now a cliché that one early Zionist leader expressed satisfaction when he heard that there were now some crooks and prostitutes in the young Jewish state. "See," he said, "we have become a normal state. We have pickpockets and crooks and prostitutes like every other state."

But there is another view, which springs from the Jewish religious tradition. Israel is to be a *model* state, a *light unto the nations,* a messenger of peace, an example to the civilized world, an expression of God's convenant with the Jewish people. In this view, Israel is a state with a Jewish majority, but whether or not it is a truly *Jewish* state depends less on demographics than on the moral qualities of its citizenry.

Has Israel demonstrated moral leadership? In many ways, yes. No other small state has brought in millions of refugees, most recently over twenty thousand black Ethiopian Jews and hundreds of thousands of former Soviet Jews, providing sanctuary to persecuted and poverty stricken people from around the globe. No other small state has displayed the cultural vitality of Israel or provided such ambitious and selfless technical assistance to the poor nations of the world—especially those in Africa. No other small society has tapped the springs of science and technology for the common good as has Israel. No other developing nation has reclaimed the desert for agriculture and committed so much of its limited resources to social welfare. None has maintained such extensive democratic institutions, free speech and free press, in the face of persistent warfare and terrorism.

But there is another side to the ledger, too. This side includes the failure to heal the "ethnic" rift between Ashkenazim and Sephardim; the second class citizenship of Israeli Arabs who are barred from the military and from a fair share of Israeli health, education, and housing benefits; the continued discrimination against non-

Orthodox Jews; the infringements on the human rights of Palestinians living in the occupied territories; the failure to provide real equality for women; a variety of economic injustices, exacerbated by the floods of new immigrants seeking jobs and housing in the Jewish state; and, above all, a failure to achieve coexistence with its Arab neighbors.

The Law of Return

The Law of Return provides that any Jew who comes to Israel can automatically claim immediate citizenship. Israel's detractors have condemned this law as discriminatory, even racist, by denying to non-Jews, including Arabs, rights that are retained by Jews.

In truth, any person *can* become a citizen under Israeli law. As in the United States, one who wishes to become a naturalized citizen must reside in the country for a period of several years before becoming eligible.

The Law of Return functions very much like the affirmative action programs described in the chapter on civil rights: a conscientious effort to overcome a history of discrimination. Upon the establishment of the State of Israel, it was determined that, in light of two millennia of Jewish dispersion and fierce anti-Semitic persecution, no Jew should have to wait to be a free citizen of the reestablished Jewish state. Thus, the principal difference between Jews and non-Jews who desire Israeli citizenship is that Jews are afforded compensation for this historic suffering—for them, the waiting period for citizenship is waived.

Israel Religious Action Center

The Reform Jewish movement has established an Israel Religious Action Center in Jerusalem to speak in the name of the Progressive movement (Reform) of Israel on such burning issues as religious liberty, Reform rights, pluralism, women's rights, Arab-Jewish relations, the environment, and consumer rights. This center has become a rallying point for Israelis from many backgrounds to lobby the Knesset, organize demonstrations, form coalitions, and seek redress of grievances.

A Real Dilemma: Should IRAC Deal With West Bank-Palestinian Issues?

When the Israel Religious Action Center (IRAC) was established in the late 1980s, it had to decide whether or not to take positions on issues such as the status of the West Bank, settlements, and Palestinian rights. On the one hand, there are few moral dilemmas facing Israel more troubling than these. To establish itself as a moral force, the center could not be silent on the divisive territorial question.

But becoming involved in this battle would preclude the center's forming political alliances with hawkish parties on domestic issues (for example, religious pluralism). Right-wing parties like *Tsomet,* for example, have liberal agendas on economic and religious rights issues that are central to IRAC's agenda. They represent votes that could be decisive in a Knesset vote on the question of who is a Jew. To have plunged into the Palestinian issue from the start would raise suspicions that the center was a disguised peace lobby.

What should the IRAC have done?

Response

The IRAC agonized over this issue, recognizing tactical and moral "rights" on both sides of the argument, and finally decided to defer dealing with West Bank issues. It did determine, however, that, when it came not to the political issues but to the *human rights* issues, it would consider involvement. Therefore, when human rights violations occur against Arabs, including Palestinians, the center has occasionally spoken out. In other cases, individual Israeli rabbis have spoken out against abuses of human rights and have demonstrated their concerns by going to the territories to witness and to protest for human rights.

The center's strategy apparently has been successful for, in a very short time, it has made a significant name for itself; built alliances across the political spectrum on a broad range of issues; been accepted by all political parties except the religious extremists; and avoided being typecast as a single-issue group. Still, some critics argue that this is a path of expediency and that the Hebrew prophets would have required a bolder and less prudent course.

The Palestinians

Modern Zionism was founded by Theodor Herzl to end what he saw as the fundamental abnormality of Jewish life—our *homelessness*. Only a homeland, he argued, could reunite the Jewish soul and the Jewish body. Until we had a land of our own, we would be subject to persecution at the whim of every ruler in search of a scapegoat. Herzl was proved correct. The Nazi Holocaust revealed that virtually no country in the world would provide a safe harbor to the Jewish victims of persecution. The State of Israel was born in the ashes of World War II and the destruction of the historic Jewish communities of Europe.

But, ironically, in solving the problem of Jewish homelessness, another people was rendered homeless. In Israel's War of Independence (1948), almost six hundred thousand Arabs fled their homes in Jaffa, Haifa, and many towns that fell within the borders of the new Jewish state. According to Arab propaganda, they were forcibly driven out by Jews; the best evidence, however, indicates that they fled either in the panic of war or under the orders of Arab rulers who told them they could return after the Jews were massacred. Some Jewish scholars suggest that Israel took advantage of this situation and, through the use of psychological warfare, orchestrated fear to prompt the Arabs to flee.

The refugees have never returned.

Kept in refugee camps as political pawns by the Arab states, raising their children on a propaganda diet rich in hatred for Israel, they yearn for the day of return to their former cities and villages. In their bitterness, many have joined Arab terrorist groups. In the 1967 war, Israel occupied the West Bank and Gaza, bringing hundreds of thousands of stateless Palestinian Arabs under Israeli control.

In December of 1987, the Palestinians in the occupied territories began the *intifada,* a bloody rebellion that has claimed hundreds of lives, mostly among Arab youths. The *intifada* demonstrated the seething fury of the Palestinians and the terrible price Israel has to pay for occupying more than a million alien and hostile people.

What should be done about the Palestinians? It is sadly true that nothing was done for the Palestinians when Jordan and Egypt controlled the West Bank and Gaza. They were not even allowed to visit Egypt, much less create a Palestinian state. Under Israeli administration, Arabs from Jordan have been accorded the right to cross "open bridges" over the Jordan River, and Palestinians from the West Bank and Gaza have been allowed to visit and to work at relatively good wages in Israel.

But, year after year, Israeli leaders refused to acknowledge that the Palestianians were anything more than refugees. "There are no Palestinians," Golda Meir said. But Palestinian nationalism—inspired by the success of Zionism and stirred by Arab countries for their own purposes—spread among the Palestinians. As one of the most enterprising and best-educated segments of the Arab world, they began to demand their rights *as a people to a national homeland of their own.* Poetry, literature, music, art, and politics converged in a new sense of Palestinian peoplehood—a common cause, a common history, a common destiny.

How then do we determine which side has the more legitimate right to establish a country on a disputed territory? On the one hand, unlike the Kurds, Basques, Croatians, and Latvians, who can recall their own former, independent national existence, there never was a country of Palestine. A distinctive Palestinian identity emerged only in reaction to modern Zionism. Over the centuries, the only people to think of the land we call Israel as their historic homeland has been the Jewish people, whose nationalistic dream has ancient roots.

On the other hand, whatever the history of the area, a generation of Palestinians has grown up to believe deeply in its gut that they have a right to self-determination in their own land. They are willing to lay down their lives for that goal and have pursued it not only through means of violence and terrorism but by creating modalities of local autonomy wherever possible. A growing number of Palestinians seem willing to give up the futile goal of destroying Israel and settle for a ministate in the West Bank and Gaza, living side by side with Israel.

How should we Jews respond to the Palestinian cry for peoplehood? Thus far, we have generally scorned it, equating Palestinians with the PLO. Are the Palestinians a people? If they were not previously, have they not clearly become one? Is it for Jews to decide how another group should define itself? Nothing in Jewish history was more insufferable to us than having the world define us in *their terms rather than ours.* Can Jews, of all peoples, be deaf to the yearning of another people for its national dignity and self-worth?

In responding to these weighty questions, one Jewish concern remains paramount: the *security* of Israel. Any political proposal must consider the ongoing threat to Israel's survival posed by Arab hostility. The memory of West Bank Palestinians standing on their roofs and cheering the SCUDs crashing into Israel during the Gulf War is seared indelibly into the consciousness of every Israeli and every Jew. Few observers doubt that, if Iraq and other Arab countries could destroy Israel militarily, they would do so. Only Israel's strength, its ability to maintain secure borders, and American support deter such a possibility.

The Options Facing Israel

But the dilemma persists. What is Israel to do with over a million and a half Arabs in the West Bank and Gaza? There are three obvious possibilities. One is to annex these areas as extremist Jews suggest, believing the territory to be part of a "Greater Israel" promised by God to the Jewish people. This course of action would inflame the entire Arab world, possibly leading to a *jihad,* a "holy war" against Israel. It would have another undesirable consequence as well. By absorbing a large Arab population with a high birthrate, Israel, in a matter of decades, might lose its Jewish majority, thus ending the Jewish character of the state.

The second alternative, first enunciated by the late Rabbi Meir Kahane and espoused by a member of the Israeli cabinet in the early 1990s, is to "transfer" West Bank Arabs to Jordan in what amounts to the expulsion of an entire people. Such a Nuremberg-style Jewish assault on an entire people based on race is an unthinkable idea. Unfortunately, some Israelis *are* thinking about it.

The third alternative is continued occupation of an alienated and embittered people who are certain to grow increasingly hostile to Jewish control of their destiny. The permanent status of occupiers would gravely threaten the spiritual and democratic character of Israel, increasing the inevitable abuses of civil liberties and human rights that *already mar* Israel's image. This, in turn, would erode Israel's standing among the democracies of the world, including the United States.

The fourth is a political settlement of the conflict.

We, in America, cannot determine which political solutions will safeguard Israel's security while accommodating, at least minimally, the claims of the Palestinian people. Only the government and people of Israel—in dialogue with the Palestinians—can decide this fateful question.

Our task as American Jews is to accept the humanity of the Palestinians, to see them as *persons* and as a *people,* and to reject anti-Arab stereotypes and slogans. To think of all Palestinians as terrorists is as logical as equating all Jews with the Jewish Defense League. To understand Palestinians, we first have to speak with them, listen to them, learn about their hopes and fears.

A Real Dilemma: Inviting Palestinians
to a Synagogue

Rabbi Douglas Krantz of Armonk, New York, invited Edward Said, a professor of literature at Columbia University and a member of the PLO National Committee, to speak from his pulpit at Congregation B'nai Yisrael one Shabbat eve. Other Jewish leaders and rabbis in Westchester severely criticized the action as did some members of the congregation, arguing that to give a platform in a synagogue to a leader of the PLO is to legitimize an organization committed to Israel's destruction.

Rabbi Krantz justified his invitation on two grounds: first, that he has the freedom to invite whomever he chooses to occupy his pulpit; second, that hearing the Palestinian viewpoint from a respected member of that community is essential if one is to form a wise and informed opinion. If Israel is ever to have peace, it must be willing to talk with its enemies; if we Jews are ever to understand the heart and soul of the Palestinian people, we must listen to them, even while disagreeing on basic issues.

Response

Professor Said appeared, made a vigorous presentation, participated in an animated question-and-answer period, and the controversy ended. Almost all who attended termed it a useful encounter.

Several founders of Zionism believed that the ultimate moral test of Zionism was whether or not it could reconcile itself with its Arab neighbors. If the French and Germans could reconcile after two world wars, if Egypt and Israel could sign a peace treaty, if Iran and Iraq could make peace, if the United States and the USSR could end their enmity, why must Jews and Palestinians remain faceless enemies forever? And what of our religious tradition that demands that we *seek* peace and convert enemies to friends? Ultimately, only a political dialogue based on mutual recognition can resolve this seemingly intractable conflict. In the watershed election of 1992, the rise of Yitzhak Rabin to the prime ministership signaled the readiness of the Israeli public to moderate the hardline policies of the Likud and to pursue every opportunity for a political settlement of the conflict.

Zionist Thought and the Dilemma of the Palestinians

The dilemmas we face today are not new. They commanded the attention of the seminal thinkers of modern Zionism. Foremost among them was Ahad Ha-Am, the architect of the vision of a Jewish state rooted in Jewish ideals and Jewish culture. He taught that a Jewish homeland must be reconciled with "consideration for the national rights of the Palestinian Arabs." He rejected the conventional wisdom of other Zionist leaders who insisted that the Balfour Declaration was a mandate for a Jewish state in all of Palestine.

Ahad Ha-Am stressed what others chose to ignore: the British pledge in the Balfour Declaration was conditioned by the clause "that nothing shall be done that may prejudice the civil and religious rights of existing non-Jewish communities in Palestine." He was haunted by the moral compulsion that the development of a Jewish homeland should not displace or degrade those Arabs who also have "a genuine right to the land due to generations of residence and work upon it." To him, Palestine was a "common possession of two peoples."

Following Ahad Ha-Am's death, his disciple, Rabbi Judah L. Magnes, carried on this difficult struggle. Magnes was a Reform rabbi who made *aliyah* in 1922 and became a founder of the Hebrew University, which he served as president until his death in 1946. He brought Arabs and Jews together to work for a binational state in which the rights of both would be protected by constitutional safeguards. "One of the greatest cultural duties of the Jewish people," he said, "is the attempt to enter the Promised Land, not by means of conquest like Joshua, but through peaceful and cultural means, through hard work, sacrifice, love, and with a decision not to do anything that cannot be justified before the world conscience."

The great religious teacher Martin Buber believed that the moral challenge to Zionism was its willingness to share the land with another people. He pleaded for the "harnessing of nationalistic impulses and a solution based on compromise between two peoples." The binational state option, once part of the formal platform of the movement, fell victim to a half-century of ceaseless hostility between Arabs and Jews and the national Jewish trauma of the Holocaust.

Arabs and Jews generally see each other through a prism of stereotypes. Only a miracle like Sadat's visit to Jerusalem can break the "psychological impasse" that prevents Jews and Arabs from recognizing each other's humanity. But such occasions are all too rare. Abba Eban once said that the "Arabs never lose an opportunity to lose an opportunity." But have we Jews in Israel and the Diaspora done all that we can to generate decent human relations between Arabs and Jews?

Peace Negotiations

On October 30, 1991, the historic Middle Eastern Peace Conference opened in Madrid, Spain. The ongoing negotiations provided the opportunity for Israel to negotiate face-to-face with its Arab neighbors in an effort to bring about peace, an opportunity Israel has sought since its establishment.

The hard realities are these: the parties did not come to the table on their own initiative but only under United States pressure in the wake of the Gulf War. Are they willing to make the necessary compromises for a settlement? Can peace be established without territorial compromise? Is there any chance for the acceptance of a Jewish state in the midst of a vast Arab sea—or a Palestinian homeland alongside Israel?

Coexistence may be the only hope. The visions of Buber, Ahad Ha-Am, and Magnes may yet prove their value in a world of militarism and cynical power politics. This particular dilemma goes deep into the Jewish past and the sources of our moral inspiration. In many ways, it will shape the nature of our Jewish future.

Can Jews Dissent on Israel's Policies?

One other vexing dilemma arises from the question: What do we American Jews do when we seriously differ with policies pursued by the government of Israel? The question is complicated by an additional problem: What American Jews say publicly frequently impacts on public opinion in the United States and sometimes even upon the policies followed by our government. The United States of America and America's Jews are Israel's most powerful and important allies, and their words and actions have a direct and crucial impact on the well-being and security of the Jewish state.

Furthermore, criticism issued out of love by American Jews can often be manipulated by Israel's enemies to validate their efforts to weaken Israel. So how should we act when our convictions differ from Israeli government policy in matters of conscience? For their part, Jews in Israel vigorously debate every major issue affecting their nation. Should United States Jews be silent partners or, worse, predictable amen-sayers regardless of Israeli policies? Many American Jews were outspoken in opposition to their own government on Vietnam, disagreeing with those who demanded, "My country right or wrong." Are we to be dissenters in America and silent spectators about events in Israel when our conscience or judgment tells us that something is wrong?

If we feel that new settlements in the West Bank seriously harm the prospects for peaceful negotiations, and needlessly antagonize the American government, should we say so? Privately? Publicly? Neither? Why?

If we feel that Israeli policy toward demonstrations in the West Bank involves excessive use of force and violations of human rights, what should we do about it? While these issues are sharply mitigated as a result of the decline of the intensity of the *intifada* as well as by the election of Yitzhak Rabin, they will remain with us in differing forms for many years.

A Real Dilemma: Breaking Bones in the Territories

In 1989, soon after the *intifada* began, then Israeli Defense Minister Yitzhak Rabin announced that the Israeli Defense Forces would "break the bones" of Palestinian militants who threw stones in violent protest of Israel's occupation of the West Bank. Rabbi Alexander M. Schindler, president of the Union of American Hebrew Congregations, was asked by reporters what his reaction was. What should he have said? No comment? Israel knows best? Violence is wrong on both sides?

Responses

Rabbi Schindler wrote a public letter to the president of Israel, condemning the threat to "break bones" as anathema to Jewish ideals and values, harmful to Israel's image, and counterproductive. Neither stones nor bullets but only negotiations can resolve the *intifada,* he said.

The New York Times ran the letter as an opinion piece, providing a readership of millions. For many Jewish and non-Jewish supporters of Israel, it was a breath of fresh air, assuring them that they could be friends of Israel and still criticize policies they thought were wrong; that they did not have to choose between their consciences and their love for Israel. On the other hand, enemies of Israel cited the letter as justification for their harsh views.

Those who support free and open discussion say that Israel is the homeland of the Jewish people, of which we are equal partners, and that the character—especially the *moral* character—of the Jewish state *is* decidedly our business. As we could not stand idly by if we saw brothers or sisters about to do harm, either to others or to themselves, so we must not stand idly by when we see Israel engage in policies or practices that we believe undermine its interests generally and, more particularly, its support in the United States. We can help Israel overcome its challenges only if we speak out frankly and involve ourselves in mobilizing support for solutions. The alternative is to create a falsely idyllic picture-postcard Israel, which encourages escape from reality rather than the necessary frank wrestling with the tough issues required of all Jews in Israel and the Diaspora.

To say we have no right to speak is to condemn ourselves to second-class status within the Jewish people, to do a disservice to Israel in assessing the impact of its policies, and to violate our own beliefs and perhaps conscience.

But the other side of the coin is that speaking out for our religious rights in Israel is quite a different matter from speaking out on matters of security and foreign policy for which the Israelis— and not we—must pay the ultimate price. They will live and die by the decisions they make. They are in the trenches; we are on the sidelines. This consideration weighs heavily on every Jew committed to Israel and to the Jewish people.

If I am committed to Israel, must I automatically defend the policies of Shamir or Rabin or whoever might be in power even if I believe they are perilous for Israel or morally wrong?

Talmudic sources highlight this discussion. In *Avodah Zara* 18a, it is written that one who feels that protest in the face of injustice may be effective and does not protest ought to be punished. With specific regard to Israel, R. Papa said, "And the princes of the exile [exilarchs or leaders of the Jewish community] are held accountable for the transgressions of the whole household of Israel. (*Shabbat* 54b)

A Real Dilemma: An Honorary Degree for Shamir?

When the Israelis, the Syrians, the Palestinians, the Jordanians, and the Lebanese representatives began the historic peace process, then Prime Minister Shamir led Israel's delegation.

A few weeks later, during a recess in the talks, Mr. Shamir came to the United States and was invited by the Hebrew Union College-Jewish Institute of Religion (HUC-JIR) in Los Angeles to receive an honorary doctorate from the college. Some thirty Reform rabbis protested this action, charging that such degrees honor the individual not the office he or she holds. They argued that Mr. Shamir had been a terrorist in the days before independence and that his hard-line policies of planting new settlements in the territories and his refusal to trade land for peace put the Soviet Jewish *aliyah* at risk and threatened the chance for peaceful negotiations. They charged that Mr. Shamir's support for changes to the Law of Return and restrictions on the rights of Reform Jews make it unconscionable to give him this honor.

The college responded that this honor was deserved because Mr. Shamir was the prime minister of Israel, and he had brought Israel to the peace table.

Should the UAHC have joined in criticizing this honor for Mr. Shamir? Why or why not?

Response

Although its leadership was deeply divided on this issue, the UAHC decided that HUC-JIR was honoring the State of Israel and the position more than the person. In addition, despite his hard-line policies, Shamir had brought Israel into the peace process and might, like Begin, yet achieve historic peace agreement with his Arab neighbors. To protest publicly at such a moment, the UAHC maintained, would seem to substantiate the Arab contention that Israel was intransigent.

It is often said that, if American Jews feel compelled to dissent, we should do so directly and privately with Israel's leadership. This may be good advice in most cases. But what if they spurn our counsel? Or what if—as in the question of the rights of Reform Jews or even the rights of Palestinian Arabs—the controversy rises to an issue of profound moral and ethical principle? Is there any way to press our viewpoint short of speaking out publicly?

If we Jews never engage in public criticism, thereby defining friendship for Israel by blind silence, will not America's non-Jewish friends feel they must choose between their convictions and their support of Israel? Do we not serve Israel better by telling Americans who support Israel we can urge Israel to change policies we feel are wrong while advocating American foreign aid to Israel and working for closer United States-Israel relations?

And what happens to our credibility if we speak out on human rights violations and social injustice everywhere in the world except when such events occur in the Jewish state?

Every thoughtful American Jew will face this dilemma at one time or another. If one speaks out, one may risk attacks on one's Jewish loyalty and even one's integrity. But a Jewish community sensitive to civil liberties must learn to respect internal dissent. Democracy, like charity, begins at home. And failure to resolve this dilemma could compromise Jewish security here and in Israel.

Crunch Time in United States-Israel Relations

In 1991, one of the most astonishing incidents in the history of United States-Israel relations took place in the battle over Israel's request for loan guarantees. Israel faced the bittersweet dilemma of a tidal wave of Ethiopian and Soviet Jewish refugees that threatened to overwhelm Israel's ability to provide jobs, education, health care, welfare services, and sufficient housing.

Israel asked the United States for assistance. In particular, the United States was asked to "guarantee" loans that Israel would take out from commercial banks: $2 billion per year for five years. The loan guarantees, which would cost the American taxpayer virtually nothing (Israel has never defaulted on a loan), would permit Israel to borrow money at the lowest possible interest rates, thus reducing the economic burden on Israel. And much of this loan money would be recycled into the American economy through the purchase of American-made products.

In May of 1991, the United States administration, which then was trying to arrange a Middle Eastern peace conference, requested that Israel hold off its request for loan guarantees until after Labor Day. Israel agreed. In September, President Bush asked for another three-month delay and let it be known that the United States intended to make the guarantees conditional on a freeze by Israel of its Jewish settlement policy in the territories occupied by Israel during the Six-Day War.

Israeli officials responded by accelerating the construction of Jewish communities on the West Bank. Earlier, Yitzhak Shamir had asserted that a greater Soviet immigration required a "Greater Israel" (code words for holding on to the West Bank and making it part of Israel). This linkage provoked an outcry from Arabs, the Bush administration, and some American Jews.

In September 1991, the Religious Action Center proposed a campaign, supported by all the Jewish religious denominations, to ask rabbis to request congregants to call their senators and representatives on behalf of the loan guarantees immediately after Rosh Hashanah. The response was overwhelming.

On September 12, a thousand Jewish leaders from communities across the country came to meet with their elected officials. In the middle of that fateful day, President Bush called an unprecedented press conference in which he made his case to the American people and, banging his fist on the podium, asserted: "I'm up against some powerful political forces. . . . I heard today there were something like a thousand lobbyists on the Hill working the other side of the question. We've got one lonely guy down here doing it."

A national uproar occurred. Although an Israeli cabinet member denounced Bush as an anti-Semite, neither the president nor his words were overtly anti-Semitic. His words were so threatening and ominous, however, that they gave aid and comfort to anti-Semites, so much so that the president felt compelled later to write a clarifying letter to the Conference of Presidents of Major Jewish Organizations. However, the president had won the day. Support for loan guarantees and for Israel plummeted. Eighty-six percent of the American public backed the president. Israel's supporters were forced to agree to further delays on loan guarantees. Mr. Shamir condemned America's change of position as destroying the special United States-Israel relationship and disqualifying America as an honest broker in the peace process.

A Real Dilemma: Loan Guarantees

The United States administration linked loan guarantees to the Israeli settlement policies, arguing that it should not be expected to subsidize building settlements in the occupied lands in violation of American policy.

Israel has maintained that to link a *humanitarian* request (loan guarantees for Soviet Jewry) with a *political* demand (stop settlements) would set a dangerous precedent. Thereafter, the United States could use this lever to pressure Israel to make concessions at the peace conference—even if such concessions endanger Israel security. The question of settlements should be negotiated in a peace conference, not imposed unilaterally by the United States as a precondition for humanitarian aid.

Should the American Jewish community accept this linkage, oppose it, or sit this one out?

Response

Most mainstream Jewish organizations, including the CCAR and the UAHC, have strongly opposed linkage in general and linkage with the loan guarantees in particular for a number of reasons.

First, such linkage violates long-standing American values and policy.

Second, the fundamental questions underlying the settlement debate (i.e., to whom the West Bank belongs) can only be decided at the bargaining table.

Third, one-sided pressure of this kind compromises the status of the United States as a fair broker and sends a clear message to hard-liners in the Arab world that they do not have to negotiate at the peace table with Israel in order to achieve their objectives. The United States clearly had made no similar demands upon the Arab parties; they can wait for the United States to deliver Israel.

Only through direct negotiations can the realities of the West Bank be changed. The incentive for Israel to halt settlements should not be humanitarian help for refugees but real compromise and peace with the Arabs.

President Bush never explained why he thought the loan guarantees would hurt the peace process. Common sense suggests the opposite. Only a secure and stable Israel is likely to bargain confidently at the peace table and be willing to take the risks necessary for peace. Nothing threatens to destabilize Israel internally more than the prospect of a million refugees overwhelming its social fabric and economic infrastructure.

It should be noted that, despite acknowledging the legitimacy of these concerns, many rabbis and Jewish leaders, concerned about the negative impact of Israel's policy of settlement expansion on American support for Israel and on the peace process, disagreed with the UAHC's and the CCAR's stand and supported linkage. They believed that nothing short of the power of the purse could change Israel's settlement policies. Both the UAHC and the CCAR oppose expanding settlements in the territories.

The election of Yitzhak Rabin in 1992 profoundly reduced the tension between the United States and Israel. Rabin drastically altered Israel's priorities, scaling back on new settlements in the territories and pledging a vigorous effort to produce a political settlement with the Arabs. In this improved atmosphere, American loan guarantees were endorsed by President Bush and welcomed by his challenger, Bill Clinton.

Reform Jewish Rights in Israel

For Reform Jews, there is a particularly nettlesome aspect of Israel's social justice agenda. After almost half a century, Israel still does not accord full religious liberty to non-Orthodox religious groups, denying Conservative and Reform rabbis the right to officiate at weddings, conversions, divorces, etc. It is a sad commentary that Israel has been wise enough to extend religious freedom to Christians and Muslims but has not done so to all Jews. The result is the persistent danger of alienation of liberal Jews whose rabbis cannot serve as full rabbis in Israel.

That the vast majority of Jews in America are Reform and Conservative—Orthodox Jews represent less that 10 percent of American Jewry—sharpens the dilemma of Israel's policies on religious liberty.

A Real Dilemma: Holding Up UJA Contributions

In 1988, a prominent "big giver" in California, who is also a deeply committed Reform Jew, contemplated saying to the United Jewish Appeal that he would no longer contribute unless it went on record opposing discrimination against Reform and Conservative Jews in Israel and ensuring that these funds were distributed equally to all streams of Judaism. The director of the Jewish Federation appealed to him to reconsider, arguing that Israel needed every cent of Jewish support to settle immigrants and to defend itself from external threats.

Furthermore, if money were withheld as a political lever on this issue, then donors would start holding up funds for their own political agendas. Others would use these political issues as an excuse to give less to the UJA generally. Besides, he said, such rights can be achieved only by struggle within Israel, not by outside financial pressure and blackmail.

The donor argued that this issue was different from other issues. This issue went to the core of his Jewishness (i.e., the efforts of the Orthodox political establishment to declare Reform and Conservative Judaism as counterfeit Judaism and its rabbis as illegitimate). UJA should not condone such discrimination by allowing the Jewish Agency (the organization in Israel that distributes UJA funding) to provide UJA funds to Orthodox institutions but not to Reform or Conservative institutions. This is particularly hurtful when one considers that approximately 90 percent of the donors and leadership of the UJA are Reform or Conservative Jews. What should the "big giver" have done? If this donor asked the UAHC to support him, how should it have responded?

Response

This donor did threaten to withhold his gift despite the decision of the UAHC not to call on its members to withhold UJA funding. Nonetheless, the threat by this and other prominent contributors led to some improvements in the Jewish Agency's distribution policies. Today, Reform and Conservative institutions in Israel do receive Jewish Agency funding—albeit still not their fair share.

Domestic Challenges

Religious pluralism is but one of a number of domestic challenges that Israel faces in the coming decades. In addition to the religious strains, Israel has been buffeted by tensions along the ethnic fault-line, particularly between Ashkenazic Jews (European in origin) and Sephardic Jews (those from Arab, North African, and Spanish-speaking countries). Israel now has a 58 percent majority of Jews of Sephardic origin, and, while it has made significant strides in the past two decades bridging the cultural and economic gap between Ashkenazic and Sephardic Jews, most top slots in economic and political spheres are still held by Ashkenazim. Economic problems are mounting with serious unemployment and inadequate housing, especially in the development towns, and those in poverty, particularly those from Arab countries, are in danger of being recycled into a second generation locked into a permanent underclass. The resentment of the have-nots is intensified by the preferential housing and job opportunities accorded to Soviet Jewish immigrants as a means of enticing them to come and to stay— a pattern that further delays improvements for other needy Israelies. Diversion of limited resources into massive settlement building in the West Bank exacerbates all these strains.

As problematic as are the tensions between Jew and Jew, they are not as severe as the growing tensions between Israeli Jews and Israeli Arabs. Israeli Arabs feel themselves to be second-class citizens in Israel. With few exceptions, they are barred from serving in the military and receive less money per capita for the health and physical infrastructure in their communities than do predominantly Jewish communities. The government does little to promote Jewish-Arab harmony on the personal level. Prejudice and antagonism were intensified by the *intifada,* the Palestinian rebellion in the occupied West Bank and Gaza, and Israeli Arab citizens feel increasingly alienated from the majority Jewish population, which in turn fears a fifth-column threat. These trends are tearing apart the civility of Israeli society, polarizing Israeli Jews and Arabs who share citizenship in the same land.

The struggle for Israel's future depends as much on its ability to address its domestic challenges as its security challenges. To those issues discussed above should be added the growing environmental threats, the issues of equality of women, and the need for electoral reform to further democratize the structure of the Israeli government.

In many ways, the vision of Israel's early *chalutzim* ("pioneers") of a society of economic equality and social justice has faded under the strains of austerity and the need to maintain a huge defense burden. As in other countries, a hunger for consumer goods has eclipsed much of the pioneering spirit of the early days, and a sense of national purpose wanes except in times of emergency.

Jews believe that only when Israel and its Arab enemies make peace and Israel can redirect the 40 percent of its annual budget from defense can it fully address its domestic concerns.

That Israel has done as much as it has for the cause of social justice is testimony to its abiding commitment to the age-old values of the Jewish people. That it has still much to achieve remains the goal—and obligation—of the people of Israel and the Jewish people around the globe. For all of us, the achievement of an Israel that becomes a light unto the nations will be the fulfillment of three thousand years of Zionist dreams.

≡ 7 ≡

PEACE AND INTERNATIONAL AFFAIRS

A Real Dilemma: Does Commitment to Israel Mean Supporting High United States Defense Budgets?

During the 1970s and 1980s, one of the central arguments of Jewish neoconservatives was that mainstream Jewish organizations particularly, and Jews in general, made a major mistake by consistently taking dovish antimilitary budget stances. A dovish position might have reflected Jewish values and interests during the Vietnam War, but after the Yom Kippur War, in which Israel was almost wiped out in a surprise assault by its Arab neighbors, Israel's very survival was clearly seen to depend on a strong American military. They argued that support for the Pentagon was vital because a strong American military would serve as a deterrent to Soviet and Arab aggressive intentions in the Middle East including threats to the security of Israel.

Neoconservatives said that support for efforts to cut the United States military budget, opposition to new weapons systems, as well as alliances with antiwar groups whom the Pentagon regarded virtually as political enemies would weaken the American military and would engender the resentment of the Pentagon. The United States government and its Department of Defense would thereby be less inclined to be supportive of Israel.

Despite the collapse of the Soviet threat, these arguments continue today, especially in the aftermath of the Gulf War. How can we ask for American funding for Israel to develop the Arrow missile portion of the Strategic Defense Initiative (Star Wars) if we oppose most other funding for Star Wars? Do we endanger Israel if we continue to push for deep cuts in Pentagon spending?

What should the Jewish community have done? What should it do now?

Response

Almost none of the mainstream Jewish organizations adopted the policies of the neoconservatives. Public opinion and voting-data analyses indicate that the Jewish community has remained as liberal as ever on both domestic and international affairs issues. The support of sixteen national Jewish agencies for the Nuclear Freeze campaign in the early eighties confirmed this conclusion. Most Jews believed that a strong military did not depend on bloated budgets as much as on sensible priorities. They believed that the stress on nuclear weapons systems not only brought the world closer to a global catastrophe but drained money from the kind of conventional weaponry that Israel needed.

Moreover, the backlash predicted by the neoconservatives never occurred. Despite the assertive liberal character of the Jewish community, much of the past two decades has seen unprecedented military alliances between Israel and the United States. And, while the Congress, including most Jewish senators and representatives, never gave Presidents Reagan and Bush the funding they requested for Star Wars—generally because they believe space-based weapons would not work and would only lead us closer to war—there has been overwhelming congressional support for the Arrow missile (a land-based defense against shorter range missiles). That support grew after the performance of the more primitive Patriot missiles used during the Gulf War. The Arrow is expected to compensate for many of the deficiencies of the Patriot and will likely be widely used by both the United States and Israel.

Jewish tradition has not glorified war or extolled the warmaker. In Jewish history, the heroes are sages and saints, rarely warriors. Rabbi Yochanan ben Zakkai is revered for his nonviolent triumph over Roman might. The historian Josephus reminds us of Jewish nonviolent resistance to the bloody Caligula. King David himself was not permitted to build the Temple because his hands had spilled blood in battle. A talmudic story depicts God rebuking the angels of heaven for bursting into songs of joy when the Red Sea closed on the drowning Egyptian pursuers: "My creatures are perishing and you want to sing praises!" (B. Talmud, *Megillah* 10b)

Likewise, Chanukah, because it originally celebrated a military victory, was virtually ignored by Jews until it was transformed into a holiday commemorating the rededication of the Temple. It is no accident that, on the Sabbath during Chanukah, Jews recite the passage: "Not by might, nor by power, but by My spirit, said *Adonai*." (Zechariah 4:6) The Book of Proverbs declares: "If your enemy is hungry, give him bread to eat; and if he is thirsty, give him water to drink." (Proverbs 25:21) And in the same spirit, "Rejoice not when your enemy falls." (Proverbs 24:17)

With the destruction of the Jewish state in 70 C.E., the prophetic vision of peace became the dream of the Jewish people. Whether by ideology or by external circumstances, Jews were almost completely nonviolent from the end of the Bar Kochba revolt in 135 C.E. to the Warsaw Ghetto uprisings in 1943. The ideal of universal peace had become the mission of the people of Israel.

The Apocrypha, the Midrash, and the Talmud place a high priority on the ideal of peace. Indeed, no subject of morality is accorded such depth of feeling and passion of conviction as the value of world peace. Jews were taught not merely to love peace but to "pursue it." Israel's majestic contribution to civilization was the inspired vision of a *universal* peace, not only for Israel but for all peoples. Micah's prophecy casts a ray of hope across the millennia of time to such peace convenants of our own times as the United Nations:

> And God shall judge between many peoples,
> And shall decide concerning mighty nations afar off;
> And they shall beat their swords into plowshares,
> And their spears into pruning-hooks;
> Nation shall not lift up sword against nation,
> Neither shall they learn war any more.
>
> (Micah 4:3)

This attitude, so basic to Judaism, was strikingly reaffirmed in the classical rabbinic period.

> Great is peace, for all blessings are contained in it, as it is written . . . *Seek peace and pursue it.* (Psalms 34:15) Great is peace, for God's name is peace. (*Leviticus Rabbah, Tzav,* 19:9) The Law does not command you to run after or pursue the other commandments, but only to fulfill them upon the appropriate occasion. But *peace* you must seek in your own place and *pursue* it even to another place as well. (*Numbers Rabbah, Hukkat,* 19:27)

But the tradition did not rest content with generalities; it was very specific about applying these ideals to daily life. Thus, for example, while Judaism does recognize the duty of a person to preserve his or her own life and defend others, it is very specific in *prohibiting the shedding of innocent blood.*

Judaism further insists that, even in the most clear-cut case of self-defense against a precisely identified assailant, the use of *excessive* violence is not to be sanctioned.

> It has been taught by Rabbi Jonathan b. Saul: If one was pursuing his fellow to slay him, and the pursued could have saved himself by maiming a limb of the pursuer but instead killed his pursuer, the pursued is subject to execution on that account.
>
> (*Sanhedrin* 74a)

The same limitation, incidentally, applied also to a bystander who, witnessing such a murderous pursuit, is enjoined to intervene on behalf of the pursued. He, too, if he needlessly slayed rather than maimed the assailant, was guilty of murder because of that excess. Even in a justifiable war, Jewish law considered killing an offense before God; a sin offering was made by all soldiers.

The limitation of violence is one of the most basic of all Jewish ethical teachings. The deployment of weapons of indiscriminate mass destruction makes it increasingly difficult to justify war from a traditional Jewish perspective.

In our paradoxical history, in which Jews dreamed of peace but frequently fought wars, how are these two realities reconciled? An evaluation of the Gulf War: Desert Storm provides an insight into the substance, and the relevancy, of the Jewish balance struck through its creation of rules regulating when wars could be fought and how they must be fought.

The Gulf War and the Jewish Community

A Real Dilemma:
Should the UAHC Support War in the Gulf?

In December 1990, the UAHC Board of Trustees met to consider whether or not to support President Bush in his threat to use force to expel Iraq from Kuwait. Organizations like the Union of American Hebrew Congregations and other Jewish bodies had vigorously opposed the Vietnam War, strongly criticized the escalating defense budgets of the Reagan years, and called for arms control agreements to reduce the number of nuclear and conventional armaments proliferating throughout the world.

For these same Jewish organizations, long identified with antiwar positions and some of which were well known in Washington as part of the coalition against such weapons systems as the B-1 bomber and MX and Midgetman missiles, to emerge as enthusiastic supporters of President Bush in his campaign to rebuff Iraqi aggression against Kuwait would be a remarkable turnaround. How could it be justified? Was it simply that, unlike the Vietnam War in which Israel was not directly involved, Israel's very survival was seen to be at stake in the Gulf conflict? And, if that was the reason for passionate Jewish support, weren't columnists like Pat Buchanan basically correct in asserting that American Jews were for the Gulf War because of their commitment to Israel?

If you were a UAHC board member how would you have voted? Why?

Response

The board voted overwhelmingly to support the United Nations vote and the leadership of President Bush in resisting Saddam Hussein's aggression. In fact, most American Jews *were* unashamedly concerned about Israel's survival in a region dominated by a dangerous tyrant brandishing an arsenal of conventional, biological, chemical, and possibly nuclear weapons and proudly affirming his plan to "incinerate half of Israel." But Jews—and non-Jews alike—also believed that fundamental American interests were at stake in the Gulf, that Saddam was a threat to all the nations in the region and therefore to the peace of the world, and that America has a duty to protect the oil supplies vital to the free world and to America itself.

Did the Gulf War make Israel safer? Probably yes. Did it, as President Bush predicted, open a window of opportunity for peace in the Middle East? The enhanced credibility of the United States with the Arab countries was certainly responsible in large measure for their willingness to engage in the peace process. But the jury is still out on whether the parties are truly prepared to take advantage of this opportunity.

Moreover, the price America has paid for this war cannot be calculated with a balance sheet. In 1991, Bill Moyers produced a powerful documentary on public television, juxtaposing our triumph in Kuwait against our tragic failures in the inner cities of America. If we could marshall the resources and the will to transport a half-million combatants halfway around the world to defeat an aggressive tyrant, why have we surrendered without a real fight in the war against drugs, homelessness, the collapsing infrastructure of America, the failure of our educational system, the scandal of our medical system, and the abandonment of the underclass? Bold presidential leadership in mobilizing the nation in a short war is easier than addressing our domestic crises, which would spell division, cost vast amounts of unavailable money, and squander political capital and popularity.

These questions are deepened by the reflection that this war might well have been avoided if United States policy prior to the invasion of Kuwait had not been one of appeasing Saddam Hussein, selling him arms and giving him credits. Some members of Congress had wanted to impose sanctions against Saddam after his massacre of the Kurds with chemical weapons, but the administration then claimed to see signs of incipient moderation and, in any event, wanted to use Iraq as a weapon against the "greater" enemy, Iran.

As the nineties unfold, second thoughts emerge about the wisdom of our policies in the Gulf War. We had believed that our war was not against the Iraqi people but only against its leader. Now it turns out that, in some ways, it was the other way around. The tyrant is still in power, defying the United Nations, stonewalling its resolutions, negotiating with world leaders, spewing venom against Israel, threatening the Kurds, and playing hide-and-seek with his nuclear assets. But the impact of the war on the Iraqi people was and is savage.

How many hundreds of thousands were killed? How many children died from hunger and disease? Exactly what did we win? We defanged Hussein for the moment and, let us hope, generated a window of opportunity for peace in the Middle East. But, for the most part, in the absence of any overall geopolitical strategy of what a new world order would look like, the euphoria has passed like a desert mirage, revealing a scene not much different from before. And the upheavals in Los Angeles pushed the Gulf onto the back burner of American attention, bringing the American domestic crisis center stage.

So was the war another Vietnam? Another false adventure, a hollow victory? Could it be a victory if Saddam is still in place? History will make its own judgment, but it will have to reckon also with some positive outcomes: Iraq's biological and chemical arsenal, which it obviously had no qualms about using against its neighbors, Arab or Jewish, was at least partially destroyed. And, while Saddam concealed some of his nuclear materials, many of his facilities were damaged. The United Nations was revived as a force for world peace and international law, and the allies intervened to provide some protection for the Kurds in the north against the Iraqi army. Hussein's position was clearly weakened, particularly in the face of continuing economic restrictions from the international community.

Some momentum was generated for arms control and restraint, particularly in the indiscriminate sale of weapons for mass destruction. The United States, in the wake of the Gulf victory, was left the only superpower with real authority, influence, and clout in the Middle East. And the only question was whether the United States could use this authority to begin shaping the new world order that President Bush envisioned as the true goal of the Gulf undertaking. The decision to sell F-15s to Saudi Arabia in late 1992 raised serious concerns. Is this a "new world order" or business as usual?

The Jewish Tradition and the Gulf War

Jewish rules and regulations of war fall into two categories: first, the different kinds of war and the justification and authority to wage them; second, the rules of how warfare should be fought. Together, these two categories of rules comprise what in Christian and secular terms is called the "just war" theory.

One of the most fascinating aspects of the Gulf War was how often the "just war" theory was invoked in discussing the war. Unlike earlier wars in this century, in which international norms were generally discussed only after the war was over, the prosecution of the Gulf War repeatedly involved justification of strategic decisions, the moral rightness of using force instead of sanctions, and the appropriate amount of force necessary to achieve various goals of the war.

In light of widespread opposition of mainstream Protestant and Catholic communities to the war in contrast to decisive Jewish community approval of the war, it is interesting to note both the similarities and contrasts between Christian and Jewish "just war" theory.

As indicated above, "just war" theory involves: (1) moral justification for *beginning* the war and (2) moral means in *fighting* the war. As to the question of a moral justification for fighting wars, both the Jewish and Christian traditions say that the underlying cause for the war must be just. Self-defense in general or defense of an innocent bystander (i.e., Kuwait) would be a valid criterion in both traditions. But one relevant contrast between the two traditions does emerge: the issue of who is qualified to declare war. Christianity presumes that competent authority to declare war can vest in the executive (king, president, prime minister, etc.) of the polity alone. Judaism requires that, in an offensive war, there must be some check on the prerogative of the military or executive authority to wage war. In ancient times, that check came through the approval of the Sanhedrin much as the United States Constitution requires the approval of Congress. In this instance, such approval was forthcoming in the "use of force" debate and vote of Congress in December 1990.

In terms of the rules on when and how to wage war, several interesting contrasts between the various traditions emerge. First, the Christian tradition advocates the use of force only as a last resort. By such a standard, the argument for giving sanctions against Iraq more time to work would have been compelling. Judaism maintains only that a good-faith effort must be made to avoid war. Some strands of the *halachah* interpret this as requiring an effort for a peaceful resolution up to at least three days before an attack; others maintain a requirement to sue for peace on three consecutive days. On this basis, repeated and much publicized

American efforts to avoid war in the Gulf clearly would appear to have met the Jewish tradition's requirements even while they failed the Christian standards.

Second, both traditions have a preeminent concern to protect civilian life. The Jewish tradition says that a city should not be surrounded on all sides so that those who wish to flee might do so. When a city is conquered, the noncombatants, particularly women and children, are given stringent protection. By this standard, the stated concern of the allied troops to protect civilian lives was in vivid moral contrast to brutal and intentional Iraqi attacks on the civilian center of cities in Israel and Saudi Arabia as well as Kuwait.

Third, Christianity requires the test of proportionality (i.e., that force necessary to achieve a military objective is permissible). Although some standards of Jewish thought seem congenial to this idea, the Jewish tradition is less concerned about proportion than it is with deciding which categories of targets are subject to attack and which are not. No force could be used against the latter (e.g., innocent civilians and fruit-bearing trees) except in specified exceptional circumstances. No limitation on force is set for appropriate targets. In this sense, the saturation bombings of *military* targets that some Christian thinkers described as disproportionately excessive might well be permitted by the *halachah*.

Fourth, Christianity seems to lack Judaism's central concern about protection of the environment through categories of targets that are totally off-limits. This begins with the admonition in Deuteronomy not to cut down fruit-bearing trees. (Deuteronomy 20:19-20) The term used is *bal tashchit* ("do not destroy"). From the prohibition against cutting fruit-bearing trees, the Talmud infers protection for any tree or plant that provides food. The halachic *midrash* expands this to include storehouses of food. The Rambam further stretches the idea of *bal tashchit*: "Not only one who cuts down fruit-bearing trees but also one who smashes household goods, tears clothes, demolishes a building, stops up a spring, or wastes food in a destructive way violates the command: 'You must not destroy.'" (*Mishneh Torah*, "Laws concerning Kings and Wars," 8-10)

Thus, anything indispensable to renewal of civilian life after a war would be exempt from destruction. On this basis, Saddam Hussein's wanton destruction of the environment through spilling millions of barrels of oil in the sea and by setting fire to hundreds of oil wells would be a gross and flagrant violation of the standards of Jewish law. However, the pulverizing allied bombing of civilian targets to cripple the economic, health, housing, electrical, and water infrastructure of Iraqi society also would be limited.

The Post-Cold War Era: United States Policies and Jewish Interests

Even before the Gulf War, the world had witnessed its most dramatic changes since the end of World War II. The Soviet international bloc had shattered; communism was disintegrating as a viable economic system in the modern world, collapsing under the weight of its own stagnation; tenuous democratic reforms swept Eastern Europe and transformed the Soviet Union itself into a commonwealth of independent republics.

The North American Treaty Organization (NATO, the West's post-World War II military alliance), devised to keep Soviet expansion in check, is in the process of reconfiguring itself into an economic alliance. Europe is preparing to join into an economic confederation in the mid-1990s and, in the process, to take a major step towards a united Europe.

In a world without either serious military threats to the survival of the United States or ideological threats to our democratic values, what is the need or justification for American intervention around the world? Is it possible to set objective standards that will determine how, in what manner, and with whom the United States should intervene to protect its interests?

What was the justification for American intervention in the Persian Gulf? Was it the violation of Kuwait's sovereignty by Iraq? Then how to distinguish between that and Iraq's attack against Iran (the United States then supported Iraq) or, for that matter, the United States invasion of Panama? Would we be justified in intervening to stop the fratricidal killing and "ethnic cleansing" in what was Yugoslavia or the tragic civil strife of Somalia?

Was our intervention aimed simply at protecting our economic interests by maintaining oil supplies? But, if that is the case, what does the United States do to defend against even stronger *economic* rivals like Germany and Japan, nations that now subscribe to democratic values? And, if our major challenge in the world is to maintain our economic well-being and influence, what policies should we adopt to offset our economic rivals?

The Breakup of the USSR

The extraordinary events of 1991 culminated in the formal end of the USSR and efforts to establish a commonwealth of republics. This hastily arranged new political order raises many problems of vital concern to the United States and to the Jewish community. Will this new commonwealth hold together or will the republics end up in strife with each other? Will democracy be the norm in these new republics or will new tyrannies of the left or right emerge? Will the ethnic strife that has already led to bloodshed between the Armenians and the Azerbaijanis tear many of these republics apart in a civil war? Will the Jewish communities of those republics survive in such an atmosphere of ethnic tensions or war?

And what of the United States? With whom does it negotiate new economic treaties and arms control agreements? In early 1992, the Russian Republic attempted to consolidate all strategic nuclear weapons under its control. Not all republics agreed and, regardless of the strategic weapons, there will still be smaller tactical battlefield nuclear weapons in many of the republics. Should the United States provide massive foreign aid packages? Will a large foreign aid package to the republics put pressure on the amount of United States foreign aid available to other countries like Israel? And will a restive American public, increasingly allergic to foreign aid, support such efforts?

Modernizing the Arms Race

The disintegration of the Soviet Union has reduced but not eliminated the threat of nuclear weapons. By 1991, the United States and the USSR had passed only two major arms control treaties: the Intermediate Nuclear Forces Treaty (INF), signed in December 1987, and the Strategic Arms Reduction Treaty (START), signed in July 1991. Such important treaties as the Comprehensive Test Ban Treaty and the Chemical Weapons Disarmament Treaty, which have been the subject of discussions for over a decade between the United States and the Soviet Union, were not completed by late 1992.

On July 31, 1991, at a summit meeting in Moscow, President Bush and Soviet President Gorbachev signed the Strategic Arms Reduction Treaty (START). This treaty marked the first actual reduction in long-range nuclear weapons and culminated nine years of negotiations. By the end of the century, over four thousand nuclear warheads will be destroyed on both sides as a result of this treaty, marking the first real steps towards disarmament.

One positive aspect of START is the reductions it mandates in Intercontinental Ballistic Missiles (ICBMs). After seven years, the USSR was to reduce its ICBM arsenal by roughly 50 percent and the United States will have roughly 35 percent fewer ICBMs. This means that each side will be less dependent on nuclear warheads that can span oceans in under an hour to reach their destination. Rather, both sides would rely more on bombers and submarines to deploy their warheads, giving more crucial time for countermeasures, hot lines, and possible emergency diplomatic solutions in case of a cataclysmic accident or mistake.

At the same time, however, START places almost no constraints on the modernization of nuclear weapons, allowing the United States and the republics to develop and deploy newer and increasingly more destructive weapons systems.

Thus, today, the United States and the independent republics of the former Soviet Union still have between them some forty-six thousand warheads—almost all of them bigger than the bomb that devastated Hiroshima. A single one of these bombs could destroy Los Angeles; the detonation of a handful could alter, at least temporarily, the climate of the earth. We must not forget that the weapons plants, labs, and scientists that existed in the USSR before the breakup are, for the most part, still there.

As the Soviet Union breaks apart into a number of rival republics, several with their own nuclear arsenals, the world could be left in a far more dangerous and volatile situation than during the bad old days of the cold war.

Furthermore, so long as these dangerous arms remain the "weapons of choice" for these powers, there is always the danger of an accidental war erupting. In the late 1980s, both the Soviet Union and the United States accidentally shot down civilian airliners, believing that they were military planes. A study in the early 1980s indicated that, on a number of occasions, United States Defense Department computers falsely indicated that we were under attack by USSR missiles, bringing the United States to the brink of war. We must use the end of the cold war to set in place new mechanisms to reduce the dangers of nuclear war, including the possibility of a nuclear accident.

The United States and the Soviet Union had for many years indicated that they were willing to live within the constraints of deterrence. Since we currently have over ten times the number of weapons necessary to destroy the other side, we could theoretically cut drastically the number of weapons without undermining our strategic position. Economic pressures have greatly increased the desire to cut deeply into the military budgets on both sides, leading to the most serious consideration of drastic reductions that we have seen in more than forty years.

A Real Dilemma: The Morality of Making Nuclear Weapons

A few years ago, a Roman Catholic bishop called upon his parishioners who worked in nuclear weapons plants to quit their jobs because the building of nuclear weapons was "contrary to Roman Catholic teaching" and because weapons of mass destruction are incompatible with moral conscience. There was deep division in the aftermath of the bishop's plea, with controversy spreading well beyond the church.

A Jewish scientist from the Northeast wrote to the Commission on Social Action: "I am a Jew, not a Roman Catholic, but I believe Catholic teachings on war and peace really derive from the Jewish biblical tradition. The bishop's statement has stirred some doubts and conflicts in my conscience—doubts that festered for years but that I allowed to be dormant in my mind until now. Can a Jew, like me, who cares about Jewish beliefs and human life, continue to devote my scientific abilities . . . to the development of weapons that, if used, would lead to mass slaughter of innocent lives? Have I been deluding myself all these years by saying that nuclear weapons on both sides have kept the peace for half a century? Even if I could justify this work during the cold war with a Stalinist Soviet enemy, can I justify it now? Should I put an end to my participation in this work and make my living in more constructive pursuits? What does the Lord require of me?"

How should the commission have replied? What would you say?

Response

As to what Judaism teaches, the commission shared with the writer what is outlined in this chapter. In particular, the extensive laws of civilian protection and of those environmental concerns aimed at ensuring the postwar resumption of normal civilian life would be seen as violated by the use of nuclear weapons per se. In addition to the enormous destruction, the irradiation of land and property would result in exactly the inability of life to resume that the tradition seeks to ensure against.

However, can the *possession* of nuclear weapons for the sake of maintaining a balance of power be justified? This is a particularly difficult question to resolve halachically. Former British Chief Rabbi Immanuel Jackobovits, who in 1962 wrote that the possession of nuclear weapons could not be halachically justified, wrote in 1982 that the very success of the balance of terror for three decades had changed his halachic evaluation on this issue.

With regard to the specifics of what he should do, the commission said that Judaism is not structured like the Church; we do not issue encyclicals, and we put a premium on individual autonomy and individual choice. Nobody except one's self can resolve so personal a dilemma. We do not wish to play God or to presume to judge other people's lives.

But his wrestling with conscience *is* very Jewish indeed, and the question of how Jewish tradition views *nuclear weapons,* with the inevitable slaughter of innocent civilians, if the bomb is used, is not settled. Israel is believed to possess nuclear weapons to protect itself by deterring aggression from the likes of Iraq, Iran, and Syria. Is possession itself immoral? Can use of such a weapon be morally justified? Under what circumstances?

Horizontal Proliferation: Nuclear, Chemical, and Biological Weapons

Despite these very genuine fears, perhaps the greatest threat of nuclear war comes not from the superpowers, present and former, but from horizontal proliferation to other countries. Even before the glasnost era, the superpowers had begun to recognize the futility of nuclear war and sought ways to manage, if not contain, the nuclear arms race.

In 1992, there were five countries in the world known to possess nuclear weapons: the United States, the Soviet Union, France, England, and China. Four others—Israel, South Africa, Pakistan, and India—either have nuclear weapons deployed or have the components that can be assembled in a short period of time. Saddam

Hussein was only a year or two away from the club before the Gulf War.

Most international experts believe that within the next fifteen years there will be as many as thirty-five nations with the capability to build or purchase nuclear military technology. Both the CIA and the Nobel Peace Prize-winning Stockholm International Peace Research Institute (SIPRI) indicate that by the year 2000 there will be at least seven more members of the nuclear "club." Among the new candidates are Argentina, Brazil, Taiwan, Iran, North Korea, Libya, and Iraq.

As Jews, we have a particular stake. The image of a madman like Saddam Hussein with his finger on an atomic bomb is no longer the stuff of overheated imaginations. Will the next round of missiles be new and improved nuclear SCUDs aimed at Israeli civilian targets? What nation will Libya blackmail with its nuclear capability other than Israel? Even the *prospect* of the use of such weapons would likely compel Israel to launch a preemptive strike, raising the possibility of another and deadlier Israel-Arab War.

What can we do?

It is impossible to stop the flow of technology. The technological capability to build nuclear weapons will become increasingly cheaper, simpler, and more accessible as time goes on. The best we can do is act aggressively to slow it down and control it. The United States is the largest purveyor of nuclear technologies in the world followed by Germany, Italy, Sweden, England, and France. That means that most of the nuclear technology in the world is sold by the United States and its closest allies and friends.

International nonproliferation legislation is inadequate and ineffective. The emptiness of such a treaty is underscored by the ironic fact that Saddam Hussein *was* and *is* a *signatory* to it. The United States should lead the world in demanding substantially tighter regulations on the sale of such technologies. It should insist that stiff international sanctions be brought against anyone who violates nonproliferation.

The United States must also stop its own obsession with nuclear weapons and reduce the role of nuclear power plants as a primary energy source.

In addition to the approximately twenty countries that are believed to be developing nuclear arms, ten are said to be developing biological weapons and thirty are developing chemical weapons. Among them are Iran, Cuba, South Africa, Ethiopia, Iraq, and Libya. Indeed Iraq used chemical weapons both in its war with Iran and on its own Kurdish citizens. It is not easy to control the spread of such weapons; the ingredients are inexpensive, relatively easy to obtain, and often also used for nonmilitary purposes.

Throughout 1990–1991, the Religious Action Center mobilized a bipartisan coalition of senators and representatives committed to the proposition that countries using weapons of mass destruction be outlawed by the community of nations and that governments and corporations assisting in the development of such weapons be exposed and subject to economic sanctions aimed at depriving them of their ill-gained economic benefits.

The president vetoed this legislation in October 1990; but, after both houses of Congress repassed the legislation by overwhelming margins in late October 1991, the president signed a bill containing very strong sanctions. In its three decades, there has been no piece of legislation in which the Religious Action Center has played a more influential role than in the passage of these sanctions.

The Cutting Edge: Energy

Our number one technological priority in the 1990s should be the development of *environmentally safe, low-cost, renewable sources of energy: sun, wind, water, and geothermal.* It is the absence of such effective energy sources, together with the high cost and political volatility of oil, that encourages many Third World countries to demand nuclear technology as a means of meeting their growing energy needs. These demands will increase as they seek to bring their people into the developed world. Furthermore, there is no line between "nonmilitary" nuclear technology and "military" nuclear technology. Once a country has the technology, it can eventually learn to adapt it to military uses if it chooses to do so.

This problem will become magnified by the growing threat of

nuclear terrorism. Plutonium waste dumped into the water reservoirs of New York City could do as much damage to the population as a nuclear bomb dropped on the Empire State Building. As technologies improve to allow for smaller explosive devices, a suitcase in the trunk of a car can be as effective a delivery system as a ballistic missile or submarine.

Democracy, Human Rights, and Jews in Eastern Europe

The democratic revolutions of 1989 in Eastern Europe were not the first such astonishing changes in the 1980s. They were anticipated by the unexpected victory of the Aquino democratic forces in the Phillipines, the restoration of democracy in Chile, Nicaragua, Pakistan, Panama, Argentina, and elsewhere. But, in each of these countries, as in the Eastern European countries, there is no guarantee that democracy will be sustained.

Unlike the United States or Western Europe, there is precious little democratic tradition in Eastern Europe or elsewhere in the world; experiments in democracy and pluralism were either short-lived or nonexistent before 1989.

Furthermore, wherever nations are wracked with serious economic crises or ethnic strife, antidemocratic demagogues and extremists strive for power on platforms that foster scapegoating and anti-Semitism. Thus, in the early 1930s, high unemployment and runaway inflation in the Weimar Republic of Germany helped breed the frustration and despair that Hitler's Nazis exploited in their rise to power.

There are, of course, particular Jewish stakes in the changing face of the Eastern bloc. Most of those nations had long been servile and virulent Soviet-bloc enemies of Israel. Within a few months of overthrowing their communist regimes, all reestablished diplomatic relations with Israel. Most joined the United States in voting in the United Nations to reverse the odious resolution equating Zionism and racism.

Furthermore, each of these countries has small and beleaguered

Jewish communities whose well-being depends in large measure on the development of democratic, pluralistic systems. The relatively few Jews remaining in the republics face new threats from nationalistic, anti-Semitic elements that had been kept in check by authoritarian communist regimes.

The Jewish communities of Eastern Europe find themselves in a paradoxical situation. Formal restrictions have been lifted, Hebrew schools begun, synagogues reopened, communities reorganized; at the same time, grass-roots anti-Semitic incidents have sharply escalated, heightening the sense of unease among Jews.

Clearly, the interest of the Jewish community can best be served by Western policies that strengthen the embryonic democratic regimes of these nations and challenge the governments to repudiate the hate groups in their midst.

What Should America Do?

A Real Dilemma: Dole—
Should We Cut Aid to Help Other Countries?

In 1990, the Republican Senate leader, Senator Robert Dole, suggested that we slash 5 percent of all existing United States foreign aid and transfer it to the developing democratic countries of Eastern Europe. This would have meant that all current recipients of foreign aid, including Israel, would have received less American assistance.

The Jewish community was committed both to helping the Eastern European countries and to maintaining foreign aid to Israel, particularly in the light of the vast influx of Soviet Jews. How should the Jewish community have responded to the Dole initiative?

Response

The Jewish community vigorously opposed the Dole initiative, insisting that United States support for the emerging democracies of Eastern Europe not be extended at the expense of other nations with legitimate claims. The Congress, thus far, has rejected the Dole approach, but the need to stabilize the economies of former communist countries requires foreign aid. This international challenge needs an international response with the United States playing a leading role. But, if it was in our interest to spend over $100 billion a year on the military in the seventies and eighties to deter the Soviets, is it not in our interest to spend a minute portion of that sum as foreign aid to stabilize democracy abroad and secure the gains to American interests and values offered by the dissolution of the USSR?

International Economic Justice

The economic inequity between the world's haves and have-nots constitutes potentially one of the most explosive ethical challenges and long-range political dangers to the world in the post-cold war era. If there is one area in which United States foreign policy has failed most abysmally in the past twenty years, it has been in the area of economic justice. Tragically, this situation is getting worse, not better.

More than half a billion people suffer from serious malnutrition and related diseases and millions of children under the age of five will die of deprivation this year. Each day *forty thousand children* in the Third World die from *preventable* disease and malnutrition.

Father Theodore Hesburgh, the distinguished former president of Notre Dame University, argues that this "systematic geographical discrimination" threatens the stability and security of "Spaceship Earth." We accept this global inequity and discontinuity with indifference each day. To paraphrase Father Hesburgh: If you are an American, you look forward to an ever-lengthening life characterized by increasing health, education, economic, and social well-being. If born in Africa, you will live a short life of illness, malnutrition, illiteracy, and hopelessness. Our children confront the frightening prospect of a glutted market of Ph.D.'s; Southeast Asian children too often never step foot into a schoolroom. We are over-fed and overweight; in South America, from the time of birth, too many suffer from systemic malnutrition that prevents their brains from developing fully. We decide where to purchase our second homes; they live in huts of cardboard or mud. We travel supersonically across this globe, even venture out into the universe itself; they grow up to bitter frustration and despair trapped in urban ghettos and rural slums whose poverty curtails their lives. We spend trillions on weapons that, if used, would destroy all of God's creation; they pray for enough resources to sustain their meager quality of life.

Peace Dividend

The startling changes that have swept the former Soviet Union and Eastern Europe offer the United States the opportunity to reshape our nation's priorities in a way not possible since the end of World War II.

If we are going to increase our economic competitiveness, move to the cutting edge of the world's technological development, house the homeless in our streets, revitalize our educational system, address the acute situation of inadequate and costly health care in the United States, protect the environment, and rebuild the infrastructure of our cities, military funds must be reallocated to civilian needs.

Plans to redistribute our resources were temporarily sidetracked by the Gulf War, the euphoria that followed it, and the newfound prestige of the Pentagon. The nation that mobilized its resources to fight and win that war is now clearly challenged to show the same kind of decisiveness, daring, and will to address and overcome the domestic crisis that is undermining America's national security. The riots in Los Angeles represented a wake-up call to this danger.

According to the General Accounting Office, up to 50 percent of the $300 billion annual military budget continues to be devoted to NATO for defending Western Europe. Some 12 to 15 percent of the Pentagon budget is spent on strategic nuclear programs— also designed primarily to counter yesterday's Soviet menace.

Regardless of the extent to which the peace dividend is postponed and whittled down, it but increases the necessity of concentration on this country's real needs. The presidential campaign of '92, albeit inadequate and frustrating, began to focus on the needs of America, our unfinished agenda. Our security depends more on the state of our cities and the status of intergroup relations than it does on B-2 bombers; as much on the health of our children and the educational standards of our schools as it does on cruise missiles and chemical weapons; more on the sense of purpose and morale of our citizenry than on ever escalating military budgets. This decade provides a unique opportunity to reassess America's priorities for the next century and, to put it bluntly, choose life over death. Abba Eban, the Israeli statesman, once wrote:

> In each of us and in every nation and every faith, there are arsenals of destructive rage, but there are also powerful armies of moral strength. The choice is ours, even as it has been since these words were addressed to our people: "See, I have set before you this day, the blessing and the curse, life and death; therefore, choose life that you may live, you and your seed after you."
>
> As we look out on the human condition, our consciences cannot be clean. If they are clean, then it is because we do not use them enough. It is not inevitable that we march in hostile and separate hosts into the common abyss. There is another possibility—of an ordered world, illuminated by reason, governed by law. If we cannot touch it with our hands, let us at least grasp it with our vision.

That is the vision to which we are called. May we have the courage to grasp it.

≡ 8 ≡

ENDANGERED JEWRY

Soviet Jewry

There have been five transcendent events in Jewish history since World War II, each warranting the claim of miracle. The first was the birth of the State of Israel, reemerging into history out of the ashes of the Holocaust and after a virtual blank of two thousand years. The second was the Six-Day War, with Israel's extraordinary lightning-quick military triumph over the vastly superior combined military force of the Arab world. The third was the peace treaty signed between Israel and Egypt at Camp David, the first peace accord between Israel and an Arab neighbor. The fourth was the breathtaking exodus of Jews from the former communist empire. And the fifth was the amazing rescue of Ethiopia's Jews— fifteen thousand alone in Operation Solomon in 1991.

Ransoming of the Captives

Ensuring the safety and well-being of our brothers and sisters in foreign lands reflects one of the oldest Jewish imperatives: *pidyon shevuyim,* the "ransoming of captives." By the early talmudic era, a body of law had developed to regulate who should be rescued, how much should be paid, and how to prevent hostage taking.

One of the greatest of the medieval rabbis, Rabbi Meir of Rothenburg, taught that everything possible should be done to ransom captives when Jewish lives were threatened; however, when persons were held captive *solely* for ransom, payment should be withheld so as not to encourage additional abductions. This responsum was written when the rabbi himself was being held for ransom. He remained in captivity to the end of his life.

The concept of *pidyon shevuyim* encompasses the idea of using political influence on behalf of beleaguered communities. Thus, in the twelfth century, when the influential Cordoban Jew Hasdai ibn Shaprut was asked to negotiate a treaty between the caliphate of Cordoba and the rulers of the Byzantine Empire, he conditioned his efforts on the Byzantine easing of oppressive regulations aimed at their Jewish community. Our unswerving efforts to save the Soviet and the Ethiopian Jewish communities are modern extensions of the ancient tradition of *pidyon shevuyim*.

The Rescue of Soviet Jewry

In the dark days of Joseph Stalin's reign of terror, the greatest Jewish writers and poets in the Soviet Union were tortured and murdered in the Lubiyanka Prison. Under communism, Jewish life underwent severe restrictions: Jewish students faced anti-Jewish quotas, the Hebrew language was banned, Zionism was condemned, and Jewish culture was torn out by the roots. The dream of emigration sustained many Jewish hearts, but it seemed an impossible dream.

After seventy years, the Communist empire has collapsed. Jewish emigration, which for decades had been cynically turned on and off like a faucet by Soviet authorities to win concessions from the United States, has now reached unprecedented heights. Indeed, in 1990, the iron door swung open and hundreds of thousands of Soviet Jews flooded through the gates, streaming into Israel and, to a lesser extent, the United States. The movement of Jews in such large numbers has powerfully transformed the Jewish map.

For Israel, the emigration of Soviet Jewry has been a godsend although the financial burdens have been overwhelming. It is a vindication of a central purpose and meaning of Zionism: the in-gathering of the exiles.

It is also a corrective to demography. Until now, the higher Arab birthrate threatened to turn Israel into an Arab state at some point in the forseeable future. No more. Moreover, the psychological and spiritual impact of this largest *aliyah* in its history has restored the nation's morale after years of adversity.

Indeed, no previous *aliyah* had brought to Israel such a pool of well-educated scientists, doctors, engineers, musicians, artists, and other professionals, perfectly suited to enhance the nation's economy and civic life.

Yet with all of its wondrous potential, much of the short-term impact of the emigration has been to cause economic and social strains.

Inadequate housing is still a problem. Israel's social service and health service infrastructure is being overwhelmed (not even the most liberal years of United States immigration policy accepted, as Israel does, all immigrants—including the sick and disabled). Massive short-term immigration intensifies Israel's water shortage problems and threatens Israel's deteriorating environmental integrity.

The most endemic and alarming problem is, of course, unemployment. Soviet (and Ethiopian) Jews will tolerate inadequate housing if they are convinced it is temporary. They are less likely to tolerate menial jobs or the lack of jobs altogether. Jobs provide hope and a future; without jobs, many immigrants will lose heart. With a general unemployment rate running at nearly 11 percent in 1992, providing job opportunities—particularly opportunities in keeping with their skills, backgrounds, and expectations—to newly arrived immigrants is a virtual impossibility.

Underlying much of this problem is the distinctly high level of educational and professional training of these immigrants. There has been no immigration like it in history:

• Approximately 65 percent are university-trained or technologically trained compared to 23 percent of the Israeli populace.

- Engineers, physicists, and architects comprise one-third of the work force—in a country that already has a high unemployment rate among its own engineers.

- Of the 220,000 who have arrived, fully 2,000 are professional musicians—enough to staff a new symphony orchestra and then some.

- Israel already has the highest proportion of doctors of any population in the world: 290 out of every 100,000 people. But the ratio of the arrivals in 1991 *was ten times that number.*

Is There a Jewish Future in Russia?

And what of the Soviet Jews who still choose to stay in their homeland? For some Jews, the promise of democracy is worth testing. Perhaps, in this new era of democracy and expanding human rights, Jewish culture and Judaism may be allowed fuller expression.

Indeed, synagogues and religious schools have reopened. A Jewish cultural center was established in Moscow, named after a Jewish artist who had been killed by the Soviets during Stalin's rule. A Jewish *va'ad* was permitted to organize as an umbrella council for the hundreds of local and national Jewish groups that had sprung up. The Hebrew language has been accepted, kosher restaurants have been opened, and Jewish rabbinical seminaries have been established. In Moscow, the nation's first Reform synagogue, Hineini, was organized in 1990 by the World Union for Progressive Judaism, the world body of Reform Judaism.

Are these developments harbingers of a genuine Jewish future in the former Soviet Union? We cannot say for certain. Popular anti-Semitism, until recently contained by totalitarian regimes, is now widespread. Indeed, as ethnic strife increases in the newly independent republics, especially Muslim republics, the potential for scapegoating and nationalist extremism rises. Anti-Semitism may no longer be official policy, but it remains the tool of the demagogues. Ultranationalists use it to stir the volatile masses. Jewish life in the republics may improve but only if the post-Communist leadership finds the courage to combat actively the growing anti-Semitism—and only if the fragile roots of these democratic experiments take hold.

The world Jewish community must continue its efforts on behalf of the Jews who choose to stay in Russia and the other republics. We need to send in teachers, educational resources, community organizers, musicians, and artists. We need to provide financial resources to support these fledgling institutions. Their religious freedom must be secured against both external restrictions from their government and internal repression from mainstream Orthodox Judaism. Until recently, the only Jewish religious option was Orthodox (particularly chasidic).

If this is the only choice, most Jews will be left in limbo. Modern liberal Judaism, adapting Jewish traditions to the real world, has much to offer former Soviet Jews eager to identify with their people through a religious faith congenial to the temper of our time. The president of the Hineini congregation in Moscow conducted the moving Jewish religious ceremonies, carried on national TV, for Ilya Krichevsky, the first hero to fall defying the attempted coup in 1991.

A Real Dilemma:
Building a Reform Synagogue in Moscow

In 1990, the World Union for Progressive Judaism (WUPJ), the international arm of Reform Jewry, faced this dilemma: Should it invest part of its limited resources in assisting the development of a Reform congregation in Moscow? We faced bureaucratic obstacles from the state in obtaining a building for the synagogue; we faced opposition from Orthodox, particularly chasidic, groups who saw us as undermining the Jewish community; and we faced the criticisms of those who maintained that the only way to secure the lives of Soviet Jews was to get them out as soon as possible. What should the WUPJ have done?

Response

After much deliberation, a firm decision was made to move ahead forcefully in the establishment of a liberal Jewish community in Moscow. Whether we liked it or not, there were Jews who were going to stay. These Jews had rights as well. Moreover, the democratic reforms in the former Soviet Union have a fighting chance to make it, and Jews who join in that fight deserve our support. Members of the Moscow congregation were heavily involved in the liberal democratic movements and many stayed up for three days and nights to face down the forces of repression during the 1991 coup attempt.

Immigration to the United States

Another prong of the miracle of Soviet Jewry is the influx into the United States. In the fiscal years 1990-1991, 40,000 immigrant slots for Russian Jews were allocated. This was a high proportion of the total of 122,000 refugees who could have been admitted into the United States in those years. Jewish organizations were under heavy pressure to lobby the American government to let more Soviet Jews into the country. But the United States was itself constrained by severe budgetary pressures. It costs the American government an average of $7,000 per refugee, and it would be unfair to ask for additional increases for a group that had another haven readily available (Israel). In addition, some 14 million refugees (in a world awash with refugees) clamor for sanctuary in the United States.

A Real Dilemma: Do Jews
Suffer from "Mitzvah Sickness"?

One of the coauthors of this book was making a speech to a synagogue audience explaining why Jewish organizations accepted the limitation (the 40,000 out of 122,000 refugees) on the admission of Soviet Jews into the United States in 1990. One angry member of the audience interrupted to say: "You people are suffering from the 'mitzvah sickness.' You should be demanding slots for *all* Soviet Jews who wish to come, not just forty thousand. No other group worries about a fair proportion of slots for *other* groups. They demand admission for their *own* people—Asians, Hispanics, Blacks—without worrying about fair shares for Jews and others. We should do the same. We have become obsessed worrying about other people and their rights. It has become our sickness."

How would you respond to this challenge?

Response

Both Jewish ethics and self-interest require us to be concerned not only with our own people but with the community as a whole. "If I am not for myself, who will be for me? But, if I am only for myself, what am I?" (*Pirke Avot* 1:14) Moreover, as a practical matter, severe interreligious and interracial repercussions could be ignited by insensitivity to the needs of others. And, as a matter of fact, in the end we did not even use all the slots reserved for our people.

Frankly, "mitzvah sickness" is not a Jewish weakness; it is our glory.

Just as Soviet Jewry may transform the quality of life in *Israel,* so Soviet Jews will have a substantial impact on American Jewish life as well. Most American Jews have contributed generously to enable Soviet Jews to settle in the United States and become part of the larger Jewish family.

But, in their first years in the United States, Soviet Jews (most of whom had not belonged to synagogues in the Soviet Union) were mostly concerned with housing, jobs, and schooling and had little time for or interest in synagogue life. Synagogues, working closely with Jewish federations, have reached out to Soviet Jewish immigrants. Many have provided complimentary membership; assisted families in finding housing, jobs, and medical care; organized English-speaking classes; and helped to integrate the new families into the community. Now, many of those who came in the 1970s and 1980s are settled enough to have become active members of the Jewish community, adding their talents and energy to enriching Jewish life.

Once, when upheaval in a European country spewed refugees all over the world, a Jewish immigration agency in America speedily and efficiently cranked up to handle the flow of Jewish refugees. Asked an official of a non-Jewish relief agency in awestruck astonishment: "How do you folks get your act together so quickly to absorb your refugees?" "Easy," came the reply. "We've had three thousand years of experience."

Ethiopian Jewry

In May 1991, almost overnight, in one of the most efficient and dramatic airlifts in history, an entire community, the black Jews of Ethiopia, were swept out of the Middle Ages and transported to a modern Jewish state. In that one stunning event, the very meaning of Zionism, Israel as a sanctuary for Jews in jeopardy anywhere in the world, was vindicated. An American journalist observed that this rescue was the first time in history that black people had been taken from one continent to another "in love, not in chains."

While Arabs were slaughtering their fellow Arabs in Iraq and Kuwait, Jews gave the world a glowing demonstration of the humanity and unity of the Jewish people. Strapped for resources, already drained by the Soviet Jewish *aliyah,* the people of Israel embraced their Ethiopian brothers and sisters, many of them ill or elderly, all of them needy. What other society would do this?

The miracle was made possible by the generous intervention of the United States. President Bush had personally signaled to the rebel leaders in Ethiopia that he wanted to see a safe harbor for the Jews. The United States Congress, especially the late heroic black Representative Mickey Leland, had kept the plight of Ethiopian Jews alive in the consciousness of the world. American Jews also played a strong role in ministering to the Ethiopian Jews during the long years of their waiting for redemption.

Organizations like the American Association for Ethiopian Jewry; the North American Conference on Ethiopian Jewry; the Joint Distribution Committee; and the Reform movement's own Project REAP (Reform Ethiopian Assistance Program), which helped to provide medical care to the Jews of Ethiopia, made the difference between life and death for thousands of Ethiopian Jews awaiting rescue. Many Israeli leaders, too, refused to turn their backs on this ancient community. And the Ethiopians themselves kept their Jewish faith alive through centuries of travail, going back perhaps to biblical days.

The absorption of these Jews into Israeli life has been bittersweet. There has never been a more enthusiastic nor more appreciative *aliyah* than that of these Jews. They have absorbed Israeli culture and modern life with amazing rapidity. Conversely, Israelis have accepted them with open arms and little prejudice.

On the other hand, the Chief Rabbinate of Israel has questioned their status as Jews and now requires symbolic conversions. Israel's economic problems and the massive immigration of Soviet Jews has depleted job, housing, and economic opportunities that otherwise would have been open to the Ethiopians. At the same time, the Ethiopian Jews are caught between their desire to be accepted and assimilated into Israeli society even while they wish to preserve their distinctive religious and cultural customs and identity. These religious and social limitations have bred growing frustrations that Israel will need to address.

≡ 9 ≡

ANTI-SEMITISM

In the decades following World War II, American Jewry experienced a glorious chapter of religious renewal, creativity, and cultural acceptance, becoming the freest, most affluent, and most secure Jewish community in the history of the Diaspora. Anti-Semitism declined significantly during this golden age, and most Jews no longer thought of themselves as guests in somebody else's home but as equal partners in a pluralistic America. Many American Jews became somewhat complacent about the danger of anti-Semitism, leaving the matter to such groups as the Anti-Defamation League, which specializes in preventing, monitoring, and containing anti-Semitism.

Quite unexpectedly, the bright sky of Jewish security in America has dimmed in recent years, with threatening thunderclouds forming over our heads, casting shadows we Jews had not experienced for decades. Perhaps no shadow was more ominous than the appearance on the American political scene of a former grand dragon of the Ku Klux Klan, one who regularly celebrated Adolf Hitler's birthday and whose entire career has consisted of exploiting racial fears and hatred. At first, David Duke was dismissed as a clownish relic of the Klan, which had gone into steep decline. Pretending to have moderated his extreme views, David Duke entered electoral politics. He cleverly pressed the hot buttons of affirmative action, welfare spending, and increased taxes. At a time of economic distress, he played on racial fears, blaming "them" for all the ills of society (e.g, crime, drugs, AIDS, welfare, and unemployment).

Armed with these buzzwords, Duke surprised everybody by winning a seat in the Louisiana state legislature. As a representative, he passed no bills in the legislature but helped to shift the agenda to target Blacks. He took colleagues to lunch to try to persuade them that the Holocaust never happened, that Auschwitz was a rubber factory, and that the sadistic Nazi doctor Mengele was a scientific genius.

In 1990, Duke ran for the United States Senate and almost won, losing to J. Bennett Johnston but winning 40 percent of the total vote and more than 60 percent of the white vote. In 1991, Duke collected a war chest from all over the United States and ran for governor of Louisiana, losing to Edwin Edwards but gaining 39 percent of the vote and more than 55 percent of the white vote in the state. In 1992, he ran for United States president but was eclipsed by another right-wing candidate, Patrick Buchanan, whose bigoted views on Jews, Blacks, women, and gays did not prevent him from attracting a large number of protest votes in many state primaries.

That a majority of white Christians in an American state would bestow their votes on Duke, a racist figure with such a sleazy background, is a cause for distress and alarm. That Buchanan's bigotry did not seem to hurt him with the electorate at large added to our anxiety. If we add to these phenomena incidents such as Crown Heights, ominous race-baiting and anti-Semitism on college campuses, and the widespread economic suffering in America, it seems that anti-Semitism in America is no longer a relic of the past. This evil needs watching; it compels a higher priority; and it is everybody's business.

Are Jews Responsible for Anti-Semitism?

Jewish behavior does not cause anti-Semitism. It was not Jewish behavior but Nazi genocidal policy that condemned six million Jews to slaughter. Hitler claimed it was the actions of Jews that made their elimination necessary: they were capitalists; they were communists; they owned all the wealth; they were an inferior breed; they were anti-Christ. Madness. If the bloody chronicle of anti-

Semitism proves anything, it is that "good behavior" does not shield Jews from blood libel accusations, religious persecution, or mass murder.

Yet such rationalizations linger. In early 1992, a poll of Germans by the prominent magazine *Der Spiegel* found that 32 percent of the Germans believed that Jews themselves are at least partly responsible for being persecuted and hated by others. This finding reflects a growing trend of anti-Semitic attitudes and incidents throughout Europe.

Perhaps this is due to the passing of firsthand memories of the Holocaust; perhaps to the prevalent economic problems of many of those countries. The "scapegoating" manifestation of anti-Semitism has been perhaps the most prevalent. Leaders faced with difficult political or economic problems have often sought to distract the masses by blaming the Jewish minority for the nation's ills. One might ask why the Jews. It is not always the Jews—but often enough to keep us vigilant.

The teachings of Christianity ignited anti-Semitism in the first place and fueled it through the long centuries of our painful history. Christian Scripture itself blamed "the Jews" for the crucifixion of Jesus, and early Christian thinkers began to speak of the crime of deicide: the killing of Jesus Christ.

Christian teaching asserted that Jews were believers in a covenant created at Sinai that God had later replaced by sending "His son, Jesus." As there was no longer a role for the old covenant, the continued role of those Jews who held to it became open to question. The refusal of Jews to accept fundamental articles of Christian faith was threatening to Christians. Jews believe in the one God that is a unity; Christians believe that God is at the same time three (the Father, Son, and Holy Ghost) *and* one. Jews believe that redemption comes from remaining loyal to God's covenant and following God's commandments; Christians believe that redemption comes from belief in Jesus. Jews believe that the Messiah could not have come because the world is still filled with persecution and bloodshed; Christians believe the Messiah once came to bring a purely spiritual redemption and will return to bring the messianic world.

When someone challenges the fundamental building blocks of your worldview, aggressive responses are common. The classic responses of Christians to Jews were attempts to convert them, to make sure that their inferior status would serve as a constant reminder of the error of their ways; to isolate them in ghettos; or to expel them from the Christian realm. This remained the norm until the so-called Age of Reason, beginning in the eighteenth century, when science, logic, and reason became the fundamental assertions of a new worldview—assertions Jews could embrace as easily as Christians. The ghetto gates opened, and Jews moved into the mainstream of Western civilization.

The record of church authorities in Jewish persecution over nineteen hundred years is more mixed than Jews commonly believe. While all too often the clergy participated in anti-Jewish activities or turned a blind eye to them, many Christian leaders intervened to save Jews and to stifle overt anti-Semitic activity. The Jewish community needs to revise its teaching of this aspect of our history to provide a more balanced and more accurate picture of Jewish-Christian relations. Nonetheless, the traditional doctrine that the Jewish religion has been superseded may have led Christians to draw the conclusion that the Jew is therefore expendable and may have indirectly paved the way toward the Nazi Holocaust.

Reform in the Church

In the wake of the Holocaust, many Christian leaders began a soul-searching reexamination of the link between Christian teaching and the darkest chapter of human evil in history.

In recent decades, interfaith relations have undergone sweeping changes, especially within the Roman Catholic church, which has formally reinterpreted some of its fundamental teachings to eliminate the anti-Semitic bias derived from historic interpretations of Christian Scripture. Moreover, after Vatican Council II, convened by Pope John XXIII in 1963, the Roman Catholic church—which had spurned interfaith contact for centuries—began to establish friendly relations with Protestants as well as with Jews.

Priests exchanged pulpits with rabbis. Roman Catholics became increasingly active in interreligious coalitions to address communal problems. Textbooks in Catholic religious schools were examined to eliminate or at least soften passages offensive to Jewish sensibilities. The Roman Catholic church in the United States established an office for the improvement of Catholic-Jewish relations to stimulate dialogue, joint action, and mutual respect.

At a historic meeting in Prague in 1990, Catholic leaders for the first time accepted responsibility for the role Catholic teachings played in the bitter history of anti-Semitism, climaxing in the Holocaust. Repentance was the theme of the meeting, which was later echoed by the Pope at a historic meeting with world Jewish leaders.

Many Protestant scholars had similarly challenged their churches to cast off the sin of anti-Semitism, arguing that the false charge of "Christ-killer" was historically inaccurate (it was the Romans, not the Jews, who crucified Jesus) and a cause of bloodshed and hatred throughout the centuries. The National Council of Churches, representing most Protestant denominations, similarly maintains a liaison office to strengthen Protestant-Jewish relations.

How Secure Are Jews in the United States?

For the past fifty years, sociologists and demographers have been engaged in fairly detailed studies of anti-Semitic attitudes and behavior. The trend shows that the number of people holding anti-Semitic attitudes has fallen steadily since the end of World War II. While this is a significant improvement, tens of millions of Americans maintain negative attitudes toward Jews. When it comes to acting out those attitudes, the number of overt anti-Semitic incidents has fluctuated over that time period but within fairly predictable limits: between seven hundred to two thousand incidents reported each year. The number of incidents reported by the ADL in 1991 represented a significant jump from recent years' figures.

Three conclusions can be drawn from these statistics. First, all the surveys indicate that the more educated the person, the less likely he or she is to hold racist, including anti-Semitic, attitudes. As educational standards, driven by the success of our public school system in America, improved in the twentieth century, anti-Semitic attitudes declined. The declining standards of American public education, as seen over the past fifteen years, may cause a reversal of this trend.

Second, the post-World War II culture of America has deemed overt racist behavior as unacceptable. In addition, an array of legislation prevents discrimination. Respect for the pluralistic character of America has demanded tolerance in our intergroup relations. Hence, the relatively small number of anti-Semitic incidents.

Third, anti-Jewish incidents often reflect more general problems in our society. Most anti-Semitic vandalism is *not* committed by members of organized hate groups but by kids out of school or out of work, looking for trouble. (Sadly, there have even been incidents perpetrated by emotionally disturbed *Jewish* youngsters.) Most anti-Jewish incidents parallel hate crimes against Catholic churches or against Blacks and other minority groups. When the economy is sound and people are confident about America, such crimes decrease. When joblessness increases and people despair, such hate crimes proliferate.

The one group that does not correspond entirely to these norms is the African American community. Among Blacks, anti-Semitism is most prevalent among the more educated individuals of the community and even among leaders. This is a source of great concern to Jews. If we are to confront it, however, we must recognize that this is a different expression of anti-Semitism from that measured by most studies. The classic form of anti-Semitism is grounded in stereotypes: Jews are greedier than others, are more powerful, and are less loyal citizens. Such caricatures generally are rejected with increased education. On such questions, anti-Semitic attitudes have fallen among educated Blacks as well.

The anti-Semitism that emerges among African American intelligentsia is a more political anti-Semitism: Jews are representatives of the white community, are economically exploiting people of color at home, and are supporters of Israel, a Western colonial outpost oppressing native populations abroad. This strain of anti-Semitism finds ample expression on many of the nation's college campuses, where Third World ideologies are commonly heard. This kind of anti-Semitism is resistant to the techniques employed in combating the more traditional variants of anti-Semitism.

A Real Dilemma: School Bus Arab Terrorism

In the 1980s, college activists began protesting South African apartheid by erecting "shanties" in the center of the campus to symbolize the squalor and despair caused by apartheid. As a vehicle of protest, shanty construction soon became a metaphor for other issues like homelessness. At the University of Michigan in 1988, a pro-Palestinian group erected a shantytown to symbolize Israeli oppression of Palestinians. After an Arab terrorist attack on an Israeli bus that year, a Zionist group called Tagar erected a mock school bus to dramatize the victimization of Israelis at the hands of terrorists. Many slogans were emblazoned on the school bus including one that read Stop Arab Terrorism!

Arab students furiously protested the slogan, saying that it was racist and contributed to the stereotype that all Arabs are terrorists. A number of antiapartheid groups joined them. In calling for the removal of the bus, they declared, How would Jewish students feel if a shanty were erected with a slogan saying "Stop *Jewish* Violence against Palestinians on the West Bank"? What should the Jewish community's position have been?

Response

True, there is much stereotyping of Arabs in the media, in American politics, and elsewhere. During the Gulf War, Arab Americans faced a great deal of harassment, some of which was even undertaken by the FBI. The UAHC joined with groups of all backgrounds in condemning such harassment.

On the other hand, Arab countries such as Syria, Iraq,

Libya, and Lebanon have clearly sanctioned or financed terrorism in many parts of the world. In the above situation, it would be necessary to take part in a dialogue with Arab Americans to understand their reaction. Would it be better for them if the sign had read PLO Terror or The Silence of Arab Nations Legitimizes Terrorism?

In many ways, America offered protections against anti-Semitism unknown to the experience of the Jews in Europe. Because of the Christian roots of life in Europe, there was a tradition of state-sanctioned, academically sanctioned, religiously sanctioned persecution of Jews. It was in this tradition that Nazi persecution of the Jews found fertile soil.

America, on the other hand, was a nation based on the enlightened humanistic beliefs of the Age of Reason. Democracy was a political system that, in theory, embodied those beliefs, particularly the equality of God's children. There was no widespread tradition of state-, church-, or university-approved anti-Semitism.

In America, academics who deny the legitimacy of the Jewish people or the truthfulness of the Holocaust are regarded as kooks. While there have always been religious extremists who targeted Jews, the mainstream religious leaders and organizations have long accepted Jews as the third of the tripartite mainstream religious categories of American life (Protestant, Catholic, and Jew). And, while there were instances of state restriction of Jewish rights well into the nineteenth century, the more common experience was the legal protection afforded by the First Amendment's promise of religious freedom and separation of church and state.

Although even the legal and political advances of America could not eradicate the legacy of centuries of popular, folk anti-Semitic attitudes, the underlying beliefs of America have offered the Jew protection and opportunities unmatched anywhere in our history. Could it happen here? Could there emerge a serious anti-Semitic movement in America? Yes. There could—and we must be vigilant. Indeed we are experiencing a surge of anti-Semitic activity today, but it would be far more difficult than in Europe for this to become a mainstream trend precisely because of our different ideological history and our constitutional safeguards.

Alan Dershowitz, a professor at Harvard Law School and author of the best-selling book *Chutzpah* believes anti-Semitism is a growing problem in America. Moreover, he believes that American Jews have allowed themselves to become second-class citizens by acting like guests in a WASP home. Indeed, Dershowitz believes our leaders are afraid to condemn anti-Semitism and to confront those who are insensitive to it mainly because we are afraid of rocking the boat. We are afraid of being accused of dual loyality— to the United States and to Israel.

Is Dershowitz right or wrong about anti-Semitism in America today? Right or wrong about the failures of Jewish leaders to speak out?

A Real Dilemma: Jonathan Pollard

In 1991, a prominent attorney, Alan Dershowitz, appeared before a committee of the National Jewish Community Relations Advisory Council, the coordinating body representing almost every major Jewish organization. He was then a leading advocate for Jonathan Pollard, an American Jew convicted of committing espionage on behalf of Israel. An intelligence agent for the United States Navy, Pollard stole a large number of top secret documents and transmitted them to Israel, arguing that he did so as a committed Zionist. He was convinced that secret data (i.e., information about Iraq's nuclear, biological, and chemical capabilities) had to be shared with Israel for its own safety and security. He pleaded guilty and was sentenced to life imprisonment.

Dershowitz argued that no American spy in recent years, even those who provided enemies with classified information vital to our security, was ever given so harsh a sentence. Israel, he pointed out, is an ally, not an enemy. Dershowitz alleged that Pollard provided only information that had been promised by the United States to Israel but had been wrongly held back. The harsh sentence, he contended, was a reflection of anti-Israel, even anti-Semitic, attitudes of some people involved in the case.

At the same meeting, the United States attorney who prosecuted the case argued that it was not the United States that had wronged Pollard, but Israel and Pollard who had betrayed the United States; that the stolen information was highly significant and compromised American intelligence agents; that this was not a Jewish issue but one of American law; and that Pollard was not Alfred Dreyfus, and Dershowitz was not Emile Zola.

Dershowitz asked the Jewish organizations to speak out publicly for a commutation of Pollard's sentence on the grounds that the punishment was excessive. Jewish self-respect requires no less, he concluded. What should those Jewish organizations have done?

Response

Most Jewish groups refused to become involved, arguing that there was no evidence of anti-Semitism and that, if the sentence were too harsh, it could be appealed properly under American law and justice. While a number of groups, including the UAHC, were willing to join in a call for rehearing the sentence, they were not prepared at that time to advocate a reduction in the sentence or to agree that Pollard had been victimized by anti-Semitism.

Several Jewish organizations, however, including the Central Conference of American Rabbis (the Reform rabbinical association), decided that the extreme harshness of the Pollard sentence suggested an anti-Israel or anti-Semitic bias. The CCAR signed a brief asking for commutation of the sentence. In fact, a judicial review of the sentence was held in 1992 and, by a 2 to 1 margin, a federal court of appeals upheld the sentence. (Ironically, both majority judges were Jewish; the dissenting judge, who called the sentence a travesty, was not Jewish.)

An underlying theme of the *Pollard* case was the so-called dual loyalty allegation, falsely suggesting that Jews are more loyal to Israel than to the United States. By acting *for* Israel and *against* the United States, no matter how well intentioned his action may have been, Pollard has added credence to this anti-Semitic canard. For Jewish organizations to rally to Pollard's support without clear evidence of an anti-Israel or anti-Jewish intent on the part of the American government would have the appearance of legitimizing these accusations. But this does not mean that pleas for mercy—parole after serving the minimum ten years—would be inappropriate.

The Rise of Hatemongering in the United States

Jews generally *feel* less secure today than they have in many years. The nervous apprehension about the growing antiforeign violence in Germany, the revival of ultranationalism in Eastern Europe, the rise of extremist groups in France, Germany, and other European nations, as well as continuing anxiety about Israel's vulnerability, has alarmed Jews worldwide. In the United States, we have witnessed the rapid rise of extremist politicians like Patrick Buchanan and David Duke; the Black-Jewish conflict in Crown Heights, New York; the increase in vandalism directed at Jewish institutions; anti-Jewish incidents on the nation's university campuses; increased efforts to deny the Holocaust really happened; anti-Jewish stereotypes in popular music and humor—all evidence of a growing anti-Semitic threat to the security of American Jews.

The expression of bigotry and meanness have indeed become more acceptable in America today—with more *overt* bigotry being expressed against Jews, Blacks, women, gays and lesbians, Koreans, and other Asians—than in the past several decades. It would also be wrong to panic and exaggerate. Most American Jewish teenagers have not experienced anti-Semitism firsthand. Discrimination is illegal in employment, housing, medical care, in virtually every area of public life. In 1991 there were more Jews in the United States Congress than ever before (thirty-three in the House, eight in the Senate), and some were elected from districts with few Jewish voters.

Few barriers remain that keep Jews out of the best universities, the most desirable neighborhoods, the rarefied boardrooms of industry, or even the most exclusive country clubs, although there are some of each (except universities) that still endeavor to keep out Jews. Jews have become presidents of colleges that once maintained anti-Jewish quotas.

All surveys confirm that Jews are widely accepted. An overwhelming majority of Americans do not object to living next door to a Jew, voting for a Jew, working with a Jew, and—more and more—even marrying a Jew. Indeed, it could be argued that assimilation, not anti-Semitism, is the real threat to Jewish survival in America. It has, ironically, been argued that anti-Semitism keeps the Jewish people viable as a distinct group.

How then should we view the increasing occurrences of anti-Semitic incidents? Anti-Semitism must be judged within the changing social trends that exist in any nation. In this light, the rise in anti-Semitism must be seen as part of a larger American social trend of accepting a certain level of prejudice. Every element of society that has a distinct identity, not just Jews, has begun to experience this reality.

The Image of the Jew

Is anti-Semitism generated by the negative stereotypes with which Jews are often portrayed in literature, in movies, on the stage, and on television? We cannot be certain.

Whatever the answer, Jews are frequently portrayed in negative terms as grasping, greedy, superambitious, vulgar, and immoral. Jews react to such images with revulsion and fear, as if looking over their shoulders to see how such negative portrayals affect the way they are viewed by their non-Jewish neighbors. We worry that such stereotypes reinforce latent anti-Jewish sentiments.

Yet, are we Jews oversensitive? Could it be that unflattering images of some Jews contain elements of truth? We seem to be comfortable when portrayed as one of society's victims, as the noble underdog, or as champions of social justice. Our self-admiring public relations image does not allow for characterizations of Jews as greedy and corrupt investment brokers or as purveyors of vulgar bar and bat mitzvah celebrations and conspicuous weddings. Yet, isn't all this part of our deepening assimilation to the contemporary American reality? Should we attribute such portrayals automatically to anti-Semitism, even if written by Jewish authors and artists?

A Real Dilemma: JAP Anti-Semitism

The term "Jewish American Princess" or "JAP" has become a hateful stereotype of Jewish women as rich and self-indulgent. At Syracuse University, students established "anti-JAP zones," which were out of bounds to any woman who displayed behavior construed as "JAPpy." At basketball games, women labeled as JAPs were publicly humiliated. Was this behavior anti-Semitic? Should the university have responded? How should the Jewish community have reacted to these incidents? If you were a student at Syracuse, what would you have done?

This issue became more complex at the University of Michigan when members of a *Jewish* fraternity printed and sold "JAP-Buster" T-shirts around campus. How should the Jewish community have responded when Jews legitimize a self-hating sexist stereotype? By speaking out publicly against the JAP stereotype, does the Jewish community turn a crude craze into a cause célèbre?

Response

In both cases, the Jewish community felt that it was necessary to respond to the Jew-baiting incidents. Increasingly, national Jewish organizations regard the JAP stereotype as a veiled anti-Semitic attack, which—like any other—must be combated. That this expression of anti-Semitism has been cast in the guise of a joke, and thus dismissed as frivolous, requires even more vigorous repudiation.

At Syracuse University, Jewish women's groups protested and called on university officials to mount a consciousness-raising effort to discredit the JAP stereotype. The university responded by sponsoring sensitivity-training workshops that addressed the JAP stereotype in the broader context of discrimination.

At the University of Michigan, the response was less public but just as concerned. Today, the JAP stereotype is frequently discussed in seminars and workshops on intergroup relations and discrimination. Hopefully, men (including Jewish men), as well as women, are becoming sensitive to the fact that JAP jokes constitute nothing less than anti-Jewish contempt whether it comes from non-Jews or Jews.

We have all faced the question of how to respond to ethnic or racial jokes.

Suppose you are sitting at a lunch table with a few of your friends. One of your friends, who happens to be non-Jewish, tells you a joke about JAPs. What should you do?

1. Respond with another JAP joke you heard.
2. Say, "I really don't think those jokes are funny."
3. Say, "I find that kind of humor offensive."
4. Listen to the "joke" coldly and say nothing and later weigh the incident in determining whether to continue that friendship.

Anti-Semitism on College Campuses

The last place one would expect to hear blasts of anti-Jewish rhetoric is on the nation's college campuses, the bastions of liberality, free speech, and pluralistic interaction. Increasingly, however, the campus has become a cauldron of racial and ethnic conflict. Some examples:

1. At Columbia University, Dr. Khalid Abdul Muhammad, a self-described disciple of Minister Louis Farrakhan, addressed a forum on Afrocentricity. Invited by the Black Students Organization, he referred to the venue as "Columbia Jewniversity" in "Jew York City" and laced his speech with similarly repellent anti-Semitic references.
2. At the University of Michigan, Steve Cokely was invited to speak by a black student organization, following the notoriety he achieved in Chicago alleging that Jewish doctors were part of a conspiracy to inject black babies with the AIDS virus.
3. At UCLA in 1990, the African American student magazine called *Nommo* published an article culled from the *Protocols of the Elders of Zion,* a classic anti-Semitic forgery. When Jewish students protested to the editors, one of them actually defended the authenticity of the protocols and attacked Jews as a "small group of European people who have proclaimed themselves God's chosen by using an indigenous African religion, Judaism, to justify their place in the world."
4. In 1991, a professor at CCNY in New York, then chair of the Department of Afro-American Studies, addressed a conference in Albany, New York, in which he denounced whites as inferior devils. He lashed out especially at Jews, charging that they control Hollywood and exploit and denigrate Blacks; they dominated the slave trade; and they conspire with the Mafia to control Blacks.

On other campuses, Palestinian students have invited speakers who blended their anti-Zionism with anti-Semitism, causing discomfort and anger among Jewish students. Anti-Israel groups also tried to have Hillel Foundations banned from the use of campus facilities on the grounds that they were Zionist and therefore racist, citing the then-existing United Nations resolution equating Zionism and racism.

Should hatemongers be permitted on campus? Why not pass a law that forbids the expression of group hatred? Unfortunately, it is not that simple.

Our courts have determined that the First Amendment was drafted to protect the expression of offensive ideas, not merely the bland and the tame. Nazis marching in Skokie, Illinois, crazies burning the American flag—both have been protected by the First Amendment of the Constitution. Better to endure the slings and arrows of occasional verbal bigotry than to tamper with the Constitution, which provides Jews and other minorities with their ultimate security. (For a more detailed analysis, see Chapter 4, "Civil Liberties.")

Does that mean we have no recourse in the face of anti-Semitic slander? No. It means we cannot stop Jew-baiting through legislation or censorship.

Anti-Semitism can be fought. University officials must be pressed to condemn anti-Semitism as well as racism when the likes of a Farrakhan appear on campus and spew their hatred.

Campus papers should be urged to speak out against the voice of bigotry. Coalitions of decency, representing all ethnic and racial groups, can organize counterdemonstrations. Truth squads can be organized to rebut falsehoods. Such means, utilized successfully on campuses, may require more effort than passing a law, but that's the price of democracy.

A Real Dilemma: Kwame Toure on Campus

In 1991, a Jewish college student at the University of Colorado called the UAHC for advice. He explained that Kwame Toure (formerly known as Stokely Carmichael), whom some considered an anti-Semite and others an anti-Zionist, had been invited to speak on campus. Jewish students were upset and not sure how to react.

Some Jewish students were demanding that the university cancel Toure's contract. Others argued that censorship was the worst solution, preferring to stage a protest that would educate the student body. What would you have advised?

Response

Anti-Semitism often appears under the guise of anti-Zionism, as evidenced by the former United Nations resolution equating Zionism with racism. The Jewish students were rightly concerned about Toure's coming to campus, but breaking the contract would not have been advisable. Freedom in this country has been protected because even individuals espousing obnoxious views have been permitted to speak their minds.

The Jewish students organized a counterevent—a "teach-in"—aimed at educating the rest of the university community about Toure's hostile views on Israel, Zionism, and Jews.

Inviting a persuasive Israeli spokesperson, or a knowledgeable American Jewish leader, at a subsequent date might be an important counteraction. Organizing a debate is not advisable because placing a bigot on the forum with a respected figure gives respectability to the hatemonger.

Is Anti-Zionism a Form of Anti-Semitism?

Since the 1970s, a new strain of anti-Semitism has appeared, masquerading as anti-Zionism or as "mere" anti-Israeli opinion. This poses a difficult dilemma for Jews. Is criticism of Israel the same as anti-Semitism? If so, how do we explain that half of Israel's population was critical of Shamir's policy on the West Bank and over half of American Jews and American Jewish leaders oppose the establishment of new settlements in the territories? Clearly criticism of particular policies of the Israeli government cannot be the same as anti-Semitism. But, does the same criticism, when it comes from non-Jews, become anti-Semitism, racism against Jews?

Racism is the assigning of negative attributes, the deprivation of rights, or the imposition of responsibility on members of a particular group of people simply because of their membership in that group. In other words, racism against Blacks consists of assigning to Blacks as Blacks negative attributes (e.g., Blacks are violent), denying rights (e.g., Blacks cannot be hired for certain jobs), or requiring certain actions not required of others (e.g., instituting difficult voter registration procedures for Blacks).

The technical term for racism against Jews is *anti-Semitism*. Occasionally one hears Arabs who engage in anti-Semitism claim: "I can't be anti-Semitic! I'm an *Arab* and *Arabs* are *Semites* themselves." This is nothing less than an intellectually insulting argument. Anti-Semitism is not discrimination against Semites; it is a "term of art" that means racism or bigotry against Jews.

One classical variant of racism is based on the religious belief of Jews. As Cardinal John Henry Newman, himself a persecuted Catholic leader of the nineteenth century, once said: "Religious bigotry is assuming that your first principles are better than someone else's first principles and you therefore have the right to impose negative attributes to others for holding the 'wrong' first principles."

Judaism, however, is more than a religion; it is a culture, a people, and a nation as well. The national expression of the Jewish people is Zionism. When we refer to anti-Zionists, it does not mean that they oppose an aspect of Zionism or a particular policy of the Israeli government; it means that they simply deny the very legitimacy of Jewish statehood. In doing so, they would deny to Jews, solely *because they are Jews,* the same right to determine Jewish political destiny that is granted to so many other peoples.

In this context, anti-Zionism is indeed anti-Semitism. The most distressing manifestation of this form of anti-Semitism occurred in 1975 when the United Nations General Assembly equated Zionism with racism. As racism in its political form is outlawed by international law, the resolution declared Jewish nationalism (i.e., Zionism) to be illegitimate and unlawful. This was not only an attack on Israel's elementary right to exist as a Jewish state but an attack upon Jews everywhere.

In the early 1990s, Israel and the United States launched a major international effort to expunge this outrageous resolution. Addressing the United Nations General Assembly on September 23, 1991, American President George Bush called on the United Nations to repeal Resolution 3379, the Zionism-Is-Racism resolution, which he described as "mocking the principles upon which the United Nations was founded." On December 16, 1991, by a vote of 111 to 25 with 13 abstentions, the disgraceful resolution finally was rescinded.

Skinheads

The ADL first learned of skinheads when a small gang of neo-Nazis from Chicago, calling themselves Romantic Violence, surfaced at a 1985 conclave of hate groups in Michigan.

The skinheads originated in Great Britain and now have a following of some eight to ten thousand there. They have counterparts in all of Europe, Canada, Australia, New Zealand, South Africa, and several Latin American countries. In 1990, several hundred rowdy skinheads demonstrated in Leipzig, Germany, screaming "to hell with Jews." The ADL reported in 1990 that, while some skinhead groups continue to menace communities across America, their overall national membership seems to have stagnated between three to five thousand. One of the reasons is vigorous law enforcement by both federal and local authorities, who have responded to the call for vigilance made by Jewish and other organizations.

Their violence is directed generally against competing gangs, but it would be a mistake to discount their lethal potential. In 1988 a group of skinheads in Portland, Oregon, brutally assaulted three Ethiopians, killing one of the victims with a baseball bat. The skinheads responsible for the attack, who call themselves East Side White Pride, were sentenced to lengthy jail terms.

Legal Steps against Anti-Semitism

While one cannot change anti-Semitic attitudes or restrict anti-Semitic speech by passing laws, one *can* use the legal system to help check anti-Semitic activity. A step in that direction was passage of the Hate Crime Statistics Act in 1990, mandating the FBI to document every "hate crime": crimes based on race, religion, ethnicity, and sexual orientation.

In early December 1991, a case challenging a Minnesota hate-crime ordinance, *R.A.V. v. St. Paul,* came before the United States Supreme Court. The case involved a teenager who was accused of burning a cross outside the home of a black family. Under a St. Paul ordinance, it is a misdemeanor to display symbols that arouse "anger, alarm, or resentment in others." In the 1942 Supreme Court case *Chaplinsky v. New Hampshire,* the Court ruled that one could be prosecuted for using language considered to be "fighting words," which "by their very utterance inflict injury or tend to incite an immediate breach of peace." There has been much debate over the implications of the *Chaplinsky* decision for the cross-burning case. *R.A.V. v. St. Paul* raises serious questions about where we draw the line between hate-crime violations and infringements on First Amendments rights. In 1992, the Supreme Court threw out the St. Paul ordinance as too broad and thus violative of the constitutional guarantee of free speech.

Consider the following composite situation based on actual situations that erupted in a number of congregations nationwide:

A Real Dilemma: A Synagogue Vandalized

Your synagogue is vandalized in the middle of the night. Ugly anti-Jewish graffiti, including swastikas, were spray-painted on the outer walls of the building. The rabbi calls you and other members of the board of the temple to an emergency meeting in his or her study at 7:00 A.M. What should we do?

The rabbi, of course, has already called the police and

reported the attack. But questions remain: Should we go public as a means of warning the community that anti-Semitic activity is taking place in its midst? Would that just blow the incident out of proportion and run the risk of copycat crimes taking place at other Jewish targets? Should we quickly have the paint and graffiti removed so as not to disturb our members? Should we call upon the neighboring churches and other faith groups to speak out on this incident as an affront to us all? Should we organize and publicize an intergroup cleanup of the synagogue? Should we play this *up,* as a challenge to the conscience of the community, or play it *down,* as an act of vandalism, and leave it to law enforcement to handle?

Response

Some congregations have chosen to play down such incidents, but all notify the police. Most have released the facts to the press. When the synagogues have reason to believe that this is the work of an organized anti-Semitic group, as opposed to an act of individual vandalism, they are even more likely to publicize the incident to rouse the awareness and concern of the community. In most cases, the general community responds quickly and visibly. In particular, churches are usually very quick to join in denouncing the attack and participate in an interfaith cleanup of the graffiti.

The Deeper Danger

The potential danger of anti-Semitism is not in the sleazy skinheads, not in vandalism, but in the future of America to solve its urgent domestic crises: the rotting of our inner cities, the despair of the underclass, the spread of poverty among children, the epidemic of drugs and of violence. Add to these inflammable conditions a full-fledged economic crisis and the potential for anti-Semitism in America would be not only serious but also imminent. So the fate of the Jew is still interwoven with the health of the total society—economic, political, and moral!

The Jewish community has every right and duty to condemn all anti-Semitism, Christian or Muslim, left-wing or right-wing, white or black. We know that, throughout our history, anti-Semitic words have often led to pogroms and even worse. But it is also important for Jews not to lose perspective.

We can find no safety in turning inward upon ourselves, severing our links with the general community. We can find safety only if we help America deal not only with the symptoms—ignorance, rage, bigotry—but with the root problems of our society—slums, powerlessness, decay of our cities, and unemployment. All these spawn the evils of bigotry and conflict. Our task as Jews must go beyond the defensive job of countering the attacks of anti-Semitism to helping bring about a just and peaceful society.

It has been said that only a person with a broken heart can be truly human. Jewish brokenheartedness has given us the empathy to understand the heart of the stranger, to share the pain. The lesson of the Holocaust is that the slogan Never Again must apply not only to Jews but to all peoples.

≡ 10 ≡

ECONOMIC JUSTICE

*A Real Dilemma: Should a Synagogue Establish
a Homeless Shelter within Its Own Facility?*

During the 1980s and 1990s, the two domestic social justice issues most frequently addressed by congregations were the problems of hunger and homelessness. Hundreds of congregations across the nation collected food for local food pantries and provided volunteers for soup kitchens and homeless shelters. As congregations became more involved, one issue came up repeatedly: Should they set up food distribution programs and even homeless shelters within their own congregational buildings?

Proponents of such measures argued that, if the synagogue was serious about social justice, it would have to do more than send volunteers to other people's shelters; it would have to bring the issue home. As the Reagan budgets cut back funding for low-income housing and feeding programs, it became incumbent upon synagogues and churches to help pick up the slack.

Opponents expressed concerns that such activity would overwhelm the congregation. By taking on the responsibility of creating a facility "in-house," they would have to ensure that the volunteers showed up and that there would be people to fill in if the volunteers missed their shifts. They would be bringing in alcoholics and mentally disturbed persons. They

165

would run the risk that someone might get hurt, thus affecting the insurance of the synagogue. They would have to devote a part of their synagogue building for the facility, possibly overtaxing the synagogue's structure and straining the budget.

What should our synagogues do? What would you have decided?

Response

This was an anguishing dilemma for many congregations. A surprisingly high number were willing to undertake the expense, the logistical difficulties, and the risks of providing just such programs. Like The Temple in Atlanta, which set up a shelter for homeless families, and Central Synagogue in New York, which set up a weekly breakfast-feeding program for the homeless, scores of synagogues opened their doors to put into practice the words of justice preached from the pulpit.

By the late 1980s, some of the more active congregations began to move beyond providing shelter, recognizing that shelters addressed only the symptom of the problem of homelessness. Some, like Temple Emanuel in Dallas, set up a child care program for the children of homeless families, thus not only serving the needs of the children but making it possible for homeless parents to mount a serious effort to find a job—without worrying about their children. Others, like Rodeph Sholom in New York City, organized programs to assist homeless families in the transition from shelters to real apartments in the community.

A number of other congregations have undertaken efforts to build affordable low-income housing. In Westfield, New Jersey, such an effort is being undertaken jointly by Temple Emanuel, a Reform synagogue, and a black church. In Los Angeles, an ambitious $7 million project was undertaken by a coalition of churches and synagogues led by an Episcopal church and the Leo Baeck Temple, resulting in the conversion of a dilapidated hotel to an affordable apartment building to house the previously homeless in downtown Los Angeles. Increasingly, congregations are exploring these types of approaches as a means to help people help themselves—the highest form of Jewish charity.

Ten Facts about Economic Justice in America

The efforts to help the poor and needy that began in the New Deal of 1930s and accelerated during the Great Society programs of the 1960s made a significant difference in lifting tens of millions out of poverty. Several factors, however, left tens of millions without resources to provide their families a minimally decent standard of living. Those factors were:

• Most welfare programs focused on providing poor people with enough resources to live better, without educating them and helping them find jobs that would lift them out of poverty altogether.

• The budget cuts instituted by the Reagan administration and steady state-level reductions in welfare benefits have undermined some of our most successful social welfare programs.

• The value of wages has eroded, especially for low-income jobs. In 1991, the average "blue collar" wage, after adjusting for inflation, was lower than at any time since 1963. In addition, the purchasing power of the minimum wage has declined sharply. A single parent with two children working full-time at the minimum wage is now about $2,000 below the poverty line. In most of the 1960s and 1970s, full-time minimum wage work would have lifted such a family above the poverty line.

• A significant shortage of low-rent housing has developed. In 1970, there were four hundred thousand more low-rent units in the United States than there were low-income renters. By 1989, there were 4.1 million fewer low-rent units than low-income renters. As a result, rents have risen sharply and most low-income renters spend very high percentages of their limited incomes for housing.

Where has this left us in terms of poverty in America? Consider these facts:

1. In 1990, 13.5 percent of all Americans—some 33.6 million people—lived below the poverty line. (The poverty line was $10,419 for a family of three in 1990.)
2. The majority of poor people in the United States are white. However, while 10.7 percent of whites live in poverty, 31.9 percent of Blacks and 28.1 percent of Hispanics are poor. In addition, the majority of the poorest of the poor is black.
3. One in five children under the age of eighteen, or 19.9 percent, lived below the poverty level in 1990. Some 15.1 percent of white children, 44.2 percent of black children, and 37.7 percent of Hispanic children were poor that year.
4. In 1990, between 18 and 20 million Americans were hungry year-round—that is, chronically short of the nutrients necessary for growth and good health. Of these hungry people, 7 to 8 million are children under the age of eighteen and 11 to 12 million are adults, about 2 million of whom are more than sixty-five years of age.
5. In 1979, cash benefits from programs such as Social Security, unemployment insurance, and public assistance lifted from poverty an estimated 18.9 percent of families with children who otherwise would have been poor. By 1987, the Census Bureau estimated, cash benefits lifted from poverty only 10.5 percent of the families who otherwise would have been poor.
6. By 1989, despite the longest peacetime recovery of the postwar period, the income gaps between both the rich and the poor and the rich and the middle class hit their widest points since the end of World War II. In fact, just the *increase* between 1977 and 1989 in the aggregate income of the wealthiest percent of the population was greater than than the total incomes of all Americans in the poorest 20 percent of the population.

7. Families with incomes below the poverty level spend, on average, 60 percent of their postshelter income on food. Nonetheless, this amounts to an average of only $277 per month for food—just sixty-eight cents per person per meal.

8. More people have died of hunger and hunger-related causes in the past five years worldwide than have been killed in all the wars, revolutions, and murders in the past one hundred and fifty years.

9. In 1989, the United States infant mortality rate was 9.8 per 1,000 births, the nineteenth highest in the world. The Washington, D.C., infant mortality rate was 22.9 per 1,000 births, higher than in many Third World countries.

10. Although the exact number of homeless people is not known, some estimates range from six hundred thousand to three million. The United States Conference of Mayors reports that the number of requests for emergency shelter rose an average of 24 percent in 1990 in thirty major cities and 13 percent in 1991 in twenty-eight major cities surveyed.

A Real Dilemma:
Should We Give Money to Homeless Beggars?

Walking home in any American city, chances are you will run into a gauntlet of homeless persons, many of them begging. You can't ignore them. What should you do? Doesn't the Jewish tradition require us to give charity to the poor? But what good will it do to hand a beggar some change? Will it be used for food or for alcohol or drugs? Yet, can you turn away without surrendering some of your humanity? Besides, even if you do want to help, isn't a handout really a cop-out? Shouldn't you be working on the fundamental problems of homelessness and poverty, of which these pathetic beggars are only pathetic symptoms? How do you resolve this dilemma?

Response

It is not a question of either/or. This unkempt and perhaps physically or mentally ill person needs the help of a fellow human being.

There are several ways to address this dilemma. First, use your instinct about giving money. If you sense they will use your money for food, give the coins; if you think they will use it for alcohol or drugs, don't offer any money. If your donation is misused, it's the recipient's fault, not yours. A second approach is to take a few minutes and actually buy food for the street person. This ensures that it won't be misused. But how many of us will really go to this trouble?

A third approach is to work with community groups who have set up mechanisms to ensure that the money given to the needy won't be misused. In Berkeley, California, a voucher system was designed to ensure that donations to homeless beggars are spent on necessities like food or laundry services. People can purchase vouchers for twenty-five cents each and offer them to the needy, who in turn redeem the vouchers at participating stores for food and other necessities. Would such a system work in your community?

However, all experts agree that taking time to chat occasionally with a homeless person, treating him or her like a human being rather than like an object to be avoided or a receptacle into which a quarter is dropped, can be as important as the money given.

Liberals vs. Conservatives:
Where Is the Jewish Community?

Beginning with the progressive reforms of the 1880s, conservatives have maintained that the capitalistic free enterprise system is inherently balanced and just. Government intervention, they argued, even when done for the best of purposes, inevitably causes more harm than good by upsetting that inherent balance and by infringing on the fundamental rights of individuals to regulate their business lives as they see fit.

Liberals take a very different approach, maintaining that our economic system is inherently neutral and therefore subject to the influence of the powerful. Since, in this society, power emanates from wealth, that influence has been used to further the interests of the privileged. In such a context, it is not only the right but the responsibility of government to intervene in the functioning of our economy and, where necessary, to regulate it to assure a more compassionate and just society for all people—the powerless as well as the powerful.

Is It Time to Say Kaddish for Jewish Liberalism?

Today, in America, liberalism is under attack. We live in a "what's in it for me?" culture, where the public mood is not interested in spending money for "them," where personal fulfillment is much more attractive than bold and costly social programs. We live in a time of political disillusionment with the efficacy of government itself and in a nation where the pressures of a staggering deficit make it difficult to contemplate expensive social innovations.

Major Jewish voices, like the magazine *Commentary,* have, for nearly two decades, exhorted Jews to abandon "knee-jerk liberalism," which they say has run out of intellectual fuel. They challenge Jews to vote their real "interests" instead of their obsolete traditions and "values." "Is it good or bad for Jews?" became the new slogan of hard-nosed pragmatism, implying that automatic support for liberal programs—subsidized housing, racial integration, church-state separation, affirmative action, abortion, civil liberties, assistance to the poor, gay and lesbian rights, etc.—is now contrary to Jewish interests.

These arguments shook and challenged a troubled Jewish community as neoconservative intellectuals began to dominate the debate on Jewish public policy. Jewish liberals went on the defensive. Unable to advance beyond the ideas of the New Deal and the Great

Society, what new ideas did liberalism offer to meet the emerging challenges? It seemed only a matter of time before Jewish liberalism would disappear.

But, as always, Jewish behavior defied all predictions. Institutionally, few Jewish organizations accepted the neoconservative line, which called for support for a stronger military, a foreign policy focused primarily on resisting communism, less government intervention in the economy, and the elimination of race-conscious remedies for discrimination. If one reviews the "Program Plan" of the National Jewish Community Relations Advisory Council, the largest umbrella organization of national and local Jewish organizations, one will see that in the past fifteen years none of these conservative positions was adopted by the Jewish umbrella group.

And it is against this backdrop that Jewish political behavior today must be viewed. Why were Jews the only white ethnic group to have consistently given a substantial majority of its votes to Democrats, joining only with America's Blacks in voting against Reagan and Bush landslides?

No other white group has displayed a similar propensity to vote against its own immediate pocketbook interests. Exit polls for twenty years found Jews more liberal than any other ethnic, racial, or religious group. Jews were most strongly in favor of abortion rights (including government aid to poor women) and civil rights for homosexuals. Jews overwhelmingly supported cuts in the defense budget and arms agreements with the Soviets, and they were far less interested than Americans generally in a constitutional amendment requiring a balanced budget. In the 1990 Council of Jewish Federations (CJF) study, 43 percent of the Jews described themselves as liberal, more than twice the percentage of Americans generally; only 19 percent of the Jews said they were conservative.

There has been persistent anecdotal evidence that younger Jews are becoming more conservative but little statistical evidence to back up such claims. Indeed, the increased social activism in Jewish youth movements belies that view. What do you think?

After two decades in which conservatism has dominated American politics, Jews remain reluctant to join the new popular mood that insists that government cannot have much impact on social problems (e.g, poverty) and that it should stop wasting our tax resources by throwing "money at problems" that can be solved only by volunteer efforts.

This is a dilemma for Jews. We, too, are burdened by heavy taxes. We, too, are angered by the waste and corruption that frequently infect government at the local and national levels, most dramatically illustrated by government failures that led to the catastrophic S & L scandal. Following on the heels of Watergate, Abscam, and Koreagate, the S & L debacle reminds us of the fundamental corruption inherent in campaign-financing practices. Yet, Jews still believe in government, still believe that government must be a primary instrument for achieving justice—and most Jews remain willing to pay taxes to support programs that work.

From where does this stubborn strain of Jewish liberalism stem? Is it a mindless, unexamined persistence in political attitudes appropriate to an earlier age? Is it a response to a widespread historic intuition that Jews are safer on the left side of the center than on the right? Is it a recognition that Jewish enlightened self-interest is best served in a harmonious, active society and that liberalism can best ensure such conditions? Is it a product of the Jewish ethical and religious heritage, which, in the context of American pluralism, is free to express itself more openly than at other times in Jewish history in the Diaspora? Is it the Jewish recognition that taxes, used well, represent an investment in the physical infrastructure and human capital of this country that secures both long-term economic growth *and* social justice? Perhaps the high level of education of Jews in America allows us to feel more secure in this more sophisticated analysis of our long-term "pocketbook interests" than less educated segments of our society. Or is it a perverse Jewish instinct to vote against our own interests? Either way, is it temporary, or is it ingrained in our group character?

Perhaps it is a bit of all of these, but there are two particularly strong explanations for Jewish liberalism. The first is an enduring conviction that, in the long run, Jewish security is safeguarded by a decent and compassionate society that actively seeks to help the disadvantaged, the poor, the handicapped, and the elderly. Only in such a stable and tranquil society can Jews be safe. Jews can never be secure in a divisive, tormented, or unjust society that can explode in rage—as we saw once again in the Los Angeles riots of 1992.

And, finally, if government doesn't care about the weak, who will? This is a clue to Jewish liberal attitudes and the Jewish belief that government must use its resources to diminish suffering and misery for those who most need assistance. Our definition of enlightened Jewish self-interest has helped to shape our social and political attitudes in democratic America.

The second explanation of Jewish liberalism goes to the heart of our religious and historic heritage. Our Jewish ethical system *compels* us to be concerned with the unfortunate and the stranger in our midst. Judaism rejects the concept of "survival of the fittest." We are not engaged in a struggle for survival against our fellow human beings. Our sages say, rather, "Not only do human beings sustain human beings, but all nature does so. The stars and planets, and even the angels sustain each other." Human life is sacred, so sacred that saving one life is considered as if someone had saved the entire universe.

Biblical ethics are permeated with laws assuring protection of the poor. Indeed, many scholars believe that the first antipoverty program in human history was spelled out in the Hebrew Bible and Talmud. Our self-interest is reinforced by profound ethical impulses drawn from a Jewish religious value system that commands us to be copartners with God in building a just and peaceful world. It does not, of course, command us to be liberal or conservative, Republican or Democrat. It does command us to "know the heart of the stranger," to care, and to *act* to improve the world.

Is the Jewish Political Tradition Liberal or Conservative?

If a key contemporary distinction between liberals and conservatives focuses on the economic role of government, the Jewish tradition is decidedly progressive (i.e., it always saw the community as playing a primary role in ensuring economic justice). As discussed in depth below, by early talmudic times, at least four communal funds, plus communal schools for children, were required in every sizeable community. These included a daily food distribution program, a clothing fund, a burial fund, and a communal money fund. By the Middle Ages, these had grown into a veritable bureaucracy of social welfare institutions. *Tzedakah* in Jewish history was a system of taxation, not a voluntary philanthropic enterprise. Since members of the Jewish community were *compelled* to support these institutions, they are analogous in our own time to government institutions, not to voluntary private charities.

Indeed, most economic relations—including landlord-tenant, worker-employer, purchaser-seller—were appropriate subjects for extensive communal regulation, not just matters of private contract law.

In the Jewish tradition, *tzedakah* was simultaneously an individual *and* a communal requirement. If the government achieved full economic justice in our nation today, *tzedakah* would still be required of all Jews. Conversely, despite the obligation of private charity, the community had primary authority and responsibility to see that the rights of all individuals, particularly the poor and the elderly, the widowed and the orphaned, were protected. While the social welfare system evolved by the Jewish rabbinic authority is obviously not the only model of an ethical economic framework, the pattern that emerged in Jewish history provides a standard against which the programs of our own society can be compared and judged.

Has Liberalism Worked?

This liberal approach has generally succeeded in contemporary American society as it did in historic Jewish communities. For America has made significant strides in the past thirty years toward achieving social justice. That is not to say that we have gone all the way or even most of the way or that there are not major reforms to be made in our economic and welfare programs. Some of the liberal *solutions* of yesterday have become the *problems* of today. But the unceasing politically inspired vilification of "liberal" programs threatened to drown the baby in the bath water.

With all the problems besetting these programs, the fundamental truth of contemporary American life is that, on the whole, liberal programs have helped make America a far more decent and compassionate society.

Consider the following: In 1959, before the birth of the modern social welfare program, 22 percent of American people lived in poverty; by 1965, it was down to 17 percent; in the 1970s, as a result of the Great Society, the rate hovered in the 11 to 12 percent range. Since 1981, the trend has dramatically reversed itself, fluctuating higher than the 14 to 15 percent range. In 1991, it was 14.2 percent. According to the Congressional Research Service, 49 million Americans would have sunk below the poverty line in 1989 if there had been no programs covering food and housing benefits, public assistance, and Social Security. Moreover, the vast majority of those in poverty were far better off than they would have been had there been no social welfare programs. Without Social Security, our elderly would be mired in poverty beyond imagining.

But there were also failures. The great failure of liberalism in the 1970s was its inability to recognize that major improvements could be made in social welfare programs, that a welfare culture was being passed from generation to generation, that there was extensive waste in some programs, and that other programs were counterproductive. The Reagan administration's efforts, however, decimated rather than reformed these programs. The economic policies of the 1980s created undue hardships for those already buffeted most severely by economic problems. Rather than protecting the weak and the vulnerable, as our tradition requires, the Reagan programs exacted cruel sacrifices from those least able to sustain them.

Women and children were hurt most. The sharpest increase in poverty in the past decade has been among *children*. The child poverty rate soared to 21.8 percent in 1983 and has since remained between 19 percent and 21 percent. For children under six, it is nearly one out of four; for Hispanic children under six,

40.7 percent; for black children under six, 51.0 percent live in poverty.

Yet throughout the 1980s, the administration sought to cut children's assistance programs. At the same time, we have witnessed alarming increases in the feminization of poverty: Nearly two out of every three poor adults are women; one-third of all single mothers live in poverty, compared with 6 percent of married couples with children; 74 percent of the elderly poor are women.

In the 1980s, billions of dollars were slashed from American social welfare programs despite the fact that assistance programs make up less than 10 percent of the budget. Because of skyrocketing deficits created by tax cuts for corporations and the wealthy, and by the nearly $2 trillion military buildup, these problems will plague us for decades to come.

While the federal programs were not eliminated entirely, many were shifted by the federal government to the states, creating considerable strain on state and municipal budgets. Unwilling, and in many cases unable, to raise new revenues by increasing taxes, most states began to impose steady reductions in welfare benefits and public services. The cumulative effect of these reductions has been severe. For example, in a typical state, benefits from the largest welfare program (Aid to Families with Dependent Children) for a family of three with no other income dropped 42 percent in purchasing power from 1970 to 1991.

Today, the gravest threats to our national security are internal rather than external. Surely the worsening quality of American life, the fate of our cities, the health of our children, the deterioration of our educational system, and the angry status of group relations are as much a measure of national security as is our military might.

We Jews have a profound stake in an America that is compassionate and whole. We are endangered by an America that is angry and torn apart. "The sword enters the world because of justice delayed and justice denied," states *Pirke Avot*.

Jewish Poverty in the United States

Poverty affects Jews directly as well. Jewish poverty is far more extensive than most people imagine. Eight and a half percent of our Jewish brothers and sisters live below the poverty line, and, in total, 16 percent, or 750,000 of our fellow Jews, live near or below poverty.

Moreover, the elderly are disproportionately hurt by poverty, and we Jews are the oldest community in America. The median age of the American population in the 1990 census was about thirty-two. The median age of the Jewish community is over thirty-six.

In addition, we Jews are the only segment of the American populace that has been practicing zero population growth for a generation, with a shrinking number of working-age people supporting an ever growing number of elderly in our community. The truth is, even if we dramatically increase our contributions to Jewish federations and charities, we cannot fully take care of our own. As Jews, we must stand together with that multiethnic coalition of decency that believes it should be a matter of national policy that those people who built our nation, fought our wars, and paid our taxes have an inalienable right to age with dignity.

Judaism and Poverty

America's concern for the poor is based, in part, on the legacy of the Judeo-Christian ethic derived originally from the Jewish Bible. Biblical ethics are permeated with laws assuring protection of the weak and the powerless. Our sages taught that poverty was the worst catastrophe that could happen to a person. "If all afflictions in the world were assembled on the side of a scale and poverty on the other, poverty would outweigh them all." (*Exodus Rabbah* 31:12) The tradition went about ameliorating the condition of poverty or, when that was not possible, the impact of poverty.

The Bible prescribes that, when a field is harvested, the corners are to be left uncut and the gleanings reserved for the poor, the stranger, the orphan, and the widow. According to the Torah, every seventh year was a sabbatical year, during which the land was to lie fallow, and that which grew of itself belonged to all "that the poor of your people may eat." (Exodus 23:11) All debts were to be canceled. Every fiftieth year was a jubilee year, during which all lands were to be returned to the families to whom they were originally allocated. The law of the fiftieth year fell into disuse in Jewish history, but its spirit was preserved.

Our ancestors realized that an unrestricted pursuit of individual economic gain would result in massive concentrations of wealth for the few and oppressive poverty for the many. They sanctioned competition, but they rejected an "anything goes" mentality. The intent of the law was to restore the economic balance, to give those who had fallen an opportunity to lift themselves up again. Land was not the permanent possession of any human being. "The land shall not be sold in perpetuity; for the land is Mine; you are but strangers and settlers with Me." (Leviticus 25:23)

"If there is among you a needy person . . . you shall surely open your hand and lend him sufficient for whatever he needs." This verse from Deuteronomy (15:7–8) also became the basis for a highly developed system of loans. Throughout rabbinic literature, the loan is regarded as the finest form of charity. "Greater is one who lends than one who gives, and greater still is one who lends and, with the loan, helps the poor person to help himself." (B. Talmud, *Shabbat* 63a) Almost a millennium after this was written, the medieval philosopher Maimonides defined the "eight degrees of charity," the highest of which is to enable a person to become self-supporting. Until modern times, every Jewish community had a *gemilut chesed* society, whose primary purpose was to grant loans to the needy without interest or security.

Jewish ethics clearly respect the institution of private property. Jewish tradition, however, never asserted that property rights take precedence over human rights—an assertion made by many in America today. Nor did Judaism accept the Puritan emphasis on the acquisition of property and worldly goods as a sign of virtue. On the contrary, for the Jew, human rights have priority over property rights. The tithe prescribed in biblical law was not a voluntary contribution but an obligation imposed on all, in order that "the stranger and the fatherless and the widow shall come and shall eat and be satisfied." (Deuteronomy 14:29)

Tzedakah

There is no word in the Hebrew vocabulary for "charity" in the modern sense. The word used is *tzedakah,* which literally means "righteousness." *Tzedakah* is not an act of condescension from the affluent to the needy; it is the fulfillment of a moral obligation. Injustice to humanity is desecration of God. "One who mocks the poor blasphemes one's Maker." (Proverbs 17:5) Refusal to give charity is considered by Jewish tradition to be idolatry.

Our sages taught that Abraham was more righteous than Job. According to rabbinic tradition, when great suffering befell Job, he attempted to justify himself by saying, "Ruler of the world, have I not fed the hungry and clothed the naked?" (Job 16:22) God conceded that Job had done much for the poor, but he had always waited until the poor came to him, whereas Abraham had gone out of his way to search out the poor. He not only brought them into his home but set up inns on the highway to give the poor and the wayfarer access to food and drink in time of need. True charity is to "run after the poor." (B. Talmud, *Shabbat* 104a)

An act of *tzedakah* is the means by which we restore the image of God to every human being. The sensitivities of recipients are to be safeguarded at all times. "Better no giving at all than the giving that humiliates." (B. Talmud, *Hagigah* 5a) "One who gives charity in secret is even greater than Moses." (B. Talmud, *Baba Batra* 9b) In the Temple at Jerusalem, there was a "chamber of secrecy," where the pious placed their gifts and the poor drew for their needs—all in anonymity. In later times, a *tzedakah* box marked *matan baseter* ("secret almsgiving") was placed in synagogues.

The sages regarded *gemilut chasadim* ("acts of loving-kindness") as being on a higher moral plane than *tzedakah:* "One who gives a coin to a poor person is rewarded with six blessings, but one who encourages that person with words is rewarded with *seven blessings.*" (B. Talmud, *Baba Batra* 9b)

Jewish Welfare

In the talmudic period, the Jewish community supplemented the obligations of private charity with an elaborate system of public welfare, the first recorded in history.

The practices and theories of Jewish philanthropy that evolved in the second century C.E. anticipated many of the most advanced concepts of modern social work. Every Jewish community had two basic funds. The first was called *kuppah* ("box") and served the local poor only. The indigent were given funds to supply their needs for an entire week. The second fund was called *tamchui* ("bowl") and consisted of a daily distribution of food to both itinerants and residents. The funds' administrators, selected from among the leaders of the community, were expected to be persons of the highest integrity. The *kuppah* was administered by three trustees who acted as a *bet din* ("court"). They determined the merit of applicants and the amounts to be given. The fund was operated under the strictest regulations. To avoid suspicion, collections were always made by two persons. They were authorized to tax *all* members of the community, including *tzedakah* recipients, according to their capacity to pay—testimony to the principle that no individual was free from responsibility for the welfare of all. If necessary, they seized property until the assessed amount was paid.

By the Middle Ages, community responsibility encompassed every aspect of life. The Jewish community regulated market prices so that the poor could purchase food and other basic commodities at cost. Wayfarers were issued tickets, good for meals and lodging at homes of members of the community, who took turns in offering hospitality. Both these practices anticipated "meal tickets" and modern food stamp plans. Some Jewish communities even established "rent control," directing that the poor be given housing at rates they could afford. In Lithuania, local trade barriers were relaxed for poor refugees. When poor young immigrants came from other places, the community would support them until they completed their education or learned a trade.

The organization of charity became so specialized that numerous societies were established to keep pace with all the needs. Each of the following functions was assumed by a different society on behalf of the community at large: visiting the sick, burying the dead, furnishing dowries for poor girls, providing clothing, ransoming captives, supplying maternity needs, and providing necessities for observing holidays. In addition, there were public inns for travelers, homes for the aged, orphanages, and free medical care. As early as the eleventh century, a *hekdesh* ("hospital") was established by the Jewish community of Cologne, primarily for poor and sick travelers. Many medieval Jewish communities in Poland and Germany adopted this pattern.

Applying Jewish Traditions to Modern Life

If the values of the Jewish tradition generally coincide with the liberal agenda today and animate the attitudes of the Jewish community, what insights does the Jewish tradition offer on specific policy issues of today?

The Jewish concern for the dignity of the poor is violated by some of the more demeaning aspects of the social welfare system in America today. For example, in Jewish tradition, those who claimed they were poor were given relief immediately and investigation of the claim came later. The reverse is done in our society.

Even the poor who were the recipients of welfare funds were taxed. This helped each person fulfill the *mitzvah* of *tzedakah* and prevented the stratification of society into two classes. Every person was a giver. Each person helped the poor.

Education

The belief in the inherent ability of each person to progress if given the proper tools led the Jewish community to develop a comprehensive system of education for boys. Moreover, through much of Jewish history, girls also were taught to read and write. "Lack of learning results in poverty," the Midrash wisely observes. If a community grew to a certain size but failed to establish a school, its leaders were subject to punishment. Regardless of a family's economic status, each male child was guaranteed a decent education. "Be zealous with children of the poor, for from them learning will come forth," states the Talmud. (B. Talmud, *Nedarim* 81a)

A lack of commitment to the funding of education is clearly a major factor in the poor condition of public education in the United States. The Economic Policy Institute reported in 1989 that the United States is fourteenth among industrialized countries in its per capita spending on elementary and high school education.

The growing problem of poverty in America compounds the challenges faced by schools. Homeless, hungry, and ill students do not learn at the same pace as healthy, well-fed, happy children. Illiteracy among minority students in some areas is as high as 56 percent. Minority students suffer disproportionately. Nationwide, they earn lower test scores than white students and are overrepresented among dropouts and suspensions.

This disparity is exacerbated by the pattern of funding schools in accordance with the relative wealth of districts. In Texas, for example, the Supreme Court noted that the state's wealthiest districts were spending an average of $7,233 per student while the poorest were spending only $2,978. Such disparities lead to a self-perpetuating cycle in which less money and poorer facilities are assigned to the already disadvantaged while the more privileged children have built-in advantages in their school systems.

A well-educated citizenry is essential to democracy and to our economic health. A work force that cannot read or write cannot compete in a global market. A commitment to education is a commitment to this country's future.

Full Employment

According to Maimonides, the highest form of charity was achieved by preventing poverty "through a gift or loan; by teaching the person a trade; by putting the person in the way of business so that the person may earn an honest livelihood and not be forced to the alternative of holding out a hand for charity." (*Mishneh Torah*, "Laws of Gifts to the Poor," 10:7–12)

While this obligation of *tzedakah* applied to individuals, we know of at least one historical moment when a community, or government, undertook efforts to promote full employment. The historian Josephus recounts what may well have been one of the first public works projects ever undertaken to alleviate the debilitating impact of unemployment. "And now it was that the Temple was finished. So when the people saw that the workmen who were unemployed were about eighteen thousand and that they, receiving no wages, were in want because they had earned their bread by their labors about the Temple, they persuaded King Agrippa to rebuild the eastern cloisters." (Josephus Flavius, *The Jewish Antiquities*, XX, 9)

It is difficult to reconcile the values of that tradition with economic policies that in the early 1980s produced the highest unemployment rates since the Great Depression—rates that after falling by the late 1980s resumed growing again in the recession of the early 1990s. Since 1980, the Reagan and Bush administrations eliminated the public service employment program CETA; eviscerated unemployment insurance for the long-term unemployed (hardly any of the long-term unemployed could receive extended unemployment benefits during the recession until Congress remedied this problem on a temporary basis in late 1991); and implemented tax policies in 1981 that, by disproportionately burdening the working poor, actually created disincentives to work.

A Real Dilemma: Mazon

One of the most remarkable Jewish responses to hunger in America is an organization called Mazon, which urges Jews to give 3 percent of the cost of a *simchah,* such as a wedding or a bar/bat mitzvah, to combat hunger. Mazon allocates funds to scores of local communities, mostly in America but also in Israel and countries worldwide. At the first meeting of the board of Mazon, someone asked, "Should these funds, which come from Jews, be limited to serving the Jewish poor or should they be distributed ecumenically across the board?" This was the first—and one of the most delicate—policy dilemmas faced by Mazon. What do you think were the arguments on both sides? How would you have voted?

Response

The decision was that Mazon, being a Jewish antihunger agency, will make combating Jewish poverty a high priority, but allocations of funds will *not* be limited to Jewish beneficiaries. In contrast to some equally admirable Jewish groups (e.g, the Ark in Chicago) that provide assistance only to Jews, Mazon gives to antipoverty interfaith and communal groups as well.

Health Care

The Jewish tradition strongly affirms the obligation of humanity to use its God-given wisdom and abilities to cure diseases. (See the discussion "Medical Ethics" in Chapter 14, "Bioethics.") The following *midrash* teaches that we should not regard sickness as the unfolding of God's plan; rather, we should intervene by fulfilling the commandment to heal:

> Once Rabbi Ishmael and Rabbi Akiva were strolling in the streets of Jerusalem along with another man. They met a sick person who said to them, "Masters, can you tell me how I can be healed?" They quickly advised him to take a certain medicine until he felt better.
>
> The man strolling with the two rabbis turned to them and said, "Who made this man sick?" "The Holy Blessed One," they replied. "And you presume to interfere in an area that is not yours?" the man remarked. "God has afflicted and you heal?" "What is your occupation?" they asked the man. "I'm a tiller of the soil," he answered, "as you can see from the sickle I carry." "Who created the land and the

vineyard?" "The Holy Blessed One." "And you dare to move into an area that is not yours? God created these and you eat their fruit?" "Don't you see the sickle in my hand?" the man asked. "If I did not go out and plow the field, water it, fertilize it, weed it, no food would grow!"

"Fool," the rabbis said, "the body is like a tree—the medicine is the fertilizer and the doctor is the farmer."

(*Midrash Shmuel* 4)

Some of the greatest figures of Jewish history, including Maimonides and the great medieval Spanish poet Yehudah Halevi, made their living as physicians. It is no coincidence that Jews represented a disproportionate number of physicians and medieval researchers of renown. Nor is it a coincidence that an amazing percentage of Soviet Jews coming to Israel are doctors!

The obligation to provide medical care to all Jews in a community was a religious obligation accepted by Jews throughout history. It is no less binding upon us today.

While the United States spends more on health care than any other nation ($600 billion annually and $2,051 per person, according to Commerce Department figures from 1989), one out of every eight Americans (35 million) has no health insurance. More than a third of these are employed, and a quarter are under the age of eighteen. Another 50 million Americans lack adequate health insurance. The United States has one of the highest infant mortality rates in the developed world, higher than that of eighteen other nations. The immunization rate for Blacks in America would rank fifty-sixth among the world's nations, behind Albania and Botswana.

At its 1987 biennial convention, the UAHC urged that state and federal legislation be enacted to (1) ensure that all Americans, whether or not they are able to provide for themselves, are guaranteed essential health care coverage; (2) guarantee affordable health care insurance covering catastrophic illness; and (3) provide for long-term health care, including adequate home health care, ambulatory day care, and health-regulated day care; assistance toward the cost of prescription drugs; changes in the deductable rule so that it is applied to each illness rather than each hospitalization, without requiring that one must be impoverished to receive governmental health care assistance.

Socially Responsible Investment: A New Expression of Tzedakah

The concept of "socially responsible investment" is an effective method of applying the values of *tzedakah* to a changing world.

The underlying idea of socially responsible investment is two-fold: (1) your financial investments should not implicate you in the activities of a corporation you consider immoral and (2) your investments should be in corporations whose activities you consider socially beneficial. Examples of the latter might include companies that produce equipment or exemplify behavior that cleans up the environment; increases health care; strengthens education in America; provides decent affordable housing; or promotes equal opportunities for all.

Seeds of this movement were planted as far back as the 1930s, but they took root in the early 1970s as concern about the business practices of some American corporations heightened. One of the first widespread national efforts embodying this concept was the campaign to encourage individuals and organizations to "divest" their investments in American corporations that conducted business in South Africa. This campaign played a vital role in the success of the antiapartheid movement.

Socially responsible mutual funds and socially sensitive consultants at major stock companies have emerged in response to investor interest in identifying appropriate companies for investment. In selecting a mutual fund, potential investors may apply certain criteria or "social screens" in making their investment decisions. For example, they may first want assurances that the corporations in the fund are not guilty of job discrimination or of polluting the environment. Rooted in the divestment tradition, this type of socially responsible investment is widely practiced. In fact, it was reported in 1989 that more than $500 million was invested in companies that had been socially screened.

The second type of socially responsible investment—proactive investment strategies—allows investors to earn money while contributing to community development banks, loan funds, and credit unions, as well as socially responsible mutual funds. An example: In 1973, the South Shore Bank in Chicago undertook a difficult, and some thought an impossible, task. It sought to help revitalize one of Chicago's toughest, most downtrodden neighborhoods. By using targeted financing, stimulating neighborhood reconstruction linked to education and employment programs, the bank has sparked an incredible comeback of a neighborhood that most people had written off. Today, the neighborhood boasts $160 million in new investments, three hundred and fifty rehabilitated large apartment buildings, and property values that are rising 5 to 7 percent each year. The community is stable, crime is down, and emerging businesses are profitable—all testimony to the power and potential of socially responsible investment. This project became a model for the community banks that have sprung up in cities across the country.

A Real Dilemma: Should Synagogues Divest from Tobacco Companies?

A large congregation in Hartford, Connecticut, was challenged by its Social Action Committee to divest its portfolio of any stocks involving tobacco companies. Some members of the board questioned whether smoking is a moral issue; still others whether it is a Jewish issue. (The Social Action Committee argued it was clearly a matter of life and death, a major health crisis and an ethical challenge to the teachings of Judaism.) How would you have voted if you were on the board?

Response

This was the first Reform congregation to adopt such a resolution. Members of the board felt this position was consistent with the spirit of a living Judaism and with the resolutions adopted by the delegates to the General Assembly of the UAHC. (See the discussion "Substance Abuse" in Chapter 12, "Life-and-Death Issues.")

≡ 11 ≡

THE CHANGING
JEWISH FAMILY

The Traditional Jewish Family

The archetypal Jewish family is the nuclear family—mother, father, and children—all of them linked to grandparents and to a large, extended family. This ideal family inspired some historian to conclude that the concept of wholesome family life, derived from Jewish tradition, may well be the crowning gift that Jews gave to world civilization. Implied in this valuation are warmth, closeness, mutual regard, intellectual and cultural aspirations, moral ideals, fidelity, religion, and integrity.

We still honor this ideal, but the reality is that the traditional nuclear family is becoming a minority segment of American families, including Jewish families. Consider the following:

- Intermarriage has surpassed 50 percent in the Jewish community.

- Jewish divorce rates approximate those for the general community; nearly one out of two marriages will end in divorce.

- Our birthrate is so low that we are not reproducing our own numbers.

- There are late marriages, with combinations of blended families from previous unions.

- The number of single-parent families is increasing.

- The number of gay and lesbian families with (and without) children is growing.

The Jewish family in America is going through drastic and startling culture shock.

The Jewish Family in Transition

Paradoxically, we who gave the world the exalted idea of marriage as a spiritual union *(kiddushin)* and of the home as a sanctuary of peace seem to be in the forefront of contemporary movements that are challenging traditional family concepts. These trends include unrestricted sexual freedom, living together without marriage, and the choice of a growing number of married couples to have only one or two children or no children at all. Add to these tendencies the zooming rate of intermarriage and divorce, easy and legal access to birth control devices and abortion, and profound changes in the role of women and gays and lesbians in our society.

None of these developments was intended to weaken the institution of the family. Quite the contrary, some—like the women's movement and abortion rights—are seen as means to enlarge freedom and thus strengthen family life in the long run. In the meantime, however, the Jewish family is in crisis as traditional values are being sharply modified.

What shape will the *Jewish* family take? In most American Jewish homes, secular values prevail. Television, sports, computers, and automobiles have more influence on Jewish family life than do Hillel, Deborah, Isaiah, and Moses. More heed is paid to the analyst than to the rabbi or even to God.

Much of the self-centeredness of American culture has seeped into the consciousness of the American Jewish family, displacing the religious and moral underpinnings of yesterday, which commanded marital fidelity and reverence for elderly parents. Similarly, alcoholism, recreational sex, substance abuse, as well as spousal and even child abuse, are no longer uncommon among Jews. The extended Jewish family has become a rarity as elderly parents often move to distant leisure villages or are placed in nursing homes far from their children and grandchildren. Are we witnessing a temporary flux or is the Jewish family becoming an endangered species?

In Jewish literature, the centrality of the family is paramount. "Honor your father and your mother" was one of the ten divine utterances heard at Sinai. The classic books of Jewish law are filled with attempts to spell out the responsibilities of children to their parents and vice versa. The practical implications of the commandments to honor one's parents are discussed in detail, and the responsibilities of parents to their children are even clearer. For example, the father must, among many things, provide for his son's circumcision, ensure that his child receives a proper education, and see that the child finds a suitable mate. All these were considered to be among the most crucial of the father's religious obligations, and any man who failed in them was regarded as a sinner.

Women

The demands of Jewish women for full equality pose a difficult dilemma for traditional Judaism. Despite Jewish heroines like Deborah in the Bible and the traditional praise of the wife and mother as a "woman of valor," it is clear that Jewish tradition casts women in an inferior position. Compared to most other cultures, however, Jewish tradition was, for many centuries, relatively more considerate toward women. Husbands were enjoined to honor their wives, to provide for their economic, sexual, and emotional needs. Jewish women were granted greater economic and legal rights than their non-Jewish counterparts in almost any other culture until the Age of Emancipation in the nineteenth century.

Nonetheless, Jewish law is plainy male-oriented. Within the framework of Orthodox *halachah,* women cannot serve as witnesses nor as rabbis. Neither can they participate as part of the *minyan,* the traditional quorum of ten people required for public worship. They may attend services only if separated from men behind a partition *(mechitzah)*.

Perhaps the most problematic aspect of family law is the dilemma of the *agunah* (a "deserted wife"). When a man leaves his wife without granting a religious divorce (a *get*), the woman is still technically married. A second marriage without a *get* would be adulterous. Children of the second marriage would be considered *mamzerim* ("illegitimate") and would be unable to marry a "normal" Jew. This situation is sad enough when a husband disappears or is killed with no witnesses, but the situation often arises where a husband tries to punish a wife by leaving her as an *agunah* or actively delays a *get* for a better deal in a divorce proceeding.

In Israel today, such matters of personal status as marriage, divorce, child custody, inheritance, and others are subject to *halachah* and are administered by the Orthodox rabbinate. It does not matter that one considers oneself "not religious"; there is no civil authority to which one can turn.

As equal rights within Judaism are demanded by women in Israel, in America, and wherever Jews live, Orthodoxy will have to resolve the dilemma between traditional law and the rising assertion of women's rights. In the Reconstructionist, Conservative, and Reform movements, this dilemma has begun to be resolved. Conservative Judaism now allows its synagogues to count women as part of a *minyan,* and they may also be called to read from the Torah. In 1985 the Jewish Theological Seminary (Conservative) decided to ordain women rabbis although its cantorial association allowed women to join only in 1991.

In Reform Judaism, the dilemma of equal religious rights for women has been largely resolved. From its inception, Reform, at least in theory, was based squarely on equality of the sexes. Men and women pray together and are encouraged to participate in all aspects of religious life. Although the promise of full equality still has not been realized, enormous strides have been made.

Women are now being ordained as rabbis; more than half of the rabbinic and cantorial students of Hebrew Union College-Jewish

Institute of Religion are women. Increasingly, women are serving as temple presidents, educators, congregational board members, and in positions of national leadership.

The picture of legal equality, however, conceals residual sexism in custom and practice that still prevents the full participation of women even in liberal Judaism. Of the two hundred members of the Board of Trustees of the Union of American Hebrew Congregations in 1991, only forty-one were women, and few heads of important committees are women.

The tension surrounding the use of masculine pronouns or terms referring to God has not yet been resolved. (The CCAR does, however, address this issue by using "gender-sensitive" terminology in *Gates of Prayer for Shabbat,* an interim prayer book published in 1992, and in the latest version of the Passover *haggadah.*)

What can be done to narrow the gap remaining between our professed aims and our practices? How can we raise the consciousness of women and men to respond to what is surely one of the most profound revolutions of our time? In the end it will be not what we *say* that counts, but what we *do.*

Zero Population Growth: Is Jewish Survival at Risk?

Jewish anxiety about the future of the Jewish family is intensified by the fear that we Jews may be a vanishing breed. The Jewish birthrate is so low (2.1 children per family) that we are not reproducing even our own numbers, much less making up for the grave loss of one-third of the entire Jewish people in the Holocaust. What makes matters worse is a growing intermarriage rate of about 52 percent and a declining rate of conversion to Judaism (the 1991 Jewish population study indicated that those entering Judaism through conversion [9 percent] and those converting out of Judaism were essentially equal). The study also indicated that, contrary to long-held assumptions, only 28 percent of children of intermarriages are raised as Jews; 41 percent are raised as non-Jews; and 31 percent are raised without any religion.

Since World War II, the percentage of Jews in the United States, in relation to the total population, has dropped from 5 percent to 2.4 percent. As a result, we are losing political and cultural influence, our communal and religious structures are weakened, our community morale diminished, and our ability to help Israel compromised.

What steps can be taken now to protect our future? Some answers are clear: strengthening the Jewish family through the teaching of Jewish parenting skills; family programming in the synagogue; expansion of outreach programs aimed at bringing intermarried families into the life of the synagogue; dynamic adult education programs; greater efforts in religious schools and youth groups to discourage intermarriage; and greatly expanded Jewish camping programs and youth trips to Israel—programs that have proven to be the most successful efforts in strengthening Jewish identity among our young people.

Other possible solutions raise interesting ethical and political dilemmas. Some Jewish leaders have recommended that communities launch a determined educational campaign to persuade young Jewish couples to have larger families. They argue that we have a moral obligation not "to give Hitler a posthumous victory," and therefore this generation must bring the Jewish population back to a level that will guarantee Jewish survival.

A Real Dilemma: Should Jewish Families Be Encouraged to Have More Than Two Children?

In 1978, the Central Conference of American Rabbis (Reform) considered the following resolution: "Reform Judaism approves birth control, but we also recognize our obligation to maintain a viable and stable Jewish population. Therefore, couples are encouraged to have at least two or three children."

Reactions were strong and divided. One feminist said of the proposal:

> I feel that what the CCAR is asking shows a lack of respect for the woman, for the child, and for the family. They are asking Jewish women to become baby machines for the political benefit of the community. Nowhere do they talk about how a woman might feel using her body in this way. Many women and mothers feel burdened and want an opportunity to do more with their lives than simply care for their children and their men. It is asking women once again to subordinate their own needs to that of the community and to become either eternal mothers and housewives or baby makers.
>
> (Mary Gendler, *Women's American ORT Reporter*,
> September/October 1976)

If the Jewish community feels it has a right to consider asking Jewish women to have more children, is it not obligated to provide day-care service to relieve the burden on young mothers who aspire to professional careers?

If you were a rabbi and a member of the CCAR, would you have voted for this resolution? Why or why not?

Response

The CCAR passed this resolution. Although undoubtedly some Jewish couples have decided to have more than two children for the explicit reasons embodied in the resolution, there has been no noticeable trend of increasing birthrates among liberal Jews. It is interesting to note that, while the Orthodox community has a higher birthrate, it has not grown either in absolute numbers or as a proportion of the Jewish community.

However, the Reform movement's Outreach program, seeking to enhance the Jewish identification of children of intermarriage, has increased our numbers by keeping within our community children who otherwise would have been lost to the community.

Intermarriage: The Big Dilemma

American Jews tend to be deeply concerned about the high intermarriage rates between Jews and non-Jews—a rate reaching above 50 percent in the 1990s.

What can be done about it? A central debate in the Jewish community has to do with rabbinic officiation at an intermarriage. Orthodox and Conservative rabbis are overwhelmingly opposed, feeling that to put the stamp of Jewish authenticity on such a marriage is to legitimize a trend that threatens Jewish survival and sends a message to young Jews that it is all right to intermarry. They feel that officiating at such a marriage is also an abuse of the trust that the Jewish community places in them at ordination and, by performing a Jewish ceremony for a non-Jew, shows a lack of respect to the non-Jewish partner who has made a conscientious decision not to convert.

Reform rabbis are split on the subject, the majority siding with their more traditional colleagues. A minority disagrees, contending that the marriage will take place anyway; that it is better not to drive the couple away completely; and that free choice also must be respected. Rabbis who do officiate at such marriages generally require that the couple agrees to raise its children as Jews.

What happens *after* a couple intermarries? Should the Jewish community reach out to the couple or write it off as lost? Reform Judaism leads the Jewish community in the effort to bring such families into Jewish communal life. The UAHC/CCAR Outreach Commission encourages programs in all Reform temples to involve the intermarried couples and to demonstrate that Judaism is a universal faith, accessible to the non-Jewish partners.

A Real Dilemma: Should NFTY Require Only Jewish Dating?

In 1991, United Synagogue Youth (USY), the youth movement of Conservative Judaism, adopted a resolution calling on all its members not to date non-Jews because interdating leads to intermarriage. The proponents of the resolution were gravely concerned about the skyrocketing rate of intermarriage. They felt that, if they were committed to the survival of the Jewish family and the Jewish people, they had to do whatever was in their power to discourage the trend towards intermarriage. The most effective way to stop intermarriage was, they felt, to stop interdating. Should NFTY, the youth movement of Reform Judaism, adopt a similar resolution?

Why or why not?

Response

NFTY refused to go along with USY, seeing it as an invasion of individual autonomy and personal freedom. They too felt that mounting intermarriage was a serious problem but believed the focus ought to be on building stronger Jewish identities, on better education about the problems of intermarriage, and on effective outreach programs to the intermarried families rather than on attempting to mandate dating patterns, which would not work anyway.

Although NFTY did not pass a resolution on this topic, leaders of NFTY did draft a statement that expressed diverse opinions about the USY resolution. The statement contains the following language:

> The concern for the Jewish community is understood and justified. However, that future rests on issues of Jewish identity rather than blood.
>
> If one interdates and ultimately intermarries, what is important is that the Jewish half of the couple does not see the marriage as cause to stop the development of a

Jewish identity . . . we feel it is important that the children be raised as Jews.

How can a community that "condemns" significant social contact with those from outside the community then turn around and be hospitable when someone from the outside wanders in?

The Rights of Jews Who Are Gay or Lesbian

The issue of gay and lesbian rights burst into the nation's consciousness in the 1970s. The question of gay and lesbian rights has "come out of the closet" and become one of the legitimate social revolutions of our time. The Kinsey Report (1952) estimated that 10 percent of the population might be gay. According to this estimate, there were about twenty-five million gay people in the United States in 1991. Thus, it can be inferred that in North America in 1991, perhaps one hundred thousand Reform Jews and five hundred thousand members of the larger Jewish community are gay or lesbian.

While there is no consensus on the origin and nature of homosexuality, there is an increasing body of law that bars discrimination on the basis of sexual orientation. In this more tolerant atmosphere, gays, lesbians, and bisexuals exert increasing political power, especially in cities like San Francisco, where they live in large numbers. National figures, including some members of Congress, have "come out of the closet," affirming their gay and lesbian identity, obviously relying on the improved climate of tolerance to safeguard them. That's the plus side.

The down side is that the AIDS epidemic, which arose in the early 1980s, has already decimated and demoralized the homosexual community. While AIDS is not a homosexual disease and increasingly strikes heterosexuals, especially intravenous drug users and their sexual partners, originally its primary path of devastation in the 1980s was young gay males. (Outside of the United States, AIDS and HIV infection are primarily heterosexually transmitted.)

As if that deadly prospect were not enough, there has been a sharp rise in incidents of gay- and lesbian-bashing, including physical violence. According to government statistics, bias-related violence against gay and lesbian people constitutes the fastest growing recognized category of hate crimes. The year 1990 saw a 42 percent increase nationwide in physical assaults, reaching as high as 114 percent in New York City and 100 percent in Los Angeles. No doubt hysteria about AIDS has sharpened the tendency to scapegoat the victim.

Indeed, despite the trend toward some city and state laws barring discrimination, there is no federal protection of gays and lesbians in terms of employment, housing, or public accommodations. In fact, homosexual relations still constitute criminal acts in twenty-five states.

The combined influence of all these threats and pressures upon young homosexuals has resulted in a high suicide rate. According to American statistics, in 1989 30 to 35 percent of all teenage suicides involved gay and lesbian youths.

Fundamentalist religious groups have joined with right-wing political forces in an effort to link homosexual rights with pornography and abortion as part of a "liberal" conspiracy to destroy traditional American family values. Against this bigotry, supporters of gay and lesbian rights have invoked the memory of Nazi persecution, an argument intended to appeal, in part, to Jewish sensibilities. They recall that, in addition to moving against Jews and other minorities, the Nazis persecuted gays and gypsies. It is bitterly ironic that, upon liberation by the Allies, many gay concentration camp inmates were transferred to civil prisons to "serve out their terms."

Jewish Views of Gay and Lesbian Rights

What about the Jewish community? Where does it stand on gay and lesbian rights? Because of the clear halachic statement that homosexuality is an "abomination," most Jewish organizations—

and especially traditional religious bodies—have been slow to address gay, lesbian, and bisexual rights.

The Reform and Reconstructionst communities confronted it squarely. As liberal movements within Judaism asserting the inherent dignity and equality of *all* God's children, they fully accepted gay and lesbian Jews.

A Real Dilemma: Should a Rabbi Perform a Wedding for a Gay or Lesbian Couple?

Two Jewish people, long active in their local temple, decide that they want to get married. Having lived together for several years, they wish to take the next step: celebrating their decision in a religious ceremony. The partners make an appointment with their rabbi. After meeting with the couple, the rabbi says that he is not sure he could perform a marriage between two women.

What could the rabbi do? After all, marriage is a legal contract between a man and a woman. Certainly, American civil law does not recognize a same-sex marriage as valid, and such a couple could not benefit from the tax breaks, health insurance, and inheritance laws that a man and woman receive. But what about a religious Jewish wedding?

The heterosexual ideal is central to traditional Judaism. If a rabbi performs a same-sex ceremony, wouldn't he or she be encouraging homosexuality? Does such a ceremony teach young people that homosexual relationships are acceptable and equal to heterosexual relationships?

Isn't marriage about creating a family with children? What about a *ketubah* ("wedding contract"), the *sheva berachot,* or the language *kedat Moshe* ("according to the law of Moses")? What would the reaction be of other congregants? The board of directors? The larger Jewish community? Should the views of congregants affect the rabbi's decision? Does this mean their anniversary will be listed in the temple bulletin or mentioned from the *bimah?*

Response

Neither the UAHC nor the CCAR has yet developed explicit policy on this issue, thus leaving it to the judgment of the individual rabbi. Hence, one UAHC staff member in 1991 in Georgia officiated at the marriage of two lesbian Jews. Upon learning of the event, the state's attorney general reversed a decision to hire one of the women as a lawyer on his staff. The woman sued, and the case is likely to become a landmark decision, raising issues of free exercise of religion and sexual preference discrimination.

At present, a few Reform rabbis perform such weddings. The overwhelming majority either oppose, have never been asked, or do not have a formal position on the issue.

Those rabbis who perform weddings between homosexuals feel that such couples are committed to creating a strong Jewish household and apply the same criteria they use to evaluate a heterosexual couple. By changing a few words of the traditional ceremony, some rabbis feel they can with integrity perform a Jewish wedding for a gay or lesbian couple.

While the majority of Reform rabbis may welcome gays and lesbians as congregational members, they cannot justify performing a gay or lesbian wedding, either because they do not accept homosexuality as a legitimate way of life or they are *not* prepared to deviate so radically from the Jewish tradition and the rest of the Jewish community.

Even within more halachically based Jewish communities, there are emerging opinions. They argue that a contemporary understanding of sexual orientation must be a new one, based on modern knowledge that simply did not exist in the biblical framework. Similarly, just as the legal and social status of other categories of people has changed as our understanding of them developed, so too we must reevaluate the biblical injunction against homosexuals. For example, deaf and disabled people were relegated to inferior status because deafness was mistaken for mental retardation, and the physically disabled were not considered whole or competent. Today we recognize the error of those assumptions and have adapted the *halachah* accordingly. So, too, the argument goes for those who regard homosexuality as abnormal or inferior.

The UAHC has formally supported both civil rights in the larger society and full integration into the Reform movement for gay and lesbian Jews. With much care and serious discussion, Reform Judaism was the first American Jewish movement, starting as early as 1974, to accept into its ranks congregations with an outreach to the gay and lesbian community.

Recognizing that much remains to be done, Rabbi Alexander M. Schindler eloquently stirred the Jewish community on this issue in his 1989 presidential biennial address to the Union of American Hebrew Congregations:

> . . . In most mainstream congregations, we have not extended our embrace to include gay and lesbian Jews. We have not dispelled the myth of the "corrupting homosexual," of the counselor and/or teacher who would fashion children in his or her sexual image. And we have not consciously included gay and lesbian parents as part of the Jewish family circle . . . .
>
> In our denial, in our failure to see one another as one family—indeed, as one holy body— we forget Jewish history, we opt for amnesia. We who were beaten in the streets of Berlin cannot turn away from the plague of gay-bashing. We who were Marranos in Madrid, who clung to the closet of assimilation and conversion in order to live without molestation, we cannot deny the demand for gay and lesbian visibility.
>
> In all of this, I am working to make the Reform Jewish community a home: a place where loneliness and suffering and exile ends; a place that leaves it to God to validate relationships and demands of us only that these relationships be worthy in God's eyes; a place where we can search— together—through the written Torah and the Torah of life, to find those affirmations for which we yearn.

In its 1987 and 1989 resolutions on gay and lesbian Jews, the UAHC affirmed its commitment to full inclusion of gay and lesbian Jews in all areas of synagogue life. The UAHC has urged all of its congregations to (1) encourage lesbian and gay Jews to share and participate in worship leadership and general congregational life of all synagogues; (2) continue to develop educational programs in the synagogue and community that promote understanding and respect for lesbians and gays; and (3) employ people without regard to sexual orientation.

The most urgent current issues regarding homosexual/bisexual rights within Reform Judaism have to do with the ordination as a Reform rabbi of a gay, lesbian, or bisexual person and employment by a congregation/organization of such an already ordained rabbi.

A Real Dilemma: Should the CCAR Accept Gay and Lesbian Rabbis?

The issue of gay or lesbian rabbis touched a raw nerve in the Jewish community. Given the special place of the rabbi as a role model and teacher, what would it mean for an openly gay or lesbian person to be ordained as a rabbi? Would this undermine the Jewish traditional view of the family by implying endorsement of an alternative lifestyle? Can the Jewish community, with its emphasis on children and historic continuity, ignore the long-range implications for future generations by sanctioning homosexuality? What impact would a decision to ordain gay, lesbian, and bisexual rabbis have on the unity of the Jewish community? How would such a bold decision be received in traditional and Orthodox circles, both here and in Israel?

Moreover, how would such a step be received by congregations? Once rabbis were ordained, would they be able to obtain employment in the Reform movement? Would selection committees start asking loaded questions in the interview process to "weed out" gay or lesbian candidates? Once knowledge of their homosexuality was known, how would that impact on their future? Would rabbis "in the closet" be moved to come out? Would closet rabbis be "outed" (exposed by other homosexuals) in this new climate?

Proponents of the ordination of gay and lesbian rabbis argued that there have always been homosexual rabbis; the real question is one of openness, dignity, and integrity. If the Reform movement was willing to take positions affirming gay and lesbian congregations, how could that same reasoning not be applied to those who wanted to pursue rabbinic roles in the Jewish community?

The CCAR was asked to decide whether or not to recommend that qualified Jewish persons who are homosexual or bisexual not be barred from ordination as rabbis. You are a rabbi and a member of the CCAR.

How would you vote?

Response

A special committee of the CCAR struggled with the question through four arduous years of debate and intense soul-searching. Its final report was submitted to the 1990 convention of the Central Conference of American Rabbis and was endorsed overwhelmingly by the Reform rabbinate. The report read in part: "The committee urges that all rabbis, regardless of sexual orientation, be accorded the opportunity to fulfill the sacred vocation that they have chosen."

While the committee agreed on that central point, it did not agree on other questions. A majority of the committee reaffirmed that "in Jewish tradition, heterosexual, monogamous, procreative marriage is the ideal human relationship for the perpetuation of species, convenantal fulfillment, and the preservation of the Jewish people."

The impact of the report is not yet clear. As of 1992, no mainstream Reform congregation has hired an openly gay or lesbian rabbi.

There were and are many honest arguments against the CCAR action—arguments based on Jewish law, on Jewish unity, on tactics of timing and publicity, etc. But some of the protests stemmed less from rational arguments than from homophobia (an irrational fear of gays and lesbians) that has surfaced so visibly in America.

Raw bigotry can target gays and lesbians as easily as Blacks, Jews, Asians, women, disabled persons, or any other vulnerable group. Just as Reform Judaism has been on the cutting edge in affirming the rights of gays and lesbians—including the right to serve as a rabbi—so, too, Reform Judaism is called upon to educate and sensitize our members to our own fears of homosexuals. We must also be more vigorous in repudiating any hate crimes, indeed any discrimination, against gays or lesbians in our own communities.

Domestic Violence

Family violence in America has reached epidemic levels. Consider the following statistics:

- One in every three female children and one in every six male children in the United States will be sexually abused by the age of eighteen. In 85 percent of these cases, the abuser is someone known to and trusted by the victim.

- One in every twenty-five elderly persons in the United States will meet with physical abuse at the hands of his or her adult children.

- In the United States, at least one million children are physically abused by their parents or caretakers every year. Two thousand die from physical abuse and neglect.

Although domestic violence plagues Jewish families with just slightly less than the same frequency as non-Jewish families, the Jewish community has been reluctant to acknowledge its occurrence. Historically, the family unit has been both the source of strength and the pride of the Jewish people. To admit that abuse occurs within our homes poses an enormous threat to our cultural identity and self-image.

Our tradition emphasizes the dignity of each human life and the sanctity of the home. Yet our tradition also defines women as the property of their husbands and fathers. We are commanded to honor our parents, but how can one honor parents who are abusive? We must confront and reconcile these contradictions and produce a coherent social framework for dealing with abuse when it occurs in our community.

Child Abuse

Studies show that child abuse can be transmitted from generation to generation; child abusers were often abused children. Many such abusers vowed that they would never subject their children to the treatment they received, yet many revert to the types of behavior that caused their own suffering.

Child abuse is found in families with varied incomes and educational backgrounds. The greatest impediment to overcoming domestic violence is denial and silence. As long as Jewish leaders cling to the assumption that child abuse is *not* a Jewish problem, Jewish children will continue to be molested, physically and emotionally, without effective community intervention.

Teachers, youth directors, and rabbis need to be trained to identify victims of abuse and provide help. They must be sensitive to those subtle types of violence that wound and tear but leave no physical scars. Although victims of abuse are certainly in need of counseling and often must be removed from abusive situations, the perpetrators of abuse are in need of help as well. We as a community must be willing to address the problem and to commit to the support and rehabilitation of all parties concerned. Hopefully we can help prevent such abuse from being passed to the next generation.

Spouse Abuse

Rabbis have recognized the problem of spouse abuse for centuries; an eighth-century Babylonian text makes specific reference to a

208 · *Tough Choices*

husband abusing his wife. Only in recent years, however, have female victims come forward and reported the crime.

Spouse abuse takes many forms, including forced social isolation, verbal harassment, sexual abuse, and battering. Studies show that, as is the case for child abuse, violence against one's spouse is as common in the Jewish population as in the general American population.

A 1980 Los Angeles study, based on more than two hundred completed questionnaires from congregants of nine Orthodox, Conservative, and Reform synagogues, reported 22 incidents of spouse abuse, 4 incidents of sexual abuse, 11 incidents of forced social isolation, and 118 incidents of violent acts toward children. In total, 30 percent of the respondents reported either having experienced or having known of violence in Jewish families.

Sadly the study also found that victims of abuse most often kept knowledge of the violence within a close circle of family and friends. A few told private therapists. Only four respondents spoke to a rabbi about the abuse.

Many abused Jewish women who call hotlines do not identify themselves as Jewish to their counselors, and many abused Jewish women can afford to and prefer to stay in hotels rather than in battered women's shelters, which remain the primary source of statistical information on spouse abuse.

Clearly, there is still a great deal of shame associated with admitting that abuse can occur within a Jewish household. A mythology seems to be at work that prevents us from addressing this unpleasant reality. Because the characteristics of a batterer or a battered woman do not fit our image of a Jewish couple, it is difficult, almost impossible, for us to believe this is a Jewish problem. The result is massive denial, even in the face of such celebrated headline cases as the fatal battering of little Lisa Steinberg in New York City by her violent father (by adoption) and the tragic story of the chasidic mother in Brooklyn who beat her son to death in 1992.

EMERGE, a men's counseling group that works with batterers, reports that one-third of the men it counsels are professionals: doctors, lawyers, even rabbis. In such cases, the wife's accusation is often met with disbelief by people in the community who know only the public image of the abuser.

As long as we perpetuate the myth that such violence does not occur in Jewish homes, the road to recovery will remain long. Even as women increasingly report their abuse, sexual assault remains the nation's least detected crime.

The sooner we engage in the debate and begin looking for the solutions to these problems, placing these issues on our communal agenda, the sooner we will bring relief to those who cower in silence and bring hope to those who are confused, ashamed, and do not know where to turn. The UAHC Committee on the Jewish Family is involved in precisely this quest.

Date Rape

In the emerging awareness of the widespread occurrence of acquaintance rape and date rape, we see a particular challenge to young adults. Date rape involves, among others, Jewish women as victims and Jewish men as perpetrators. In fact, because of the particular focus on college campuses and the disproportionate number of Jewish women and men attending higher educational institutions, there is a specific Jewish dimension to this issue.

Consider the following hypothetical situation, taken from an article, " 'Friends' Raping Friends," published by the Association of American Colleges:

Phil and Cindy: The Same Story, but Two Different Points of View

Phil: I still don't know what happened. Cindy and I had been dating for about two months and, while we had not slept together yet, I had certainly made it clear that I was very attracted to her and eventually expected to have sex with her. We were supposed to go to a party and, when she showed up in this sexy low-cut dress, I thought maybe this was her way of saying she was ready. At the party we drank some beer, which made her sort of sleepy and sensual. When she said she wanted to go lie down and have me come snuggle with her, what was I supposed to think? Of course I thought she wanted to have sex. Granted, she did grumble a little when I started to undress her, but I just figured she wanted to be persuaded. Lots of women feel a little funny about being forward and want men to take responsibility for sex. I don't know. We had sex, and it was fine. I took her home from the party, and I thought everything was OK. But ever since then she refuses to talk to me or go out with me. I thought she really liked me. What happened?

Cindy: I'll never forget that night as long as I live. Phil and I had been dating a while, and he had always acted like a perfect gentleman. Well, we had done our share of kissing, but he never gave me any reason not to trust him. The night of the party I wore this gorgeous dress that I borrowed from my roommate. It was a little flashier than I normally wear, but I thought it was very flattering. At the party I had some beer, and it made me tired so I wanted to lie down. Maybe I shouldn't have suggested we both lie down together, but it felt wierd to go upstairs by myself and leave Phil all alone. The next thing I knew he was all over me, forcing me to have sex with him. It was horrible. I didn't want to scream and make a fool of myself with all those other people in the next room, but I tried to fight him off. I guess I was just too wiped out to be very effective. Needless to say, I never want to see Phil again. He seemed like such a nice guy. What happened?

Was this rape? Date rape? How could Cindy and Phil see the same experience in such shockingly contrasting ways? The best way to avoid such misunderstandings is to set one basic ground rule in sexual relations: when one partner says no, *at any time,* the decision of that partner must be fully respected.

Youth Suicide

Suicide is the third leading cause of death among young people between the ages of fifteen and twenty-four. In the United States, eighteen young people commit suicide every day. For each of these successful suicides, there are a hundred unsuccessful attempts. There are an estimated five hundred thousand attempted youth suicides annually in the United States. Almost every student in high school or college today knows at least one person who has attempted suicide. Although precise statistics are unavailable, it appears that these figures apply proportionally to the Jewish community as well. Teen suicide has increased 200 percent since 1964. This trend is a tragic indication that many young people are feeling deeply alienated from their families and other support systems in our society.

Why do young people choose to commit suicide? Often, they believe that their feelings of loneliness and stress are unique and hopelessly irresolvable, and they will not be understood by others. While an individual is unlikely to commit suicide in response to a single incident, such factors as the death of a sibling, the strain of dealing with a parent's financial failure, a breakup of a romantic relationship, or concern over homosexual feelings may elevate stress in teens to the point of contemplating suicide. Although divorce per se has not been shown to be a direct factor in adolescent suicide, "pathological divorce," in which parents fight over the children or use them as pawns, may in some cases be such a factor. It is, therefore, important for young people to learn how to deal with stressful situations and feelings without becoming so overwhelmed that they consider suicide as a solution.

The UAHC has responded to this frightening trend in a variety of ways. In 1985, its Task Force on Youth Suicide Prevention was formed. The task force was created under the auspices of the *Yad Tikvah* ("Hand of Hope") Foundation with the goal of encouraging congregations, camps, and youth groups to become involved in the vital work of suicide prevention. In 1985, the UAHC Press published Sol Gordon's best-selling *When Living Hurts,* an in-depth book on suicide prevention geared especially to young people. The UAHC also distributes a suicide prevention kit that includes programming options for religious schools, camps, and youth groups. The kit was sent to rabbis to implement suicide-prevention programming in their temples.

How can friends as well as adult supervisors of children (parents, counselors, teachers, rabbis, youth directors) help? Primarily by being observant and willing to listen. While signs of depression, of sudden appetite loss, of sudden changes in sleeping patterns, of repeated unexplained bruises, of crying jags, of a sudden decrease in concentration or deterioration of grades might well have varied—and often innocent—causes and explanations, they should never be ignored! They are all symptoms that *may* mask more serious problems: physical abuse, drug and alcohol use, and emotional problems that could lead to suicide. A responsible adult should be informed, and that adult should look into the matter. Above all, even passing references to suicide should never be considered idle chatter but should be addressed directly and caringly by a responsible adult.

In addition to its proactive emphasis on preventative programming and counseling, the task force has published a booklet, *It's Not Over When It's Over: The Aftermath of Suicide,* which is a guide to rabbis on how to comfort suicide survivors. Often, the sense of shame, guilt, and anger surrounding the suicide makes the grieving process especially difficult for its survivors.

The recent epidemic of suicides and attempted suicides is especially disturbing because of the immense value our religion ascribes to human life. Traditional Jewish law views the taking of one's life as *chet* ("sin")—morally wrong and prohibited. A suicide is traditionally buried on the periphery of the Jewish cemetery, a significant distance from the other grave sites. In addition, no mourning rites are traditionally observed for one who commits suicide, unless the individual is considered mentally incompetent.

Although Reform Judaism concurs that suicide is wrong, we think that the Jewish tradition emphasizing compassion and concern for the surviving family supersedes other considerations. Therefore, in Reform tradition, rites of burial and mourning customs are observed for the deceased who has committed suicide, and every effort is made to avoid attaching stigma to the victim and the family.

≡ 12 ≡

LIFE-AND-DEATH ISSUES

This chapter deals with several controversial life-and-death questions that are sure to roil the national as well as congressional agenda in the coming years: abortion, capital punishment, gun control, AIDS, and substance (drug, alcohol, and tobacco) abuse.

Each one of these volatile issues has become a buzzword in American politics, with the power to excite extremists to the heights of demagoguery and to seal the lips of nervous politicians who vote with a finger to the wind.

More than mere political hot potatoes, they are urgent moral issues that cannot be omitted from the Jewish agenda.

Abortion

A Real Dilemma: A Rabbi's Choice

In 1990, the state of Louisiana adopted a sweeping and highly repressive antiabortion law. A young rabbi in Shreveport, Michael Matuson, had strongly opposed the bill, arguing that the law violated women's rights and privacy. The night the law was enacted, an official of the American Civil Liberties Union (ACLU) visited the rabbi, asking him to be one of the defendants in a law suit to enjoin the implementation of the law that would criminalize doctors and health care workers as well as women seeking abortions. Rabbi Matuson agreed.

The local newspapers plastered the story of the rabbi's role on the front page. Community repercussions were severe. Indeed, the local KKK group came to the parking lot of the temple in full regalia and threats to the rabbi's life were received daily.

The congregational leadership was upset that, in a small town in the South with a tiny Jewish population, the rabbi had placed them in the eye of the storm without consulting them in advance. If you were a member of the temple board, what would you have said when an emergency meeting was called to discuss the matter?

Response

The board responded that they respected the rabbi's freedom of the pulpit and admired his courage. However, they said that the next time the rabbi should inform the board before, and not after, making such a controversial decision and involving the synagogue in a heated public dispute.

This is a difficult decision for rabbis. On one hand, rabbis have the same rights to express and act on their personal beliefs as do others. They have an obligation to provide leadership for the Jewish community based on their understanding of the values of the Jewish tradition. They are not merely the mouthpiece for the majority view of the temple board or membership. They have complete freedom of the pulpit. On the other hand, rabbis derive some of their authority from the perception that they speak for their synagogue and the Jewish community. When a pulpit rabbi speaks out, the rabbi thereby implicates the synagogue.

Rabbis walk a tightrope, balancing their conscience and leadership role with their community relations responsibility. Trust must be placed in the rabbi's judgment on this. While tying the rabbi's hands by requiring approval of the board on specific issues would undermine the integrity and authority of the rabbi, informing the board in advance of controversial positions helps prepare the board members for questions from congregation members and affords an opportunity for gathering support. Both the UAHC and the CCAR commended Rabbi Matuson for fulfilling the resolutions adopted by the Reform movement and for his courage in upholding unpopular views.

Several months later, when this rabbi led the community in opposition to David Duke, sixteen members of the clergy, including the Roman Catholic bishop, joined the rabbi on the *bimah* for Sabbath services to express interfaith solidarity.

In the political climate of the United States today, few issues are more divisive than abortion. This is true particularly in the wake of the *Webster* decision by the United States Supreme Court in 1989 (upholding state restrictions on when, where, and how women can exercise the right to abortion guaranteed in *Roe* v. *Wade*), the *Rust* decision in 1991 (essentially "gagging" doctors and counselors in publicly funded clinics from even mentioning abortion), and the *Casey* decision in 1992 (upholding requirements for parental notification, a twenty-four-hour waiting period, the reading of a prepared statement by the doctor concerning the risks of abortion, and a narrow definition for medical emergency exemptions).

A firestorm of protest after the *Webster* decision by pro-choice Americans changed the political balance of power on the abortion issue in many states and in the Congress. Earlier, responding to the clout of the single issue pro-life organizations, both the Reagan and Bush administrations had made the fight against abortion a kind of moral crusade, and both tried to use views on abortion as a litmus test of eligibility for the federal judiciary. For both administrations, purity of opposition to abortion was part of the heavy price of support by the Religious Right and the potent antichoice groups.

But, from 1989 on, as pro-choice forces demonstrated exceptional political muscle and savvy in many states, many antiabortion "true believers" were seized by sudden attacks of pragmatism. The Republican party in New York State came out for "reproductive rights" in 1990, and candidates with long records of vehement opposition either modified or switched their positions, however uncomfortably, or frequently went down to electoral defeat. Public opinion polls showed much confusion on the morality of abortion, but an overwhelming majority believed that it is the woman—not a politician—who has the right to choose.

More decisively than any other group in America, Jews favor the right of free choice in abortion. Some 87 percent, almost twice as high a percentage as non-Jews, support abortion rights. Of the half-million supporters of abortion rights who gathered on the Mall in Washington, April 5, 1991 (the largest such demonstration in American history), fully 21 percent were Jewish, according to a *Washington Post* poll. Nonetheless, there are differences even among Jewish groups, as there are among Protestants and Catholics. Reform and Conservative Judaism have taken a clear stand in favor of free choice for women, and rabbinic and lay leaders of these branches play prominent roles in groups like the Religious Coalition for Abortion Rights. Orthodox Judaism sides with the Roman Catholic church in condemning abortion—albeit rejecting efforts to define human life as beginning at conception, a view incompatible with *halachah*.

In a testimony presented by Rabbi Balfour Brickner before the House of Representatives in 1980, the UAHC said:

> The Supreme Court holds that the question of when life begins is a matter of religious belief and not medical or legal fact.
>
> We recognize the right of religious groups whose beliefs differ from ours to follow the dictates of their faith. We vigorously oppose the attempts to legislate the particular beliefs of those groups into the law that governs us all. This is a clear violation of the First Amendment . . . .
>
> We oppose bills aimed at halting Medicaid, legal counseling, and family services in abortion-related activities. These restrictions severely discriminate against and penalize the poor who rely on governmental assistance to obtain medical care to which they are legally entitled, including abortion.
>
> We are opposed to attempts to restrict the right to abortion through constitutional amendments. To establish in the

Constitution the view of certain religious groups on the beginning of life has legal implications far beyond the question of abortion. Such amendments would undermine constitutional liberties that protect all Americans.

But Jewish dilemmas remain. Jewish tradition generally holds that a fetus may be destroyed to save the mother's life. More liberal strands of the tradition would justify an abortion simply to protect the mother's health. But is it not stretching the tradition to assert that it would support abortion on demand? Can Jewish tradition really sanction abortion on economic, psychological, or social grounds?

Arguing for the right of free choice in the matter of abortion does not necessarily mean that the grave decision to abort a fetus is either ethical or wise. Abortion may be, and should be, a free choice, but it must be seen as one of the most serious moral decisions a person can ever face. Perhaps, as writer Roger Rosenblatt has urged, a moral position for America would be to permit but strongly discourage the practice of abortion. Consider the following fictional situation, a composite of real-life situations that happen across America every day:

Imagine you are sixteen years old. A month ago, your "boyfriend" forced you to go further sexually than you wanted to. It was a situation of "date rape." You were embarrassed and scared and didn't tell anyone—particularly your parents, who would punish you severely. Your mother drinks a lot under stress and, when she does, she hits you. Your father demands you meet his view of moral purity and always warned you against sexual activity, saying he would punish you severely if you had intercourse before marriage. You are miserable but decide to focus most of your energy on your schoolwork. You figure that there is a way out: you will go away to college and escape the pain.

You don't get your period on time. You don't know what to do. Panic strikes. You go to the drug store and buy a home pregnancy test. You are pregnant. What are you going to do?

You know you are not prepared to be a mother. You don't

know whom to ask for advice. You definitely can't tell your parents, who would probably say skeptically, "If you were raped, why didn't you say anything until now?"

You finally decide to tell an older friend. She takes you to the nearest family planning clinic three hours away. You talk to a counselor there. The two of you finally decide that abortion is the best option. Although the procedure terrifies you, becoming a sixteen-year-old mother in an unsupportive family is even more frightening.

The counselor tells you that, in West Virginia as in twenty-three other states, before the doctor can perform an abortion on a minor, one parent must consent. In some states, she tells you, *both* parents must give their permission.

What are you going to do? You wish you were able to tell your mother, to have her hold you in her arms and tell you that everything is going to be all right. However, you know that this is not going to happen in your family.

You explain the situation to the counselor at the clinic. She explains that the Supreme Court has decided that, in any state with a parental consent clause for minors in their abortion law, there is a "judicial bypass" mandate. This allows the pregnant teenager to go to a judge, who will determine if she is mature enough to make this decision on her own. If the judge decides that she is, she can get an abortion. Of course, the counselor explains, this is a complicated and time-consuming process. The longer you wait, she tells you, the more complicated the abortion would be.

Your head is swimming. You never wanted to have sex in the first place. You were raped. And now your entire life seems in danger. What should you do?

The UAHC passed a resolution at its General Assembly in 1981 supporting minors' access to reproductive health care and, in 1989, endorsed a resolution proposed by the National Federation of Temple Sisterhoods that included this clause:

> [We] support minors' access to reproductive health services, including contraceptives and abortion, unrestricted by parental notification, parental permission, or court order requirements.

There are several reasons why most Jewish organizations believe that this is the responsible stand to take.

First, laws that mandate parental consent do nothing to improve parent-child communication or to prevent sexual activity among teenagers. Second, they can create dangerous delays in the decision-making process. Although the risks of legal abortion never even approach the risks of childbirth, after the first eight weeks of pregnancy the risk of major complications from abortion increases about 15 to 30 percent for each week of delay. A study in Minnesota indicated that the parental notification law increased the percentage of minors who obtain second trimester abortions by 26.5 percent.

Even more tragically, there have been cases in which women who feel they cannot go to their parents actually resort to attempts at self-abortion or rely on back-alley practitioners who use unsafe methods. This has resulted in great physical harm to the mother, at times even death.

Most young women *do* turn to their parents when they find they are pregnant. When else are they more in need of parental love, support, and guidance? Some 55 percent of the minors who obtain abortions at clinics have already talked with at least one parent about their pregnancy; some 75 percent of young women under the age of fifteen talk with at least one parent about their pregnancy.

Although good communication benefits both parent and child, we believe that compassion must be shown toward those young women who come from families that fail to nurture, and even terrorize, their children. Therefore, the UAHC opposes all parental consent or notification laws, even with judicial bypass.

Abortion presents other grave dilemmas both for opponents and proponents. Opponents, claiming fidelity to the *right to* life for the unborn, often care little about ensuring a decent *quality of* life for these children either before or after birth. They often show scarce concern for children on such matters as prenatal nutrition and health care programs, Headstart, and child care and job programs for parents. They have not distinguished themselves in passionate concern for "life" beyond the womb on such issues as capital punishment or gun control. They frequently help to elect politicians who vote "right" on abortion no matter how wrong they may be on everything else.

Similarly, those who wage war against abortion also tend to fight measures to *alleviate* the abortion crisis: sex education, free birth control clinics, and the support services required by poor pregnant women. Certainly, all Americans who do not have moral objections to birth control, whether they are pro-choice or anti-choice, should agree that we have a moral obligation to do everything possible through the dissemination of birth control technology and education about birth control options to avoid putting women into the position where they need to choose whether or not to have an abortion.

On the other hand, some proponents, for their part, have created an environment in which abortion, regarded as a profound and grave personal decision by most women and men, is almost made into an amoral decision. Today there are 1.6 million abortions performed annually in the United States. Sometimes abortion is used as another form of birth control by people who are somehow casually confident that the first manifestations of human life can be disposed of at will. It is one thing to defend the right of free choice; it is another to make a moral good of abortion. As has been the case with every woman who has had to consider abortion, all of us must pause and reconsider the moral and human implications of this persistant and painful dilemma.

A Real Dilemma: Operation Rescue

Operation Rescue, a militant antiabortion group, which argues that abortion clinics are the equivalent of Nazi death camps, believes it has a moral and religious obligation to prevent women from going ahead with abortions. In this effort, the group takes extreme actions, including hurling their bodies in front of cars, blocking entrances to clinics, and frightening women with threatening shouts and pictures of bleeding fetuses.

In 1991, in Wichita, Kansas, several hundred activists launched a militant campaign to shut down two abortion clinics. Judge Patrick Kelly, a federal judge, ordered the activists to "cease and desist" from interfering with the legal rights of the clinics and their patients and threatened to sentence offenders to prison terms. The United States Department of Justice challenged the judge's ruling on technical grounds, in effect siding with the demonstrators. The judge denounced the government's intervention as a "political agenda" and said he was "disgusted" by its action, which he charged undermined respect for law and order.

Columnists on both sides argued that the incident paralleled the civil rights conflict in the South. Do you think that such antiabortion tactics are the modern equivalent of civil disobedience by civil rights demonstrators? Was the judge the modern equivalent of the federal judge who ordered desegregation in Little Rock when southern whites tried to stop black children from exercising *their* rights to attend an integrated public school?

The UAHC issued a statement. What should it have said?

Response

Here is the press statement the UAHC released:

Two organizations associated with the movement of Reform Judaism today criticized the Bush administration for joining forces with an antiabortion group that is fighting a federal judge's effort to keep open abortion clinics in Wichita, Kansas.

The Union of American Hebrew Congregations and the National Federation of Temple Sisterhoods, in a joint statement, commended United States District Judge Patrick Kelly for his courage in upholding the law and for distinguishing between legitimate protest and actions that go beyond the law, such as seeking to close down a lawful institution.

Regardless of the political agenda of the White House, which clearly opposes free choice in abortion, American women still have a constitutional right to choose an abortion, as protected by the decision in *Roe* v. *Wade*.

That United States Supreme Court ruling means that the government has a solemn duty to assure law and order and to prevent violence and anarchy. It is outrageous that the Bush administration, in pursuit of its political agenda, should intervene in behalf of lawbreakers, thereby encouraging them to continue to unleash—in the words of Judge Kelly—"mayhem and distress" on the city of Wichita.

Judge Kelly deserves support for standing up in behalf of lawful process against threats to close down the abortion clinic. He should be congratulated. The Justice Department should be condemned.

Death Penalty

In 1976, the Supreme Court, reversing a trend of decisions that virtually barred the death penalty, gave the green light to the states to resume capital punishment. By July 1991, one hundred and fifty persons had been executed. Studies show that those executed are disproportionately poor minority persons and that, in cases of murder, it is the race of the *victim* more than the race of the *defendant* that affects juries: cases of whites slain by Blacks elicit the death penalty far more often than Blacks slain by Blacks or whites by whites.

The many national Jewish organizations opposed to capital punishment were shocked by the results of a 1989 poll showing that 74 percent of all Jews oppose abolishing the death penalty. Jews, traditionally regarded as particularly liberal and humanitarian, voting in favor of capital punishment! What was going on?

Jews were demanding tougher measures to crack down on increased drug-related shootings, violence in the schools, and muggings on the streets. Some measure of law and order on the streets of our cities and safety in our homes had to be restored.

It is not "illiberal" to demand an end to such savagery. Like others, Jews are no longer content to articulate theories that the criminal is the product of society's failures and that reconstructing society is the surest way to reduce crime. Life and property are in jeopardy now. Daily life has become too anxiety-provoking.

Exasperated by the failure of other solutions, even Jews are tempted by politicians who exploit these anxieties. Reinstitution of the death penalty has become the vote-getting response of many politicians pandering to the public cry for law and order.

In many elections, politicians compete for the "bloody shirt" honor of promising to subject more criminals more quickly to the death penalty than their opponents. In 1991, the Senate passed a bill by a 71 to 26 margin expanding the death penalty to include over fifty new federal crimes, half of which do not involve murder. This trend is exacerbated by a 1991 Supreme Court decision drastically limiting the right of appeal by those on death row. The increasing frequency of executions has desensitized us and disappears into the back pages of newspapers, but there is no evidence whatsoever that state-sanctioned killing reduces crime.

Capital Punishment in the Jewish Perspective

In Judaism, the religious justification for the death penalty is found in the Hebrew Scriptures ("an eye for an eye"), but evolving Jewish law came to abhor the death penalty.

In early Hebrew society capital punishment was instituted for crimes that later generations considered trivial. But those later generations could not simply repeal the ancient laws of divine origin. They could, however, create conditions whereby enforcement of the law became impossible. According to Deuteronomy 21:18-20, for example, a "stubborn and rebellious son" could be turned over to the elders of the city who had the power to sentence him to death by stoning. Despite this law, there is not a single case cited in all of rabbinic literature of a "rebellious son" being executed.

That law, as most legislation pertaining to capital punishment, remained purely theoretical.

Only deliberate murder was punishable by death, and proof of culpability had to be nearly absolute. Intent to commit the murder, treacherous lying in wait, and the use of a deadly weapon had to be proved. The murderer had to be warned specifically of the nature of the act and the severity of punishment—prior to committing the crime. To establish guilt, two witnesses were required to give *identical testimony* against the accused in the commission of the murder. Such impediments to capital punishment reflected the dominant rabbinical view.

The most famous talmudic exposition on the limits of capital punishment appears in *Mishnah Makkot* 1:10.

> A Sanhedrin that executes [a criminal] once in seven years is known as destructive. Rabbi Eleazar son of Azariah says: Once in seventy years. Rabbi Tarfon and Rabbi Akiva say: If we had been members of the Sanhedrin, no man would ever have been executed. Rabbi Simeon son of Gamaliel says: They [Rabbi Tarfon and Rabbi Akiva] would have been responsible for the proliferation of murderers in Israel.

As campaigns mount to restore the death penalty, we must recall that, in its origin, capital punishment was conceived as revenge. Modern advocates of this practice stress it as a deterrent to other murderers and capital offenders. This contention was already challenged in 1923 by Dr. George W. Hirchwey, a renowned penologist: "On June 21, 1877, ten men were hanged in Pennsylvania for murderous conspiracy. The *New York Herald* predicted the wholesome effect of the terrible lesson. 'We may be certain,' it said, editorially, 'that the pitiless severity of the law will deter the most wicked from anything like the imitation of these crimes.' Yet, the night after this large scale execution, two of the witnesses at the trial of these men had been murdered and, within two weeks, five of the prosecutors had met the same fate." Some deterrence!

Capital punishment by hanging was practiced in England up to the eighteenth century and often became a public spectacle. There was no evidence that the crime rate lessened. Pocket-picking became so prevalent among the audiences gathered to watch the public hangings of pickpockets that these spectacles were suspended.

There seems little, if any, correlation between the severity of punishment and the frequency of crime. Minnesota and Michigan were just as safe as Iowa and Illinois even when the former two states had outlawed capital punishment.

Most problematic morally, the possibility of judicial error cannot be overlooked. Our system of justice is fallible because human beings are fallible. In 1955, in New York, Louis Hoffner, who had been convicted of murder and had already served twelve years of a life sentence, was pardoned on the basis of new evidence that had become available. Such grievous errors occur. But what if Hoffner had been given death instead of life imprisonment? Since 1900, approximately three hundred and fifty innocent people have been sentenced to death; of these, twenty-three were executed.

Some have argued that gas, electrocution, and lethal injection have made execution painless. Others reject this assertion and point out that, even aside from the physical pain, the mental torture preceding supposed "painless death" is beyond calculation. In addition, they point to the torment and stigma inflicted upon innocent relatives of the executed. Perhaps worst of all is what capital punishment does to society itself: it brutalizes the human spirit and arrogates to society God's lifetaking power.

Until 1979, when Florida executed John Spenkelink, capital punishment seemed to have been fading from American life. No person was executed in the United States between 1967 and 1973; every state awaited the Supreme Court's decision on the constitutionality of the death penalty. Finally, in 1972 the High Court determined that the unequal application of the death penalty, which is usually reserved for the poor and minority group members, did represent "cruel and unusual punishment" and was unconstitutional. It left open the question of whether the death penalty itself is unconstitutional.

Today, as advocates of capital punishment push the death penalty as a quick-fix answer to mounting crime, many states have drawn up laws that pass the Supreme Court's strictures. The debate will continue in every state and community until such time as the Supreme Court decides that the death penalty is unconstitutional. Meanwhile, the door is now open to a virtual bloodbath of condemned men and women currently on death row.

Gun Control

Every two minutes a gun is used to kill or wound an American citizen. Since 1900, three-quarters of a million people have died in the United States by guns—through murder, suicide, and accident. This is two hundred thousand more than the number of Americans killed in all our wars.

A 1990 Gallup poll showed that a significant majority of adult Americans are (and have been for the past thirty years) in favor of firearms control legislation, including the registration of all guns. Yet, the wishes of the majority for a sensible control of firearm sales have been stymied by the formidable lobbying effort led by the National Rifle Association (NRA) and various gun manufacturers.

The proliferation of guns in the hands of Americans, abetted by easy access and availability, has been cited as a major cause of the soaring crime rate in our country. Then why, in light of this harsh reality, has so little been done over the years to control the ownership of guns?

Rabbi Jerome K. Davidson, religious leader of Temple Beth El of Great Neck, New York, is one of many Americans who brought the following 1979 incident to the attention of *The New York Times.*

> To the Editor: Brenda Spencer, a San Diego sixteen-year-old, last week momentarily diverted our attention from the big news made by strife in Iran and visitors from China. She did it by opening fire with a .22-caliber rifle on an elementary school, killing two and wounding nine, including children ranging in age from seven to twelve. "I don't like Mondays. This livens up the day. I just started shooting for the fun of it. . . ."

There is no excuse whatsoever for a .22-caliber rifle, with five hundred rounds of ammunition, to have fallen into that girl's hands. She didn't steal it. It isn't a trophy someone brought home from the war. She received it for Christmas! Someone gave it to her as a present.

Such tragic occurrences are not rare. Who does not recall the college student who gunned down forty-five people, killing fourteen, from the top of a tower at the University of Texas? Have we already forgotten the mass killing in New Rochelle by an American Nazi whose apartment contained an entire arsenal? Have we pushed the ugly memory of the "Son of Sam" killings out of our minds? Or the Brooklyn high school student who murdered two fellow classmates in the hallway? The TV evening news in most metropolitan areas is replete with such tragedies, day after day.

These shattering events reflect the unwillingness of Americans to admit to the real danger that the private possession of guns represents to our very lives. There are 40 million handguns alone in the United States. One is sold every thirteen seconds. Twenty-five thousand people are shot to death each year, sixty-nine each day. But, it is evidently not enough to cause the American people to overpower the National Rifle Association and demand the enactment of effective controls.

It has already been said, "With all the violence and the murders and the killings we have in the United States . . . we must keep firearms from people who have no business with guns." Yet, we do not heed the words despite the dramatic fact that they were spoken by Robert F. Kennedy five days before his assassination.

A few weeks after Rabbi Davidson wrote his letter to the *Times* demanding gun control, the gun lobby bought paid advertisements in several Long Island newspapers: an open letter signed by another rabbi. It read, in part:

> . . . The solution to the problem of violent crime cannot possibly be found in any panacea like gun control (prohibition) legislation.
>
> Firearms have often been the only hope of oppressed and persecuted peoples. With but ten pistols, the Jews in the

Warsaw Ghetto chased out the mechanized Nazi German war machine and forced the German army into house-by-house combat and the burning down of that ghetto in order to conquer it. Later in Budapest in 1944, the Nazis realized that they could not then afford a repetition of the Warsaw uprising.

For that reason they waited in their extermination of the Jewish community of Hungary until they were able to enlist the cooperation of the Hungarian Jewish leadership. This the Nazis were unfortunately able to do, to reassure the Jews and persuade them to go quietly to their extermination by keeping the horrible destination a secret. The Nazis perceived that armed resistance by even a handful of pistol-toting Jews in Budapest would necessitate house-to-house combat with troops they could not then afford.

Historically, Jews and other minorities have much to fear from gun control laws—laws that have been selectively enforced, inevitably against ethnic, religious, and political minorities all over the world. Therefore, any additional legislation on this subject must be approached with great reservations.

So the issue was joined. Which rabbi is most in accord with Jewish values? Would the possession of guns by Jews in Germany and Hungary really have prevented the Holocaust from taking place? Is gun control good or bad for the Jews?

Handgun Control Legislation

A background paper on firearms legislation, prepared for the Commission on Social Action of the Union of American Hebrew Congregations (UAHC), will help to clarify this issue:

What are the arguments of the opponents of firearms control legislation?

1. They maintain that the right "to keep and bear arms," guaranteed in the Second Amendment to the Constitution, would be violated by such legislation.

2. They are afraid that gun control laws would hurt the responsible sportsperson who uses guns for hunting and marksmanship.
3. They claim that the legislation would not lower crime rates as criminals would still be able to obtain firearms illegally.

These arguments are unfounded.

1. The Second Amendment states: "A well-regulated militia being necessary to the security of a free state, the right of the people to keep and bear arms shall not be infringed." This obviously was written in order to guarantee each state a militia, and the Supreme Court has stated many times, in upholding the constitutionality of gun control laws, that it does not apply to individual citizens bearing arms. In 1939, in *United States* v. *Miller*, the Court held that "the Second Amendment applies only to those arms that have a reasonable relationship to the preservation of efficiency of a well-regulated militia." Furthermore, the courts have established that rights given by the Constitution are not absolute and have recognized the government's power to limit such rights in the face of compelling interests of the general welfare and domestic tranquility. The right to bear arms must be subordinated to the right to life. There may be a legal right to own an automobile, but the automobile must still be registered and anyone who wants to drive it must be licensed.
2. Sensible gun control legislation would not in any way interfere with the legitimate use of guns by the responsible hunter or marksperson. In nations with strict firearms laws, hunting still thrives. After the enactment of the laws controlling the purchase of guns in many states, the sale of hunting licenses increased. Legislative measures that would help eliminate the irresponsible firearms owners and set standards of competence for firearms usage should indeed increase the prestige, and certainly the safety, of gun sports.

    The purpose of gun control legislation is not to prevent legitimate ownership of firearms but to keep such arms from those who would misuse them. Furthermore, over the last few years, much gun control legislation has been aimed at stopping the proliferation of automatic weapons.

3. No one claims that gun control legislation is the neat and total solution to violence and crime. But, the fact is that it does cut down both the incidence of crimes in which guns are involved and the general rate of violent crimes. In states with strong firearms laws, the percentage of homicides in which guns are used is significantly lower than in states without such laws. A comparison of our country with other nations that have stringent gun control is even more revealing. In 1990, handguns were used to murder 13 people in Sweden, 91 in Switzerland, 87 in Japan, 68 in Canada, 22 in Great Britain, 10 in Australia, and 10,567 in the United States.

What Rabbi Davidson could have only imagined in 1979—that the American public would stand up to the powerful NRA lobby—finally took place in the early 1990s. The NRA's opposition to legislation barring so-called cop killer bullets actually cost them the support of law enforcement agencies. The NRA opposition to legislation banning even assault weapons caused a severe backlash in public opinion.

The "Brady Bill"

In 1991, both houses of the United States Congress approved the "Brady Bill," handing the gun lobby a major defeat. However, the "Crime Bill" to which the "Brady Bill" was subsequently amended had not yet passed by September 1992.

The history of the "Brady Bill" illustrates the tragedy of our failure to have enacted gun control legislation earlier. On March 30, 1981, when John Hinckley, Jr., attempted to assassinate President Ronald Reagan, he shot and forever changed the life of the president's press secretary, James Brady.

Today, Mr. Brady is permanently brain-damaged and partly paralyzed—doctors say that he will never walk again. Since the shooting, his wife, Sarah, has courageously led the fight in lobbying for legislation named after her husband, which would impose a national seven-day waiting period before the purchase of a handgun. The intent is to give people, who seek to buy a gun in a moment of anger, time to cool off, as well as to provide time for gun shop proprietors to check if the prospective purchaser has a criminal record or is mentally ill.

After former President Ronald Reagan himself, reversing his oft-repeated position against gun control, declared his support of the "Brady Bill," the measure was approved and, despite initial threats to veto it, signed by President Bush.

In recognition of their heroic leadership in support of this legislation and their ability to overcome personal adversity to mobilize the public conscience, the UAHC bestowed upon Jim and Sarah Brady the Maurice N. Eisendrath "Bearer of Light" Award at its 1991 biennial convention in Baltimore, Maryland.

AIDS

Another issue of life and death, which emerged only a decade ago, acquired immunodeficiency syndrome (AIDS), has already afflicted more people in the United States and throughout the world than have all of America's wars.

A Real Dilemma: Condoms at Kutz

The UAHC/CCAR Joint Committee on AIDS was asked to take a stand regarding a proposal to combat AIDS by distributing condoms at all Reform Jewish camps in which teenagers, as campers or staff, participate. There are strong feelings on both sides of the issue.

The proponents of distribution argue that AIDS and other sexually transmitted diseases pose a serious risk to sexually active young people. To deny that our teenagers are sexually active is naive. As Jewish educators, we have a responsibility to educate our young people so that this generation has the real possibility of being AIDS-free. The distribution of condoms would take place only in the context of discussions of Jewish sexual ethics and responsible behavior.

Others argue that the distribution of condoms implies approval of sexual license at camp and youth group activities. Parents might not send their children to a summer camp that distributes condoms. It might be perceived that the camps are even encouraging sexual promiscuity.

What should the committee have recommended?

Response

By the camping season of 1992, the UAHC/CCAR Joint Committee on AIDS determined that it was not yet prepared to make a recommendation but is intensively studying the issue. In the meantime, programs on sexual ethics and AIDS remain part of the youth movement's educational activity.

The public response to AIDS was transformed overnight when Magic Johnson, the basketball superstar, told a stunned world that he was infected with the human immunodeficiency virus (HIV) that causes AIDS. In an instant, for millions of people, the AIDS crisis was moved from the margins of public attention to the center of public concern.

The national habit of denial—"this is not my problem; it is a problem for homosexuals and drug users"—was challenged in an extraordinary moment of truth. Magic's courage and honesty illuminated one of America's most urgent and misunderstood problems.

That everybody is at risk from AIDS, that only abstinence and safe sex can begin to curb the escalating horror of AIDS, that a hedonistic lifestyle of casual sex can be lethal, that much larger public funding is needed—all these truths came forward like a full court press when this gallant and smiling superhero addressed the American people. The Johnson story is a vivid reminder of the limitless power of one individual to make a difference in the world.

The Reform Jewish movement, partly upon the plea of its gay

and lesbian congregations, has responded strongly to the AIDS crisis. A Jewish quilt panel, honoring Jews who died from AIDS, was unveiled at the 1989 UAHC biennial convention.

Reform Judaism was the first national Jewish body to confront the challenge of AIDS. Its high-level commission of doctors, scientists, and care-givers serves as a resource committee for the movement and a conscience to the Jewish community. The commission presses for greater public funding; opposes discrimination against PWAs (people with AIDS); and trains rabbis and others in counseling AIDS patients. The Jewish values that drive this concern—*pikuach nefesh* (the "saving of lives") and *bikkur cholim* (the *mitzvah* of "visiting the sick")—resonate eloquently in one of the earliest sermons given on this issue (1985) by Rabbi Robert Kirschner, then at Temple Emanu-El, San Francisco, California. The sermon led to the establishment of an AIDS relief fund in the congregation, raising significant monies for AIDS service agencies.

> Usually, when a rabbi quotes his ancient predecessors, he does so with approval, even reverence. Our sages of blessed memory were remarkably wise and perceptive, noble and compassionate. But not always. I quote from an ancient *midrash* on the thirteenth chapter of Leviticus, dealing with the subject of leprosy. The sages are discussing what they do when they see a leper. R. Yochanan says: I go no closer to a leper than four cubits. R. Shimon says: If the wind is blowing, I go no closer than one hundred cubits. R. Ammi and R. Assai say: We do not even go near a place where lepers are known to live. R. Eleazar b. Shimon was still afraid: If he heard that a leper was in the vicinity, he would hide. Then there was the great sage Resh Lakish: When he saw a leper, he would throw stones at him shouting: "Stop contaminating us and go back where you came from!" (*Leviticus Rabbah* 16:3)
>
> I am not proud of this passage. I quote it now because I think it has something to teach us on Yom Kippur, when we ask forgiveness for our sins. Scholars have shown (*Encyclopaedia Judaica* 11:38) that, by the time this passage was written, the segregation of lepers enjoined by the Bible was no longer required. In a case where a rabbi himself came

down with leprosy, the decision was handed down that he could enter the synagogue together with everyone else.

No, the hostility of our passage does not arise merely from the fear of contagion. After all, to avoid a leper is one thing; to throw stones at him is another. In rabbinic literature, lepers are accused of everything from murder to incest, idolatry to robbery, perjury to blasphemy to slander. In the days of our sages, to be a leper was not only to be afflicted with a disease but to be despised for it. It was not only to die a terrible death but to be accused of deserving it.

Today, leprosy is called Hansen's disease, and those who suffer from it may walk among us without fear. No longer must they bear—as if their illness were not enough—the crushing weight of anathema. But now there is a new multitude of sufferers to fear and to shun. Theirs is the new dread affliction, the new mark of doom: AIDS.

The condition now known as AIDS, acquired immunodeficiency syndrome, was first recognized in 1981. Patients with AIDS have developed a severe loss of their natural immunity to disease, leaving them vulnerable to lethal infections and cancers. To date, no treatment has been able to restore the immune system of an AIDS patient to normal function. Almost 75 percent of the people who have developed AIDS are dead. [Ed. note: These statistics represent the figures in 1985, when the sermon was written. As the life expectancy is increased with medication, the percentage of those living with AIDS has increased. There have been 182,834 documented cases of AIDS in the United States as of August 1991. Of these 115,984 have died. There are an estimated one million people in this country who are HIV positive.]

Like the ancient rabbis, we prefer to keep our distance from the victims of this illness. Like them, we are afraid of catching it. But, according to the medical experts, those outside the high-risk groups are highly unlikely to do so. [Ed. note: While, to date, the majority of AIDS cases and related deaths are among gay and bisexual men and intravenous (IV) drug users, the fastest growing group of new HIV infection is among primarily poor, heterosexual women of color and their children.]

Only 1 percent of all reported cases involve a transfusion

recipient or a child born with the mother's infection. Of over thirteen thousand cases nationwide, not one has been attributed to casual contact with AIDS patients. Of those caregivers who are constantly exposed to AIDS and frequently tested for it—doctors, nurses, hospital workers, family members—few outside of the high-risk groups have caught it and those only after exposure to the blood of a carrier.

Yet, despite the evidence, we are still afraid. Not enough is yet known about AIDS. The fear of contagion is itself contagious and likely to persist. It explains, in part, why we stay away from people with AIDS. But, as in the case of the ancient lepers, it does not explain it all. Our aversion, too, goes beyond the fear of infection. We shrink from people with AIDS not only because they are sick but because we don't like how they got sick. When it comes to homosexuals and drug addicts, our sympathy for their affliction is diluted by the suspicion that they deserve it. Like the ancient leper, the AIDS patient suffers not only the torment of illness but the stigma of it. The patient's life and now death are alike regarded as a kind of disgrace.

Tomorrow afternoon, traditional Jews around the world will read the eighteenth chapter of Leviticus. This is where homosexuality is described as an abomination (18:22) punishable by death. (20:13) But Reform Judaism departs from the Torah on occasion. We do not stone adulterers; we do not ostracize children of forbidden marriages; we do not sprinkle lepers with blood. Such biblical legislation, we believe, is the work not of divine but of mortal and fallible hands, and we consign it to the antiquity from which it came.

The divine content of the Torah, we believe, is found in its transcendent vision of justice, peace, and compassion. The God we revere is the One who, as R. Akiva taught (*Mishnah Avot* 3:18), creates each of us because He loves us, who as the *Mishnah* says (B. Talmud, *Sanhedrin* 4:5) considers each life to be worth the life of the whole world. The God we revere is the One who, as the Torah itself insists, sides not with the mighty but with the forlorn, who hears the cry of the helpless and defends the defenseless. (Exodus 22:21 ff.) The God we revere is the One who loved us when we were the unwanted, the unwelcomed, the exiled, and the outcast.

A belief in this God, to my way of thinking, simply cannot be reconciled with a judgment of anathema upon homosexuals, or lepers, or any other of God's children. "Blessed are You, O Eternal One," says our prayer book, "who has made me according to God's will."

Each of us, in our unique being, is the work of God's hands and the bearer of God's image; each of us—even someone with AIDS. . . .

. . . A friend of mine, Father Michael Lopes, told me something that happened on a visit to ward 5B at San Francisco General Hospital. This is where the most desperately ill AIDS patients are treated and comforted before they die. Father Lopes walked into one of the rooms on the ward. The blinds were closed; only a little shaft of light penetrated the darkness. The patient lay in bed in agony. His entire body was covered with purple lesions of the cancer called Karposi's Sarcoma. His face was terribly swollen and disfigured and his mouth was infected with fungus. So appalled was Father Lopes that he could hardly bring himself to come near. But, just then, the patient turned in his bed, and the little shaft of light came to rest on his eyes—bright blue eyes, clouded with pain but now suddenly filled with gratitude at the sight of his visitor. Looking into those eyes, Father Lopes said he remembered that beneath the mass of lesions was a person, a human being, hurting so badly that the mere presence of a visitor was a benediction.

My friends, surely as God is in heaven so is God with the patients on ward 5B. As surely as God's light shines above this ark, it shines above their beds. But God has no other hands than ours. (Dorothee Soelle, *Suffering* [Fortress, 1975], pp. 149, 174) If the sick are to be healed, it is our hands, not God's, that will heal them. If the lonely and frightened are to be comforted, it is our embrace, not God's, that will comfort them. The warmth of the sun travels on the air, but the warmth of God's love can travel only through each one of us. . . .

. . . I return this time with great pride to the teaching of our ancient sages. "Where," they asked, "shall we look for the Messiah? Shall the Messiah come to us on clouds of glory, robed in majesty, and crowned with light?" The Talmud (B. Talmud, *Sanhedrin* 98a) reports that R. Joshua b.

Levi put this question to no less an authority than the prophet Elijah himself.

"Where," R. Joshua asked, "shall I find the Messiah?" "At the gate of the city," Elijah replied. "How shall I recognize him?" "He sits among the lepers." "Among the lepers!" cried R. Joshua. "What is he doing there?" "He changes their bandages," Elijah answered. "He changes them one by one."

That may not seem like much for a Messiah to be doing. But, apparently, in the eyes of God, it is a mighty thing indeed.

AIDS Testing and Civil Liberties

The ability to test for the AIDS virus has introduced new ethical and legal dilemmas over how to balance public health concerns with the right to privacy.

AIDS tests have the potential to save lives when their results are used responsibly to help prevent spread of the virus. However, when the test results are made public, the person who has tested positive for HIV antibodies often faces severe discrimination by the fearful general public, by employers, and by health insurance companies.

One set of questions revolves around whether or not doctors and test centers should be required to report positive HIV tests to public health authorities, who would treat the virus like a sexually transmitted disease, contacting all former partners and suggesting they be tested. While this might help alert some people, AIDS public interest groups and civil liberties advocates such as the ACLU emphasize the importance of privacy in AIDS testing.

They claim that, although people should act responsibly to take precautions against spreading the virus, there should be no law requiring the mandatory reporting to health authorities of test results. Some health care experts point out that such mandatory reporting would, in fact, scare people away from voluntary testing programs, making it more difficult to curb the spread of the virus.

Most testing programs are aimed at individuals at high risk of

AIDS—individuals who are in minority groups, distrustful of government and fearful of further discrimination should they be discovered to have AIDS. In states that have instituted mandatory name-reporting legislation, there have already been drop-offs in the number of people being tested. The ACLU also argues that, once the government has a list of the names, addresses, sexual orientation, and other information about people who test positive for the AIDS virus, the list would be an irresistible target for insurers, school systems, or any state agency that might gain future access to the list.

The reverse side of this argument concerns people's "right to know" information that would allow them to make educated decisions about protecting their health. This has recently become a burning issue as it relates to health care workers who test positive for HIV. Of the more than one hundred eighty thousand AIDS cases known in the United States, there has thus far been only one documented report of a health care worker passing on the AIDS virus. This occurred when a Florida dentist infected five of his patients. One, the late Kimberly Bergalis, publicly demanded a law forcing health care workers to divulge to their patients their HIV status.

A Real Dilemma:
Testing Health Care Workers for HIV

Is it a patient's right to be informed if his or her doctor has tested HIV positive? If so, is this information only relevant if the doctor will be performing operations in which bodily fluids might be exchanged, or does this right apply to all health care professionals?

This case has stimulated much public hysteria as well as extensive media coverage on the issue of health care workers with AIDS. Although the Center for Disease Control released guidelines on the subject, which did not recommend mandatory testing legislation or mandatory reporting of results, Congress considered legislation in 1991 that would have imposed maximum criminal penalties of ten years in prison and a $10,000 fine for health care workers with the AIDS virus who do not inform their patients of their condition. The legislation would have required all surgeons and dentists who perform certain high-risk operations to be tested for the AIDS virus and, if found positive, to stop performing them. It was strongly opposed by the medical profession as well as civil liberties groups and eventually dropped in a House-Senate conference.

Should the UAHC have supported or opposed passage of the law in 1991?

Response

The UAHC joined with the medical profession and civil liberties groups opposing this legislation for the reasons stated above. Also, if a doctor must divulge, why not a *patient?* And what would be the effect on both doctor and patient?

Substance Abuse

At least 5.7 million Americans may have serious drug problems. The National High School Senior Survey reported that 47.9 percent of high school graduates have tried an illicit drug. About 500,000 Americans presently use crack; the number of people using cocaine daily increased from 292,000 in 1988 to 336,000 in 1990 before turning downward. Each week, from 2.2 million to 2.4 million Americans use cocaine. In the United States, 600,000 are addicted to heroin.

Our nation's drug policy is impotent at best. Some 70 percent of the federal drug-control budget is spent on law enforcement, border interdiction, and international antinarcotics activities. Only 30 percent is spent on prevention and treatment. As a result, as many as 6 million Americans in need of drug treatment are unable to receive proper treatment and rehabilitation care.

The age at which young people begin experimentation with beer, wine, and alcohol has dropped sharply. While the abuse of drugs has diminished slowly over the past few years, individual lives are distorted and sometimes wrecked by alcohol abuse, and legions of families are torn asunder by the spiraling conflicts set in motion by this abuse. The challenge of growing up in America is to ignore media hype and the seduction of advertising and to develop a life-style that is healthy and positive.

Of course, it is naive to expect slogans like "Just Say No" to make a difference. But, in a culture that is permeated with reliance on drugs (from valium to aspirin) and that suggests in its advertising that whatever feels good must be morally OK, it is necessary to take charge of one's own life at an early age—and choose life! That applies to the choices we make about our own bodies—including drugs, alcohol, sex, and tobacco.

A Real Dilemma: Using the Synagogue for Alcoholics Anonymous Meetings

An Alcoholics Anonymous group asks permission to utilize the facilities of the synagogue. The proposal is submitted to the board. Some board members urge that the group be admitted just as other outside groups are able to use the synagogue facilities. One member of the board says this will look bad for the synagogue, their presence will "detract from the dignity of the institution," and, besides, very few Jews are alcoholics.

You are a member of the board, what do you say?

Response

Many synagogues welcome Alcoholics Anonymous and Narcotics Anonymous groups. Jewish alcoholism rates are only slightly less than those of the general society and participants of both groups include Jews. The presence of such groups in synagogues affirms the concept that the synagogue is an accepting and relevant institution to help members of the larger community, both Jews and non-Jews, receive the kind of support they need to overcome their addictions.

Smoking

Most Americans agree that the problem of drug addiction is one of the most serious confronting the country today. Nevertheless, when people speak of drugs, they usually fail to mention or even recognize one of America's deadliest drugs. Tobacco is directly responsible for, or is a contributing factor in, the deaths of an estimated 390,000 Americans annually. *More Americans are killed by smoking than by all other illicit drugs, AIDS, alcohol, automobile accidents, homicides, and suicides combined!* Though still generally accepted in society, cigarettes represent, according to former Surgeon General C. Everett Koop, "the most lethal and addictive drug known."

Such societal acceptance has allowed the tobacco industry to flourish. In the process, it has established itself as a multibillion-dollar industry that will not easily disappear, regardless of the harm it leaves in its wake. Each year, the tobacco industry spends in excess of $3 billion dollars on cigarette advertising. For the welfare of the tobacco industry, this is money well-invested, as indicated by the annual sale of 30 billion packs of cigarettes. As for the nation's welfare, smoking contributes to medical bills and lost work hours, costing the country a staggering estimated $65 billion dollars annually.

Judaism and Smoking

Cigarette smoking endangers not only the life of the smoker but also those who come into contact with the smoker, including children.

Still, there are those who say, "When I smoke, the only life I endanger is my own." Even if it were true that smoking causes no harm to others, it would still be difficult to reconcile with Jewish law. The *halachah* reflects a value system in which the intrinsic worth and preservation of human life is of paramount importance. Thus, it is forbidden to harm any human being including oneself.

The Union of American Hebrew Congregations has taken a strong stance against smoking, banning the use of tobacco products in all its buildings. Many UAHC congregations have prohibited smoking in their facilities. In addition, congregations like Beth Israel of Hartford, Connecticut, have resolved not to invest in tobacco companies. (See the discussion "Socially Responsible Investment" in Chapter 10, "Economic Justice.")

In taking a long and hard look at the issue of smoking, the UAHC adopted the following resolution intended to bar smoking at its meetings, to mandate an educational campaign to raise the consciousness of Reform Jews on this issue, and to call upon its Religious Action Center to lobby against subsidizing the tobacco industry:

> In our time, cigarette smoking is the single most preventable cause of death and disease. Each year over three hundred thousand Americans and seventy-five thousand Canadians die from causes associated with the use of tobacco. The American Cancer Society and the Surgeon General of the United States concur: smoking one or two packs of cigarettes a day decreases a smoker's life expectancy by at least six to eight years.
>
> Nonsmokers are also put in danger by the smokers around them. Indirect smoking . . . can cause disease, including lung cancer in healthy nonsmokers. Infants and children exposed to tobacco smoke have increased respiratory infections and specific changes in lung function. The simple separation of smokers and nonsmokers in the same airspace does not decrease the hazards to nonsmokers.
>
> *Therefore be it resolved* that the Union of American Hebrew Congregations
>
> 1. ban smoking entirely at all its meetings, functions, and workplaces, and urge its affiliates and congregations to do likewise.

2. establish educational programs that discourage the use of smoking and nonsmoking tobacco products, and make those programs available to its congregations for use in their religious schools and youth group programs.
3. support enactment of legislation to protect nonsmokers in public areas and workplaces.
4. urge the United States and Canadian governments to phase out subsidies to the tobacco industry with steps taken to cushion adverse economic impact.
5. urge parents who smoke to refrain from smoking when they are with or around their children.

The last item (#5) was an amendment proposed on the floor by the teenage delegates of the North American Federation of Temple Youth.

A Real Dilemma: Should Owners of Tobacco Companies Be Leaders of Jewish Organizations?

In 1990, a prominent and respected social activist came to the Religious Action Center with a generous but most unusual offer: he would contribute over $100,000 as an endowment fund to support the work of the center, provided that its leadership would agree never to allow as its chair, and never to honor in its events, any person who was an officer of a tobacco company. The first reaction was shock, mixed with irritation.

How dare he put such strings on his gift! What right did he have to dictate to an organization who its leaders should or should not be? And what kind of cockamamy condition was this man trying to impose? Why smoking? Why not also alcohol, adultery, income tax fraud, drugs, or any other on a long laundry list of personal and social sins?

Not so fast. The contributor explained the thinking behind his offer. Smoking is a *unique* problem, he argued. The tobacco industry is *sui generis* ["in a class by itself"]. It is the only legal industry whose products are almost always addictive; smoking cannot be used safely and kills millions.

Recent statistics show that smoking is related to nearly four hundred thousand deaths in the United States each year. The number of deaths and disabilities that are connected to smoking throughout the world makes this a larger death industry than war itself.

Is it not a supreme moral contradiction that the smoking industry is legal? As Jews, given our commitments to life and health, we must at the very least withhold our moral sanction from those whose profits tempt the unknowing into a habit that leads only to death and tragedy. Jews should be in the forefront of efforts to end smoking, but at the very least we should not put our endorsement on this social evil by honoring its leaders. In any case, doesn't he have a right to insist that, before his name is attached to an endowment to the center, he ensure that it not be associated with people involved in an industry he believes to be anathema to the values of the center?

What would you have decided if you were a commission member and had to vote whether to accept this gift?

Response

The Commission on Social Action rejected the offer, not because it disagreed on the evil of smoking, but because it felt it wrong to allow any donor to impose such strings on a *gift* to the Religious Action Center. We wanted to avoid even the appearance of being "bought." Some members felt that as long as tobacco was lawful the tobacco official's other good deeds should be weighed into the decision. Each case needed to be evaluated individually; no categorical limitation was appropriate. The donor, while disappointed with this decision, accepted it and has since contributed to specific programs of the center, but he did not proceed with the endowment.

≡ 13 ≡

THE ENVIRONMENTAL CRISIS

The earth is *Adonai*'s and the fullness thereof . . . .
                                                    (Psalms 24:1)

We do not inherit the world from our parents, instead we borrow it from our children.
                    (Anonymous contemporary rabbi—but borrowed
                            by the authors who have the *chutzpah*
                            to pretend it is an ancient *midrash*)

These two compelling moral concepts remind us that the earth has been lent to us as a "trust" by God on the condition that we care for it, protect it, and ensure that future generations will benefit from its bounty.

The traditional Jewish view of our stewardship of earth is conveyed in the following *midrash* on the story of creation:

> In the hour when the Holy One created the first human being, God took Adam before all the trees of the Garden of Eden and said: "See My works, how fine and excellent they are! All that I have created I have created for you. Think upon this, and do not corrupt and desolate My world; for, if you corrupt it, there is no one to set it right after you."
>   (*Ecclesiastes Rabbah* 7:28)

All the evidence indicates that we are doing exactly what the tradition warned us not to do. As a result of the breakthroughs of the twentieth century, we are the first generation capable of pol-

245

luting the environment to such a degree that we face the real possibility that our planet might no longer be hospitable to human
existence.

The First Twenty Years of the
Environmental Movement: Good News, Bad News

A college student once published the following satirical obituary:

> Michigan, Lake. Memorial services for Lake Michigan will
> not be held as such; however, visitation will remain in effect
> indefinitely. The lake, age 23,031, died recently after many
> years of abuse, stemming primarily from pollution. The lake,
> once a popular sports and recreation area for millions of
> people, is survived by Lake Superior and Lake Huron. Lake
> Michigan was preceded in death by Lake Erie and Lake On-
> tario.
>
> David M. King
> University of Illinois

The postmortem to this obituary notice on the environment is one
of good news and bad news. The good news is that Lake Michigan
and others have been significantly detoxified and reclaimed in the
past two decades. We are also making great progress through international cooperation in dealing with global environmental
problems. In the United States and across the globe, political "green"
parties and environmentalist groups have gained unprecedented
power and influence. State and federal agencies, corporations, and
individuals have had some positive impact as well.
   Consider:

1. In the mid-1980s, Weston Birdsall of Osage, Iowa, inspired the
   town of 3,600 to make a concerted commitment to conservation. By implementing simple energy-saving mechanisms (e.g.,
   plugging leaky windows and insulating walls and ceilings) and
   making energy-conscious capital improvements, the town was

able to cut its overall natural gas consumption by 45 percent, saving an estimated $1.2 million.

2. 3M, the Minnesota Mining and Manufacturing Co., has reaped monetary benefits by instituting a variety of environmentally conscious waste cleanup measures. By using fewer toxic chemicals, separating out reusable wastes, and substituting alternative raw materials for hazardous substances, 3M cut its waste generation in half and saved $420 million in a single year.

3. During the 1970s, so contaminated was Lake Erie that officials feared it would catch fire. Alarmed by the extent of the lake's degradation, the state of Ohio implemented drastic cleanup measures. Today, the once flammable lake has been restored as a popular recreation site on Ohio's northern coast.

4. Clean water acts passed by the United States Congress in the 1970s and 1980s set the stage for massive waterway cleanups from the Jersey Shore to the Mississippi River.

5. The 1990 Clean Air Act, the most comprehensive environmental legislation ever passed, includes important provisions that force power plants to cut in half by the year 2000 their acid rain, which causes sulfur dioxide emissions. Other elements of the legislation require oil companies to develop new, cleaner-burning fuels by 1995.

6. According to the research group Public Citizen, in the past decade, Arizona, California, Colorado, New York, and Vermont have improved energy efficiency dramatically. If the other states were to reduce their per capita energy consumption to the level of these five, the United States would decrease its energy use 35 percent.

7. McDonald's, the world's largest fast-food chain, switched in 1990 from ozone-damaging styrofoam take-out containers to paper containers.

As the above items indicate, we are winning many battles. The bad news is that we are losing the war. For every lake that is reclaimed many more lakes "die"—their water so polluted that they cannot sustain life. If we fail to reverse this trend, the planet's ability to support life as we know it will be greatly reduced.

How bad is bad?
Consider:

1. A hole in the ozone layer over Antarctica has now grown larger than the United States. In the past two years, a similar hole has begun to open up over Greenland. Ozone protects us from ultraviolet rays that cause skin cancer in human beings and damage to plant and animal life.
2. Scientists estimate that every day another 100 species of living organisms become extinct. The current rate is over a thousand times faster than ever before in the history of the earth.
3. Every Sunday, more than 500,000 trees are consumed to produce our newspapers, 88 percent of which are not recycled.
4. Americans go through 2.5 million plastic bottles every hour, only a small percentage of which are now recycled.
5. We throw away enough glass bottles and jars to fill the 1,350-foot twin towers of New York's World Trade Center every two weeks.
6. The world's forests are being destroyed at the rate of one acre per second.
7. While eastern Canada contains more than one million lakes, acid rain has sterilized 14,000 and severely damaged another 150,000.
8. The National Academy of Sciences estimates that $5 billion or more in damage is done every year by acid rain in the eastern United States alone.
9. The world's population is doubling once every thirty-five years, reaching 5 billion in 1990 and heading for 6 billion in the year 2000.

Judaism, Ecology, and the Environment

The prophet Jeremiah, using God's words, could have been speaking to us when he warned his contemporaries: "And I brought you into a land of fruitful fields to eat the fruit thereof and the good thereof; but, when you entered, you defiled My land and made

My heritage an abomination." (2:7) Everyone who reads—or even looks around— can see how badly we, in our time, have defiled the land and ravaged God's earth.

Long ago in Jewish history, ecological ideals were translated into specific regulations. Tanneries, which produced odor pollution, were sharply restricted in their proximity to residential centers. The location of threshing floors, which produced significant dust pollution, was likewise restricted, as were businesses that caused noise pollution. Communities were obliged to keep public streams, water supplies, and roads clean and in good repair.

Even wartime military camps were obliged to follow waste disposal procedures. Soldiers had to carry shovels and dispose of their human waste outside the camp so "the camp will be holy." (Deuteronomy 31:15) From this, our sages argued "how much more so" should care apply to residential encampments in times of peace.

The Levitical cities had to have a *migrash* (a "pasture" or green area) around them. Maimonides extended this requirement to all cities. The Jerusalem Talmud instructs: "It is forbidden to live in a city that does not have a green garden." (J. Talmud, *Kiddushin* 4:12)

Concern for the perpetuation of species of animals, represented by the story of Noah, is reflected in laws in the Torah (e.g., one should not kill a cow and its calf [Leviticus 22:28] or a bird and its young [Deuteronomy 22:6]). According to the medieval commentator Nachmanides, one who kills mother and children on the same day or takes them while they are free to fly away is considered as if that one destroyed the species (commentary on Deuteronomy 22:6).

The concept of *hamafkir nazakav hayav* (i.e., one who leaves a dangerous article in a public place is responsible for any damages that may result) could well apply today to those who dispose of toxic waste in a manner that endangers the environment and human health. Similarly, the basic concept of liability for damages caused by the negligent control of an inherently dangerous condition (e.g., a pit or a fire) establishes the principle that one who owns something environmentally hazardous bears responsibility for its elimination. If there is no alternative to engaging in hazardous activity, then all reasonable steps must be taken to mitigate the resulting risks to people and property.

Ecology poses profound religious, theological, and moral questions: Has God endowed us with dominion over nature? Is competition or cooperation the nature of our relationship to one another? Are human beings inherently greedy? What is our responsibility to the generations yet unborn?

Some say the despoiling of our world is rooted in the Hebrew Bible. They cite Genesis 1:28: "Be fruitful and multiply and populate the earth and conquer it. Rule over the fish of the sea and the birds of the heavens and over all living things on earth. I have given you all the grass and trees for you and all other living things to eat."

Jewish tradition, say its defenders, makes it clear that our "dominion" over nature does not include a license to slaughter indiscriminately or to abuse the environment. *Bal tashchit* ("do not destroy") is the basis of the talmudic and post-talmudic laws that prohibit willful destruction of natural resources or any kind of vandalism even if the act is committed by the property owners themselves. One must not needlessly destroy or waste anything that may be useful to others. (See the discussion on *bal tashchit* in Chapter 7, "Peace and International Affairs.") "The earth is *Adonai*'s and the fullness thereof" (Psalms 24:1) implies that we are the stewards of nature, obliged to cherish and preserve it.

This view is eloquently expressed in the following passage from rabbinic literature:

> Woe to one who stands on the earth and does not see what one sees, for in every drop of water in the sea and every grain of dust in the earth have I created its own image. . . . Of everything God created nothing was created in vain, not even the things you may think unnecessary, such as spiders, frogs, or snakes. . . . Human beings were not created until the sixth day so that if their pride should govern them it could be said to them, "Even the tiniest flea preceded you in creation." . . . Why did God appear to Moses in the lowly bush? To teach us that nothing in creation is without God's holy presence, not even the commonest bush. . . .

Creation in Crisis

Five of the most pressing worldwide environmental issues are global warming, ozone depletion, acid rain, overpopulation, and the loss of biodiversity. Below is a brief question and answer section on these threats.

1. *What is global warming and the much discussed "greenhouse effect"? Can they really destroy the world?*

The "greenhouse effect" is a global-warming trend resulting from a distortion of the natural warming mechanism of the planet caused by certain types of pollution. Normally, the earth is blanketed with a layer of various "greenhouse gases" that serve to trap some of the sun's heat around our planet. Since the beginning of the industrial revolution, however, the layer of gases around our planet has been thickening as industrial emissions increase, trapping more heat around the planet.

The two primary contributors to global warming are carbon dioxide (CO_2) and chlorofluorocarbons (CFCs). Carbon dioxide (50 percent of greenhouse gases) results primarily from the burning of fossil fuels, like coal, oil, and natural gas, in our factories, automobiles, and power plants. CFCs (20 percent) are industrial chemicals widely used in air conditioners, as solvents, and in the production of plastic packaging and foam insulation.

The buildup of greenhouse gases from automobiles and factories could bring far-reaching changes to the world's climate. Evidence of this massive climatic transformation continues to mount. According to calculations made in 1992, the six warmest years of the past century have been, in decreasing order, 1990, 1991, 1988, 1983, 1987, and 1989. It is predicted that, if current trends continue, the average global temperature could rise from three to nine degrees within the next century.

If, as a result, sea levels rose by as much as five to seven feet from the melting of polar ice caps, approximately one-half of the world's population would be affected. Of America's coastal wetlands, 30–80 percent could be submerged by such a rise in sea level. Some scientists have predicted that America's agriculturally rich Midwest would experience a major decrease in rainfall, transforming productive farmland into arid grassland or even desert.

Only by attacking the root of the problem can global warming be stopped. The nations of the world must cooperate in reducing emissions of greenhouse gases. The most feasible strategy towards that goal is to reduce dependence on fossil fuels and eliminate use of CFCs.

2. *How serious is the problem of ozone depletion? Can it really cause cancer?*

High above our planet in the upper atmosphere, ozone functions to reduce the sun's hazardous ultraviolet radiation from reaching Earth. This layer of protective ozone is now being destroyed by the release of CFCs into the atmosphere. Upon release, CFCs rise to the upper atmosphere and deplete ozone. Serious holes and tears in the ozone layer have been detected above Antarctica, Greenland, and the Arctic region.

If this depletion goes unchecked, the Environmental Protection Agency (EPA) predicts the development of millions of skin cancer cases in the coming decades. Increases in ultraviolet radiation will compromise the human immune system and could also cause the loss of billions of dollars worth of crops.

3. *With all the debate on acid rain, what is it and how bad is it?*

Acid rain is formed when sulphur dioxide and nitrogen oxide, released into the atmosphere by coal-burning power and industrial plants, mix with clouds to form diluted sulphuric and nitric acids. Acid rain has already destroyed significant portions of Germany's forests and threatens to do the same in North America. When acid rain falls on soil, it releases naturally occurring aluminum into water systems.

This increase in aluminum levels is sufficient to kill the aquatic life in lakes. Three hundred lakes in the Adirondack

Mountains (or one-quarter of the total number) are already so acidic they no longer support life; the fish in another three hundred lakes in the area are seriously endangered. Off the Louisiana coast, nitrogen deposits caused by acid rain have led to proliferation of algae, which limits the oxygen available to other marine organisms.

4. *Will the exploding populations of the world overwhelm our resources? What relation does overpopulation have to global warming?*

Every day the world population increases by two hundred and fifty thousand. At the present rate, an additional billion people will be born from 1991 to 2000, an amount equal to the present population of China. The bulk of the population growth will occur in poor countries already ravaged by mass hunger and severe housing shortages. The problem of overpopulation not only has created terrible economic strains on the developing countries, it has also forced them to adopt policies that accelerate the environmental degradation such as strip mining, the cutting down of rain forests, and rapid industrialization. Developing countries now account for 60 percent of the overall increase in energy consumption. That means the burning of more coal, oil, wood, and natural gas. Continuing this scorched-earth strategy will not ultimately lead to development but to poverty—unless effective measures are taken to control the birthrate in the developing nations.

Family-planning programs have been met with varying degrees of success because they often run counter to traditional cultural and religious practices. Furthermore, the United States government's refusal in the 1980s and early 1990s to fund international programs that make abortions available has made world population control hostage to Washington's antiabortion policy.

5. *Why can't we see the forest for the trees? Is our profligacy costing us forms of life?*

Covering 7 percent of the earth's surface, tropical rain forests are home to at least half of the world's species of plant and animal life. These forests are a source of medicines and foods and act as an important bulwark against erosion. Nevertheless, the world's rain forests are being destroyed at an alarming rate.

Approximately 40 percent of the earth's rain forests in the last thirty years have been destroyed. As rain forests are particularly efficient in breathing in carbon dioxide and breathing out oxygen during photosynthesis, such extensive losses significantly contribute to the greenhouse effect through the buildup of carbon dioxide in the atmosphere. Deforestation has caused the destruction of native cultures and the daily extinction of as many as one hundred species of plants and animals.

On our domestic environmental scene, we are wrestling with issues of waste disposal and reduction, water pollution, and transportation.

1. *Are we Americans trashing our nation?*

In the United States each year we generate nearly a ton of trash per person; 90 percent of this ends up in local landfills. We are generating 230 million tons of trash a year—an amount that has nearly doubled in thirty years. Despite the mountain of garbage we generate, environmental concern rightfully has forced municipalities to stop burning refuse in landfills. Many landfills have been filled to capacity. Since 1978, 14,000 solid waste landfills have closed. Today there are only 6,000 landfills left, and one-third will be filled in five years. Incineration as an alternative has been widely opposed by environmental activists who contend that burning garbage causes toxic pollution.

The most environmentally sound and cost-efficient way to alleviate the crisis is to reduce the amount of waste we generate in the first place. Recycling is another environmentally responsible approach to decrease the amount of waste. But, while unprecedented numbers of people today participate in local recycling programs, the economic viability of these programs is now being called into question. In some areas, it is much cheaper to haul waste to landfills than to recycle it. This is forcing many economically strapped communities to limit or discontinue their recycling projects.

2. *Is it safe to drink the water and breathe the air?*

In the United States, more than half the population drinks ground water, 40 percent of which comes from untreated, contaminated wells. Industrial and agricultural pollution, underground injection of waste disposal, and chemical wastes from mining and petroleum production are steadily accumulating in our water.

Air pollution and water pollution threaten the lives of millions. For example, some metals corrode almost a hundred times faster in the unhealthy air of some of our major cities than in places where air is still relatively pure. The EPA estimates that about four of every ten Americans live in areas where air is often unhealthy to breathe. Air quality in America is contaminated by many pollutants, most notably the poisons that pour out of our automobile exhausts.

3. *Should we reexamine our love affair with the automobile?*

Though it provides a quick and easy way to get from place to place, the private automobile constitutes a major threat to the environment. Carbon dioxide-laced exhaust contributes to the global greenhouse effect; lead emissions cause brain damage; asbestos from brakes winds up in the water supply. Our cars and trucks cause more than 70 percent of air carbon monoxide pollution; 50 percent of hydrocarbon pollution; 45 percent of nitrogen oxide pollution, resulting in as many as half of all cancer deaths linked to toxic emissions.

Increasing use of oil to fuel auto engines further increases pollution. All alternatives to the automobile—ranging from passenger trains and planes to telephone and computer link-ups—are more energy-efficient than the car and much safer to the environment.

Raising automobile fuel-efficiency is one of the most effective single steps that can be taken to curb global warming and ensure a safe energy future for America. Over 40 percent of the oil that we use goes into our automobiles. More fuel-efficient cars would reduce our dependence on oil and would lower levels of carbon dioxide in our air. The current Corporate Average Fuel Economy (CAFE) standards, passed in 1975, have gone a long way toward this end. These standards require that new cars average 27.5 miles per gallon (mpg). Raising the CAFE standards by another 40 percent, as many members of Congress have suggested, would save our country millions of barrels of oil daily, preventing hundreds of millions of tons of CO_2 from entering the earth's atmosphere. A 40 percent increase in CAFE translates into 2.5 million barrels of oil saved each day. In addition, each gallon of gasoline saved would reduce the amount of CO_2 pumped into the atmosphere by nineteen pounds.

Critics of this approach argue that raising CAFE standards requires building smaller cars, which would result in higher accident death tolls. Supporters respond that new safety technologies and new construction techniques can achieve the same standards with minimal loss, or no loss in safety standards.

Ecology and Justice: The Ecojustice Movement

While in the long term environmental problems affect us all, in the short term their impact is greater on the underprivileged. Ecojustice requires the linking of environmental concerns with the desire for economic justice. Consider the following facts:

1. Forty-four percent of urban black children are at risk of illness from lead poisoning—four times the rate of white children, according to a federal study. The lead comes from paint chips and from soil and dust contaminated by leaded fuel residues.
2. By 1984, some 313,000 farm workers suffered from pesticide-related illnesses. Some 80 to 90 percent of the migrant work

force is of Mexican descent, with Blacks making up the next largest group.

3. Three out of five waste incinerators in the United States are located in poor or minority neighborhoods.
4. The United States exports millions of tons of hazardous and nonhazardous waste to Third World nations each year.

Perhaps most urgently, from a moral standpoint, it ill-becomes the developed world to demand that Third World countries make efforts to protect their environment at the expense of condemning the vast majority of the world's population to poverty and hunger. Justice demands the development of environmentally safe energy and industrialization processes to ensure that these nations have the technological capacity to lift their people to a higher standard of living.

Israel: A Fragile Environment in Deep Trouble

Though a small country, Israel consists of many ecological habitats (desert, tropical, and alpine). Massive reforestation (190 million trees), initiated and managed by the Jewish National Fund (JNF), has created groves of trees where land once lay barren.

As Israel has reclaimed deserts, swamps, and other neglected areas, its population has grown from 600,000 in 1948 to more than 4 million today. On the negative side, this massive infusion of immigrants has occasioned tough environmental dilemmas in such areas as air and water quality, toxic and solid waste disposal, and future conservation.

One environmental concern exceeds all others: water. Israel receives most of its water from rivers that extend far up north into Syria, Lebanon, and Turkey. Much of that water is diverted by those countries for their own use. What reaches Israel is a highly valued commodity.

About 65 percent of Israel's annual renewable water sources (from rain) are collected in three major reservoirs, the coastal aquifer, the mountain aquifer, and Lake Kinneret. Water experts have determined the operational reserve capacity for each reservoir in terms of an upper and lower threshold level. If the upper level is exceeded, overflow will result; if the lower level is reached, both water quality and quantity will be threatened. At the start of 1991, the level in each of the major reservoirs was at or below the "red line." That is why the relatively large water supply (40 percent of reserves) that lies beneath the West Bank is of great importance, economically, politically, and strategically.

The precarious location of these precious water supplies, the growing population in the region, and the ever-present danger of drought promise to lead to a conflict in the future unless a comprehensive regional water use treaty is agreed upon. The next war in the Middle East may be not over oil but over water. This makes a comprehensive political settlement more difficult but also more urgent.

The Energy Crisis

Even the most fervent environmentalist must face the awesome challenge of the energy crisis. Few issues facing our nation rival our energy policy in complexity. Without a comprehensive and coherent energy policy, possible ruinous economic, social, and political consequences could threaten our free institutions, limit our diplomatic independence, curtail our standard of living, despoil our environment, and divide us internally by regions and classes.

The 1973 oil embargo and the resulting economic and political crises led this nation to formulate three policy conclusions:

1. Establish a major strategic oil reserve to free the United States from dependence on drastic oil price and supply fluctuations.
2. Find alternative energy sources.
3. Implement effective conservation measures.

Sadly, we have done poorly in each of these areas.

As gas prices dropped and the gas lines receded, so did our sense of crisis—and with it our determination to take those steps necessary to achieve our stated goals. The original strategic oil reserves set up by Congress in 1975 called for a reserve of 750 million barrels. In 1992 the reserve contained only 586 million barrels.

Second, the alternative fuel policy (aimed at reducing our dependence on gas, coal, and oil) under President Carter emphasized such renewable, clean forms of energy as sun, wind, and geothermal power. It shifted under President Reagan to processing oil shale, opening up oil exploration offshore and in the Alaska wilderness, and substantially increasing nuclear energy sources. Each fell victim to its own problems in the 1980s: solar, wind, and geothermal to technical limitations and decreasing tax incentives; oil shale and nuclear energy to technological problems that threatened availability in one case and safety in the other; and increased oil exploration to a growing environmental consciousness. The result has been that gas, coal, and oil remain an even larger component of our energy picture than they were in 1975.

Finally, we need to take further steps in the conservation of energy. While we comprise less than 5 percent of the world's population, we use 25 percent of the energy consumed.

Although we made enormous strides in improved conservation in the seventies, which led to reductions in our imported oil, the loss of the sense of crisis, combined with ten years of deregulation, resulted in almost no improvement in our energy consumption in the 1980s.

In 1977 we imported 6.2 million barrels (35 percent) of oil from OPEC; by 1985, it had dropped to 1.8 million barrels (11 percent). By 1990, it had rebounded to 4.3 million barrels (25 percent).

A Real Dilemma: Alaska Wilderness vs. Dependence on Arab Oil

In the late 1980s and early 1990s, one of the most contentious environmental debates centered on the opening of the vast Arctic National Wildlife Refuge (ANWR) to the oil and gas companies for development. Proponents argued that, if the United States is to minimize its dependence on Arab oil, it must develop all of its resources. Its largest untapped oil and gas resources are in this region. Opponents argued that this would be catastrophic for the ecology of the nation's largest remaining wilderness area. Earlier development of other regions in Alaska had resulted in systemic ecological damages. The Exxon Valdez oil spill disaster dramatized the danger before the world.

This issue was clearly of concern to the Jewish community. No group feels more strongly about the need to reduce American dependence on Arab oil.

Proponents recognized the special concerns of the Jewish community sufficiently to enlist the assistance of the former director of the American-Israel Public Affairs Committee (AIPAC) to lobby for the opening of the wilderness area. Environmental groups, likewise, lobbied the Jewish community to publicly oppose the opening.

Should the Jewish community have supported the opening of the Alaska wilderness area or opposed it?

Response

The UAHC was the only national Jewish organization to oppose the opening of the wilderness area.

It believed that, by acquiescing in this environmentally risky proposition, the United States would send to our own citizenry and to the other nations of the world the wrong message, setting back the possibility of an environmental consensus in America for years. Furthermore, the energy sources to be produced in that region would, at best, total the equivalent of American energy needs for three years—and it would take eight to ten years to bring any of those sources on line.

Diverting the money and political energy necessary to accomplish this task would only delay the United States in developing a more comprehensive energy plan in which conservation and renewable energy sources would be major components. Our natural allies in this fight are the environmental groups. The tactical need to keep a close relationship with them further convinced the UAHC it could not ignore this issue and sit on the sidelines.

In light of President Bush's National Energy Strategy in 1990, which focused almost entirely on the expansion of nuclear energy and the development of fossil fuels—particularly in the Alaska wilderness and the equally ecologically vulnerable offshore oil drilling areas—the UAHC stepped up its opposition. At the writing of this book, it is not known what the final disposition of the Alaska wilderness area will be. Stay tuned.

The Nuclear Dilemma

Advocates of nuclear energy say we have little choice but to expand our nuclear power facilities to meet the growing demand for electricity. They insist that nuclear energy is safe, produces less pollution, and is less expensive than other fuels. However, many experts still have grave doubts about the safety of nuclear power stations and the unresolved problem of safely disposing radioactive waste. Others doubt the economic wisdom of investing heavily in this form of power, even if it is safe.

The terrifying accidents at the Three Mile Island nuclear power plant in 1979 and in Chernobyl, Soviet Union, in 1985 cast a heavy shadow on the future of nuclear power. The Japanese, however, forged ahead with their ambitious nuclear power campaign, one of the world's largest, hoping to receive 43 percent of their electricity from nuclear power by 2010. Their plan may be slowed down by the 1991 accident at a nuclear plant in Japan, which required the use of the emergency cooling system to prevent a meltdown.

Radioactive Wastes

Even if the health and environmental threats of nuclear power plants themselves were eliminated, a basic problem of nuclear power would remain: radioactive wastes. The American military has been the largest producer of such wastes. There are fifteen nuclear weapons facilities in the United States. At the Hanford facility in Washington, the Department of Energy has identified over a thousand radioactive and toxic waste sites containing over 1.2 million cubic yards of radioactive waste (enough to fill a hole the size of a football field that is seven hundred feet deep). The cost of cleaning up these weapon facilities alone, where wastes have been stockpiled for the last forty years, has been estimated at over $200 billion. Finding a technically safe and acceptable method of storing radioactive waste for thousands of years now seems more difficult than the government had realized.

Burying the waste, throwing it into the ocean, blasting it into outer space—all these are being considered as options for nuclear waste disposal, but the safety and practicality of any of these methods has yet to be established.

A Real Dilemma: A Rabbi Tries to Stop a Nuclear Power Plant

A massive demonstration was being organized to oppose the construction of the Seabrook, New Hampshire, nuclear power plant. Rabbi Arthur Starr of Manchester, New Hampshire, was asked to join other clergy in the protest as part of the interfaith contingent.

Should he accept? Whom would he represent? A Jewish voice? Himself? His congregation? Should he publicly oppose a project that promised to give the region an economic boost and provide for its energy needs?

Response

Rabbi Starr decided to attend the protest as part of the interfaith delegation. He participated as an individual, not on behalf of the Jewish community. Though he did not address the crowd of twenty thousand who attended, he became a visible and active community voice against the Seabrook power plant. His leadership inspired others in the Jewish community to join the campaign.

The UAHC adopted this resolution on nuclear power in 1979:

> The near-disaster at Three Mile Island . . . has provoked profound concern and has resulted in a justifiable reassessment of the safety and future of nuclear energy. We, therefore, believe that any further expansion of nuclear energy should await a resolution of presently unanswered questions regarding safety and nuclear waste disposal. We further call for continued investigations and efforts to increase security and safety in current operations. . . .

A Real Dilemma: NFTY and Styrofoam

The North American Federation of Temple Youth (NFTY) developed a multipronged effort to fight pollution. In one case, a youth group went to the temple board to ask them to ban styrofoam in the synagogue. They pointed out that styrofoam is one of the primary products that contain chlorofluorocarbons (CFCs), which contribute to the destruction of the ozone layer. Considering the ultimately dire consequences of ozone depletion and the Jewish moral imperative not to destroy the environment, they argued that styrofoam use should be banned in the synagogue.

At first, many of the board members were reluctant to take such steps, contending that their actions would be insignificant in the broader scheme of things and that such concerns did little but inconvenience the congregation. One board member ridiculed the idea as faddist and claimed that the use of other substitute materials such as plastic and paper could be destructive in other ways.

Response

Most board members took the debate over styrofoam seriously, resulting in the board's launching an initiative that made the temple more environmentally friendly. Styrofoam and other environmentally destructive materials were replaced with recyclable products. After an energy audit, the temple replaced all incandescent lights with compact fluorescents and fully insulated the building. These actions proved to be both cost- and energy-efficient.

It is sometimes difficult to substantiate the specific benefit of a particular step. Which pollutes more, a particular form of styrofoam or the dense paper product used to replace it? Which uses more energy, recycling products or making new ones? Few of us are expert enough to evaluate these arguments (although we should try to choose policies that we are convinced will be environmentally useful and should keep an open mind to arguments critiquing such policies). But, when the evidence is not totally clear on one side or the other, if we are to err, does not *bal tashchit* require that we err on the side of creating habits of recycling, on the side of using products that are biodegradable?

Needed: A Radical Change

The disasters at Chernobyl, Three Mile Island, and Bhopal, India, where thousands of people were killed or injured as a result of a poison gas leak from a chemical plant, are ominous storm warnings. They compel us to reexamine our divinities. We have made an idol of technology, believing it can solve all human problems.

We must stop worshiping at the altar of consumption; now, in order to survive, we must value human life above all and establish that fellowship among the peoples of the world for which Judaism spoke at the beginnings of history.

In 1931, Albert Einstein addressed the California Institute of Technology and asserted, "Concern for man and his fate must always form the chief interest of all the technological endeavors. . . . that the creation of our minds may be a blessing and not a curse to mankind. Never forget this in the midst of your diagrams and equations."

≡ 14 ≡

BIOETHICS: THINKING
THE UNTHINKABLE

The Impact of Modern Technology

Several factors make the ethical challenges posed by modern technology the most formidable humankind has ever faced.

Above all is the tremendous pace and rate of technological advance. Because of the rapid pace of technological change in recent decades, it is no exaggeration to say that there has been as much change during our grandparents' lifetime as there had been during the entire previous history of civilization: transportation has been transformed by the jet plane; entertainment by VCRs; and business by the computer and the Fax—all within the lifespan of most of our high school students. In a generation that has learned to split the atom, crack the genetic code, and pierce the veil of outer space, the question no longer seems to be what *can* we do but what *should* we do. And this is, essentially, a moral question about which the Jewish tradition has much to say.

Our moral dilemmas are further exacerbated by the *rate* of technological change. Each new invention, developed to solve a specific problem, tends to produce a series of new problems for which other innovations are needed. The result is a geometric expansion of technological development. In contrast, ethical thought, the development by society of humanistic or religious values, is a relatively glacial process. As a result, we face the central dilemma of our era: By the time society has realized the deepest implications of the technological innovation and sets for itself the task of formulating an ethical response, the innovation may already be firmly entrenched or even obsolete.

Jewish Ethics

In its biblical and rabbinic periods, Judaism never developed a systematic theory of ethics. Where Aristotle writes in the realm of abstractions, the prophets, the most authentic spokespersons for Jewish ethical ideals, speak about such mundane categories as widows, orphans, and the poor. When Jewish expression did give rise to a more abstract formulation, it produced not a coherently reasoned theory but a pithy sentence that condensed everything to a few short words: "It has been told to you . . . what is good, and what God requires of you: Only to do justly, to love mercy, and to walk humbly with your God." (Micah 6:8) or "The world is founded upon three things: upon truth, upon justice, and upon peace." (*Pirke Avot* 1:18)

Nevertheless, fundamental principles can be derived from the sacred Jewish literature of these periods—principles that speak to the issues of technological and biological ethics: human freedom, the infinite dignity of the human being, the supreme importance of human life.

Medical Ethics

In the Jewish view, God allows human beings to be partners in creating a better world and has given us the freedom of choice to do so.

We are expected to use our God-given wisdom to help create a better world. The philosopher-physician Maimonides in essence wrote: "God created food and water; we must use them in staving off hunger and thirst. God created drugs and compounds and gave us the intelligence necessary to discover their medicinal properties; we must use them in warding off illness and disease." (Maimonides' commentary to *Mishnah Pesachim* 4:9) But to what lengths must a doctor go to save a life *(pikuach nefesh)?*

Organ Transplants

Although the rabbis of the Talmud could not have imagined the transplantation of human organs, there seems little doubt that the Jewish commitment to the preservation of life would generally have approved such an advance in healing the sick. In analyzing the issue of organ transplants, the Jewish tradition brings to bear certain considerations that are distinctive from our modern secular perspective. Foremost among them is the assertion that each of us is made in the image of God and that our bodies, being created by God, are not ours to do with as we please. From this principle we derive the prohibitions against substance abuse, asceticism, and suicide.

Even in death, we must treat the body as God's creation. This justifies the requirements for the immediate burial of corpses and the prohibition against desecrating a corpse. Nor are we permitted to derive economic benefit from a corpse. No body parts may be extracted and sold, not even hair for wigs.

On the other hand, almost any law may be broken to save a life. This commitment to *pikuach nefesh* ("saving a life") would seem to justify one's voluntary decision to donate an organ if it can be done at a minimum risk to the donor, and it would seem to condone the removal of organs after death for the purpose of transplantation. Thus Orthodox scholars permitted cornea transplants, the first such technique perfected by medical science. The application of *pikuach nefesh* to the question of transplants is, however, limited in Jewish law by two other concepts: *holeh lefananu* (to justify transplants "we must have a sick person before us," i.e., someone for whom *emergency* treatment is needed) and *refu'ah bedukah* (the procedure must offer a good chance for success).

These two rules suggest that one may not remove organs solely for research purposes or when the life of the recipient is not threatened. These considerations underlie the prohibition of many Orthodox scholars against allowing autopsies except in a situation where there will be immediate benefit derived for the living (e.g., during an epidemic).

Increasingly, however, Orthodox scholars are joining their Reform and Conservative counterparts in recognizing that, in a world where organs can be transported by jet across the globe in a matter of hours, where medical advances and breakthroughs are happening at breakneck speed, the old understanding of "an immediate need for the organ" must be reinterpreted more leniently.

Nevertheless, the progress of medicine in this area creates burning ethical questions. So far, the law is clear that the donor must consent to the transplant or, if the donor is dead, the next of kin must consent. Will this principle always be applied? Are there any conceivable circumstances under which someone might justifiably be pressured to give an organ against his will?

What if a person is dying because both his kidneys are diseased, and the only way to save his life is through the transplant of a healthy kidney from his brother? (A person can function normally with only one kidney.) And what if this brother with two healthy kidneys refuses to act as a donor? Is the brother morally or legally obligated to donate one kidney? Is it conceivable that an alternative to imprisonment for criminals might be to offer them the option of donating a kidney or a lung to save the life of another human being? Would such a deal be moral? Is it conceivable to find justification for the removal of a healthy kidney from a deeply retarded person, who lives in an institution at taxpayers' expense, for use in saving someone's life?

Conversely, do people have the right to be donors if by so doing they seriously endanger their own lives or even end them? If someone has an incurable disease but a strong heart and wants to donate the heart to save the life of a loved one, should the person be permitted to do so? If the principle of human dignity conflicts with *pikuach nefesh*, where should the balance be struck?

Fetal Tissue Transplants

Similar questions arise in response to fetal tissue transplants. In 1988, a University of Colorado researcher transplanted "ten tiny bits of fetal brain tissue, sliced from a single piece the size of a grain of rice" into the right side of a patient with Parkinson's disease. That news burst on a country already embroiled in an intense debate over abortion. Opponents of abortion charged that such procedures would justify abortions as a means of obtaining human tissue for experimentation or transplant purposes.

Proponents of fetal tissue research and transplants responded that several formerly intractable diseases, including Parkinson's disease, diabetes, blood disorders, leukemia, and even AIDS, might be cured through the use of fetal tissue. Fetal tissue is particularly suited to research and transplants because it multiplies extremely fast; it grows easily in the laboratory; it does not have an immune system and therefore will not be rejected in transplants; it can be used to achieve an extremely accurate evaluation of new vaccines and the toxicity of drugs; it can be used to produce large quantities of human growth hormone, insulin, and anticancer substances.

The first fetal-to-fetal tissue transplant was performed in April 1991. A couple who had already suffered two stillbirths because of a defective gene learned that the expected child would have the same malady. This time there was recourse to a new procedure that offered hope. The doctors performed an *in utero* operation in which the five-month-old fetus was injected with the tissue of an aborted fetus in the hope that the healthy cells from the aborted fetus would cure the rare illness.

Even if one agrees in theory that these procedures should be allowed, problems arise: Who will regulate the process? Can individuals designate the recipients? Will mothers be permitted to sell the tissue of aborted fetuses?

In the spring of 1991, Mary Ayala gave birth to a baby girl, Marissa, with the hope that bone marrow from the newborn would be transplanted into Anissa Ayala, her nineteen-year-old daughter dying of leukemia. Fortunately, the bone marrow type was a perfect match and was promptly transplanted. But what would have happened if prenatal testing had found Marissa to be an imperfect match? Should ethics have allowed Mary Ayala to have an abortion so she could try again? What do you think?

Euthanasia

On a cold January night in 1983, a twenty-five-year-old, lively woman named Nancy Beth Cruzan lost control of her car on a country road in Missouri. The car rolled over several times, and Nancy was hurled thirty-five feet. She landed face down in a water-filled ditch. When paramedics arrived on the scene, they found no detectable respiratory or cardiac function. At the scene the paramedics were able to restore Nancy's heartbeat and breathing by using medicine, a respirator, and heart massage. She was transported in an unconscious state to a local hospital. Doctors at the hospital determined that a fifteen-minute lack of oxygen had caused Nancy Cruzan to suffer permanent brain damage. She was in a "persistent vegetative state," which means that, while she was able to exhibit motor reflexes like breathing and circulation, she showed no indication of cognitive function. Completely oblivious to her surroundings, the parts of her brain that once thought, felt, and experienced sensations had deteriorated drastically and were continuing to deteriorate.

According to Nancy's doctors, the remaining cavities of her brain were filling with cerebrospinal fluid, and her cerebral cortical atrophy was "irreversible, permanent, progressive, and ongoing. Nancy would never interact meaningfully with her environment again and would remain in a persistent vegetative state until her death." Because she could not swallow, doctors implanted a tube in Nancy's stomach to deliver her nutrition and water.

Three years of treatment followed to no avail. After it had become apparent that Nancy had no chance of regaining her mental faculties, her parents requested that the hospital terminate the artificial nutrition and hydration procedures by removing the feeding tube. Because the hospital refused to honor the request without court approval, Nancy's parents went to the state trial court. The authorization to remove the feeding tube was granted. However, when the Supreme Court of Missouri reversed the lower court's decision, the matter reached the United States Supreme Court (1990) in the now-celebrated case of *Cruzan* v. *Director, Missouri Department of Health*. For the first time in American history, the

Supreme Court was presented with the issue of whether the Constitution grants an individual the right to die.

Prior to the Supreme Court ruling in *Cruzan,* a number of cases had been decided in lower courts. Most of these dealt with the continuation of medical treatment, not feeding as in the *Cruzan* case. Consider how you might have ruled if you were the judge in the following cases:

• Karen Anne Quinlen in New Jersey slipped into a persistent vegetative state after ingesting a combination of sleeping pills and alcohol. Her parents and doctors concluded she would never recover and wanted her disconnected from the respirator that was keeping her alive. The Supreme Court of New Jersey allowed it. Although expected to die immediately, she lived without the respirator for nine more years, never regaining consciousness.

• Abe Perlmutter was in the advanced stages of amyotrophic lateral sclerosis (Lou Gherig's disease) when he sought to have his own respirator disconnected. Only after a lengthy court battle, during which he suffered excruciating pain, did the Florida court decide. They allowed him to have the life support machines removed and permitted him, in his words, to die "with dignity."

A Real Dilemma: Justice and Mercy—
Roswell and Emily Gilbert

Roswell and Emily Gilbert had been married for many decades when Emily began to suffer from Alzheimer's disease and the degenerative bone disorder osteoporosis. Over the years, the pain and suffering became unbearable for Mrs. Gilbert, who finally begged her husband of fifty-one years to put an end to her agony and terminate her life. On March 4, 1985, Mr. Gilbert, following what he believed to be Mrs. Gilbert's wishes, shot and killed her.

Two months later, a jury found Mr. Gilbert guilty of first-degree murder. Judge Thomas Coker, Jr., sentenced Gilbert to twenty-five years in prison with no chance of parole. Judge

Coker summarized the feelings of many when he said, "I am not without sympathies, but I am sworn to uphold the law."

Was this, as Roswell Gilbert testified, an act of love? Or was it simply murder, subject not to the fuzzy sentiment of human emotion but to the clear statutes of the state? If you had been on the jury, how would you have decided? The UAHC was asked to intervene to request a lenient sentence. What should the UAHC have done?

Response

In the aftermath of this decision, many people have looked carefully at this case and the very real dilemmas it poses. In fact, the case received such widespread notoriety that it became the subject of a 1987 television movie, "Mercy or Murder," which focused national attention on the killing of a loved one.

The Commission on Social Action decided that Mr. Gilbert had been treated unfairly, saying the situation required justice *and* mercy, but the court had applied only the letter of the law. The UAHC did not contest the verdict in the light of the law and Jewish tradition's general opposition to euthanasia. However, the UAHC did become part of an effort to commute Mr. Gilbert's sentence, an effort that contributed to Mr. Gilbert's being granted clemency in 1990 by Florida's Governor Bob Martinez.

Against this backdrop, the *Cruzan* case came to the Supreme Court. The *Cruzan* case was different because, while there was no hope for recovery, there was no disease or sufficiently grave injury from which she would die. By halting the intravenous feedings, she would slowly starve and dehydrate to death. Was this dying with "dignity"?

The Supreme Court ruled: A competent person did have the right to refuse lifesaving hydration and nutrition. With an incompetent person, however, there had to be clear and convincing proof of that incompetent person's wishes not to be kept alive. While Nancy

Cruzan had made some verbal statements to that effect, there was no formal statement of such intent, and, therefore, the Supreme Court would not authorize the removal of the feeding tube. This decision stirred millions of Americans to prepare a living will, affirming their wishes if they were ever to find themselves in Cruzan's situation.

Arguments for and against Euthanasia
The basic argument for euthanasia—the purposeful hastening of death in order to end extreme suffering—rests in the commitment to the concept of individual autonomy: as long as an individual's choice does not infringe on anyone else's right, that person should be able to decide whether to accept or to refuse medical treatment. Others question whether a life that must be lived out with increasing pain and suffering, with no hope of reversal, as in a vegetative state, should be valued as preciously as a more "normal" life. Finally, on an economic basis, the cost of maintaining life through exorbitant treatments can be staggering, quickly wiping out a family's savings.

Those who oppose euthanasia argue that personal autonomy is secondary to the value of preserving life. They believe cutting a life short for any reason is tantamount to murder or suicide. Furthermore, there is the "slippery slope" argument: if society decides that the lives of the terminally ill or vegetative patients are worth less than other lives, who else might be considered unworthy of life—the retarded, the elderly, homosexuals, the disabled, gypsies, Jews?

A Real Dilemma: Initiative 119

In the fall of 1991, the state of Washington held a referendum called Initiative 119 that affirmed the right of a terminally ill patient to reject treatment and permitted doctors to participate in "aid-to-dying." If a rabbi from the state were to ask the UAHC Bioethics Committee for an opinion on such an initiative, how would you expect the committee to respond? What would your response be?

Response

In fact, the UAHC Bioethics Committee is in the process of considering such initiatives. The General Synod of the United Church of Christ is the first national religious group—Jewish or Christian—to endorse suicide for the hopelessly ill. For Jews, the tradition's abhorrence to suicide places a check on any who would argue that the humanity of the tradition would justify mercy killing. On the other hand, the reality is that many people are becoming *more afraid of dying than of death*. Has technology so changed the consequences to human dignity and freedom that we now need to reevaluate how best to apply the values of the Jewish tradition? This would be the first such legislation legalizing euthanasia.

The Washington Initiative 119 was defeated by the narrow margin of 6 percent—53 percent voted against and 47 percent were in favor.

Jewish Perspectives on Euthanasia

The two summary statements on euthanasia in the Jewish tradition are summed up in the sixteenth-century code of Jewish law the *Shulchan Aruch* (which was authoritative in the Sephardic Jewish communities) and in the commentary on the *Shulchan Aruch* by Moses Isserles (which was the authoritative equivalent in the Ashkenazic communities):

> Even if a patient has agonized for a long time, and he and his family are in great distress, it is forbidden to hasten his death by, for instance, closing his eyes, or removing a pillow from under his head, or placing an object such as feathers or a synagogue key under his head.
>
> (*Shulchan Aruch, Yoreh Deah,* 339:1)

> However, if there is an obstacle that prevents the departure of the soul (death), such as noise outside or salt present on

the dying person's tongue, we may stop the noise or remove the salt so as not to hinder death.

(Commentary of Rabbi Moses Isserles
to *Shulchan Aruch, Yoreh Deah*, 339:1)

These passages essentially differentiate *active* and *passive* euthanasia. While one should do nothing to actively kill someone, one is not required to begin treatment if death is imminent.

In Jewish law, these strictures referred only to one who is classified as a *goses* (i.e., someone who is likely to die in the next few days). In ancient times, there was no way of knowing if someone's disease was irreversible until they were visibly near death. Today, we can know long in advance that someone's disease or injury is irreversible or irremediable. A major debate among Jewish scholars today is whether passive euthanasia should be allowed when death is certain—even if it is not imminent. The *Cruzan* case provides a variant of this dilemma. She clearly would not die for a long time; yet there was no hope whatsoever for a recovery.

New medical techniques have made it possible to prolong life even when the disease is incurable and irreversible and the pain is excruciating. Does Judaism's commitment to the preservation of life imply an obligation to use every available technique of medical science to keep a patient alive under all circumstances? Is it ever permissible to allow a suffering patient to die even if that patient could have been kept alive for days, months, years?

And who should make the decision? The doctor? The family? A government committee on life and death? The Jewish halachic tradition, as interpreted by Orthodox Judaism, would suggest that such questions should be decided by a rabbi in accordance with *halachah* and that the family of an irreversibly comatose patient has no special role in the decision-making process. Given what we know about modern medicine, does the traditional Jewish approach make sense to you?

The Definition of Death

Halachah generally defines death as the cessation of the heartbeat for several minutes (most variants include cessation of breathing).

We know today that cessation of the heart no longer means that the person is dead. Even after the heart has stopped beating, a person can be revived, and, if this is done within a very short period of time, there may be no ill effects. In other words, death is no longer considered to be a point in time but rather a process. The end of the process seems to be the absence of all electrical activity in the brain.

Among other obvious concerns, the point of death is a critical consideration in regard to organ transplants. In order for the heart to be transplanted, for example, to avoid damaging the organ, it must be removed from the body considerably before the end of the process. Some have argued that taking the heart before "brain death" is a kind of murder. Where is the end of the responsibility to keep alive the dying person, and where is the beginning of the responsibility to save the recipient?

Traditional Jewish sources require that, while nothing may be done to hasten the death of the patient (like giving him an overdose of sleeping pills), there is no obligation under such circumstances to take extraordinary measures to prolong the dying patient's life. This is sometimes described as prohibiting "active" euthanasia but allowing "passive" euthanasia. Is this distinction clear in all cases? Under what category would stopping intravenous feeding fall? What about turning off a heart-lung machine once it has been in operation? Who has the right to decide?

A Real Dilemma: Supporting Agudas Israel on Time-of-Death Legislation

In the mid-1980s, Agudas Israel, a theologically and politically far-right Orthodox Jewish group, approached state legislators in California in an effort to block a proposed law that would have changed the definition of death—a definition to bring it into line with modern science. The old definitions were ambiguous and outdated. The proposed new definition, based mostly on "brain death" (with some provisions to allow for organ transplants), contradicted the halachic definition of death: the cessation of breathing and heartbeat for a period of time.

Without consulting any of the mainstream Jewish agencies or the Jewish Community Relations Councils (CRCs), Agudas told legislators that this proposed legislation violated "the rights of Jews" and was opposed by the Jewish community. The Los Angeles CRC criticized the effort of Agudas to have its religious definition of death enacted into law, calling it a violation of church-state separation.

The CRC called the Religious Action Center to ask its advice. What should it have recommended?

Response

Despite the general hostility of Agudas to the values and activities of Reform Judaism, the center's staff recommended that the mainstream community groups should try to accommodate Agudas Israel's viewpoint. While the proposed legislation was better from both a public policy and a medical point of view, there should be a legal exemption providing for religious groups whose definition of death differs from that provided by the California law. The state could define death as the cessation of brain activity and, where Orthodox Jews request such treatment, still recognize their definition based on the cessation of heart and breathing activity as an additional requirement. In this manner, the state would never declare death only on the fulfillment of the halachic definition; it would always have to wait for cessation of brain activity.

Asking for legal exemptions to accommodate differing religious beliefs, it should be noted, is not the same as imposing one's religious belief on the entire population. There are some downsides to this approach. In a number of situations, the additional time lag (and attendant deterioration of internal organs) in waiting for cessation of heart/breathing activity would eliminate the possibility of organs from that body being used for transplants even if the patient had indicated that intent. Furthermore, this doesn't resolve the dilemma of when to turn off heart-lung machines where someone is brain dead and the religious exemption applies. This raises keen moral problems when there are others waiting for the machine necessary to keep them alive.

At the same time, however, the center's staff felt strongly that Agudas had erred by not consulting the larger Jewish community. It thus precipitated a situation where the organized Jewish community felt it had been misrepresented by Agudas which suggested that their view was "the" Jewish view. Thus the opportunity to evolve a common position on an important matter of public policy was lost. Since Judaism has a fairly well developed body of law regarding medical and biological ethics, the need for such consultation is vital, lest we repeatedly face similar bioethical decisions that become needlessly divisive for the Jewish community.

Who Shall Live and Who Shall Die?

Every day hospital staffs must decide whom to keep alive and whom to let die. There simply are not enough dialysis machines, heart-lung machines, or transplant donors to accommodate everyone who might need them. Who should be saved? Jewish tradition teaches: "You shall not render an unfair decision: do not favor the poor or show deference to the rich; judge your neighbor fairly." (Leviticus 19:15)

In addressing this issue, Rabbi Solomon B. Freehof, the most influential twentieth-century Reform Jewish interpreter of traditional Jewish sources, drew on a section in the Talmud (*Avodah Zarah* 27b): When there is a chance for a cure for a dying person, we are allowed to risk the patient's last hours to try out a new remedy that has the prospect of curing the patient or of adding a significant amount of time to the patient's life. Rabbi Freehof then summarized a number of responsa, concluding that a physician must strive to decide whether or not to save a patient solely on *medical* grounds rather than considering the personal situation of the patient. The doctor must select the patient who has the better prospect of survival and of leading a relatively healthy life. (*Modern Reform Responsa* [New York: Ktav, 1971], pp. 204–216)

Again, who should decide? And on what grounds should the decision be made? Should we choose to cure people who are rich because they have the money to pay for what is very expensive treatment? Who should pay the treatment costs for poor people who cannot themselves afford it? Should we choose to give care to those who hold the most responsible positions in society? Should we choose the middle-aged person in the prime of life or a young person on the threshold of life? Should the choice be random—a kind of life-and-death roulette—or based purely on medical grounds? Is it possible to arrive at a consensus that is objective or would the chosen criteria inevitably reflect the prejudices and self-interest of the determining group?

Ethical Dilemmas in Altering Life

Genetic Engineering

Perhaps the most far-reaching moral dilemmas in technology concern advances in genetics. No other technology so allows us to "play God." By altering the genetic structure of bacteria, plants, and animals, we can actually create new life forms, today even altering human life itself.

Genetic engineering began in the 1950s and 1960s with the lower organisms. By altering their genetic structure, scientists could "engineer" bacteria that consumed oil, fertilized plants, or killed harmful insects.

Moving up the evolutionary ladder to plants and animals, researchers genetically altered plants to produce more fruit and cows to give more milk.

While using genetic engineering to increase the world's food supply promises great benefit, the critics of this technology fear that it could lead to a catastrophe. Could we be certain that a newly engineered bacterium would not accidentally start a new disease in human beings—a bacterium that would multiply so fast we couldn't contain it? While scientists feel far more confident today than a decade ago of their ability to control such problems, we can never be sure. By the time we know enough about what the potential damage of a new technological development might be, it may be too late to prevent it.

Take just one analogy: If we knew sixty years ago what we know about nuclear energy today, would we have deployed it as a power source? If we knew the destructive potential of nuclear weapons in advance, would we have developed the atom bomb? If we could magically put the nuclear genie back in the bottle, should we do it? If so, it would likely be at the expense of nuclear medical technologies that save lives; at the expense of basic research into subatomic structures, which have vastly expanded our understanding of the universe; and at the expense of an energy source that, in fact, provides a significant percentage of the world's energy sources. Could we ever have prevented the development of such new technologies, or was it just a question of the United States developing them first or letting someone else do so—someone who would not have cared as much about human life as we do?

In 1980, Genetech, a leader in the field of genetic engineering, developed a new strain of microorganism and applied for a patent at the United States Patent Office. The application was challenged and the case reached the United States Supreme Court *(Diamond v. Chakrabarty)*. The Court subsequently upheld Genetech's right to "own" the new life-form it had created. What does it mean to "own" a new form of life? Or, to reap all the financial benefits from the production and use of that life? If it applies to bacteria, should we also allow corporations to own new forms of plant or animal life? How do we draw these distinctions? Do corporations have the right to "play God"?

Consider "cloning," a process by which an entire organism is replicated from the original and contains the exact genetic makeup. This has been done with lower forms of life and may some day be applied to human beings. In theory, it is not inconceivable that, from a single living cell of Beethoven or Einstein, a new Beethoven or Einstein could be produced. The same would, of course, apply to Attila the Hun or Hitler.

Recent advances in biochemistry and genetics have presented

various possibilities of controlling birth defects and deformities. Artificial insemination allows a woman to have a child by an anonymous donor whose sperm had been tested for genetic health. Today, for the first time, it is possible to detect genetic defects at a relatively early stage of pregnancy, allowing for the possibility of curing the fetus by replacing or repairing defective genes, aborting the fetus, or, at least, giving parents time to prepare for proper care after birth if the other two options are not acceptable or available.

This would lead ultimately to the possibility of constructing whatever genetic makeup the parents might want. The fertilized egg with the appropriate genetic constitution could then be inserted in the uterus or even nurtured in the laboratory.

The idea of avoiding genetic diseases is not entirely new. In the Talmud (B. Talmud, *Yevamot* 64b), we are instructed that one should not marry into a diseased family (e.g., a family in which three people have suffered from leprosy or epilepsy). While today we know that both diseases are treatable or controllable, this was clearly an early effort to avoid diseases that were thought to be genetic. The *Mishnah*, however, reminds us of limits in the altering of nature: A person may not pray to God that his pregnant wife bear a male child. Such prayers are considered *levatalah* ("wasted for foolish purpose") since the sex of the fetus has already been determined at the moment of conception. (*Mishnah Berachot* 54a)

Have we gone too far? Should we try to impose limits on human genetic experimentation?

Germ-Line Experimentation

Some critics of genetic engineering distinguish between altering genes related to a specific genetic disease and altering the genetic structure of a human being in such a way that the altered trait itself would be passed on through reproduction to the next generation. The latter, the critics say, is to be prohibited because changing the "human germ line" through experimentation is truly "playing God." If, God forbid, we should make an error when changing the genes of an individual, the impact of that error is contained; when changing the germ line, that error will spread through generations and expand as those people have children. Proponents of germ-line research respond that, by correcting a genetic malfunction and allowing that correction to be passed through generations, we can eliminate the need for genetic surgery on the future generations of children who would otherwise carry that genetic trait.

What do you think?

Privacy and Genetic Engineering

In the 1990s, scientists in the United States are engaged in an extraordinary scientific research project. In what is commonly referred to as the "Human Genome Project," scientists are attempting to map out the entire genetic structure of the human being. If they succeed in doing so, this information will make it possible to understand completely, and perhaps even alter, the genetic structure of human beings—more accurately and completely than scientists even ten short years ago could have dreamed about.

This raises an entirely new set of dilemmas involving individual privacy.

A Real Dilemma: Genetic Research and the Right to Privacy

If we begin to do regular genetic checkups on people to find out if they have diseases or if they have the genetic makeup that might possibly lead to diseases, how will that information be used? Some types of genetic problems always lead to certain results. Many others indicate the possibility of a particular result. For example, people who have a parent who died of Huntington's Chorea disease have a 50 percent chance of contracting the disease. Thus, without very sophisticated genetic testing, we don't know who will live a healthy life. Who should have this information? Should it be given to insurance companies, which would be unlikely to provide a life or health insurance policy to such people—even though 50 percent will never have a problem. Should information about a propensity to alcoholism be given to a potential employer? Should information about a genetic tendency to emotional problems be given to a university admissions office?

What could the UAHC do to address these issues?

Response

In the late 1980s, several key UAHC leaders were part of a small coalition of prominent religious and scientific figures who began to raise ethical concerns regarding the intense pace of genetic research and application of such research. This coalition urged that testing and implementation of genetic research be slowed enough to ensure that these experiments are considered not only by scientists but by public officials, ethicists, and average citizens. The coalition was criticized, in turn, for using scare tactics and trying to delay valuable genetic research.

On the privacy issue, both "fast-track" and "slow-track" advocates of genetic research generally have given their support to a bill, introduced in 1990, called the "Human Genome Privacy Act" that would ensure that no genetic information about an individual could be released to the public, including employers, educational institutions, insurance companies, or other public agencies (except in cases of medical emergencies or criminal investigations), without the written approval of the individual. The bill had not passed by the end of 1992.

Jewish Genetic Disorders

The likelihood of Jewish parents passing on one of a number of inherited genetic disorders to their children has been one of the most alarming medical issues to face the Jewish community worldwide. The fatal consequences of many of these diseases make recent advances in the field of genetics and genetic screening particularly important to Jews.

Specifically, there are six genetic diseases that are primarily, but not exclusively, found among Jews. Among the most prevalent:

- Bloom's Syndrome stunts its victims' growth.

- Torsion Dystonia is a muscle seizure disease.

- Gaucher's Disease can result in blood abnormalities such as anemia, easy bruising, and impaired blood clotting.

- Tay-Sachs, the most well known of these diseases, is carried in the genes of some Jews of Eastern European descent. The disease causes paralysis, blindness, and severe mental retardation, followed by death at the young age of three or four. The disease occurs in one out of 2,500 children born to Ashkenazic Jews.

Genetic Screening and Counseling

Until recently, these diseases were unpreventable. Every birth brought with it the risk that the newborn's life would be scarred by a debilitating genetic disorder. Today, however, a variety of screening measures can detect these genetic signals both in the parents and in the fetus. For example, a simple blood test given to anyone of reproductive age can identify carriers of the Tay-Sachs genetic disorder. Further, during pregnancy, an *in utero* diagnosis can be made through amniocentesis. If the fetus is affected, the pregnancy may then be terminated and the parents spared the agony of having a Tay-Sachs child.

Today, genetic screening tests give doctors the ability not only to predict who will be born with one of the known four thousand inherited disorders but also which infants will be born with genes that are associated with—but do not necessarily result in—the more common illnesses like cancer and heart disease. And genetic screening will move from testing fetuses to testing children or adults and predicting who has a propensity towards diseases like cancer or certain types of mental illness.

This remarkable advance in medicine has already proven to be a potent weapon in fighting disease. After an intensive genetic screening program in New York, the incidence of Tay-Sachs, the fatal disease that hits the Jewish community hardest, was dramatically reduced.

A number of obvious moral and ethical dilemmas come to mind

regarding genetic screening. In addition to the concerns about privacy, society must now deal with other questions. For example, once the genes for alcoholism or Alzheimer's are discovered, should an airline pilot at risk for the disease be forced to stop flying? How about surgeons or nuclear power plant operators? Should insurance companies be allowed to charge higher rates to those at risk?

What happens when it is determined that a baby has genes associated with early heart disease? Should society invest in the child's education or professional career?

And what if the couple (or the government) is permitted to monitor embryos so that any with an "undesirable" genetic trait may be aborted? Is this social progress or the first step towards creating Hitler's master race through eugenics (i.e., preserving only genetically "superior" people)? What if tests show there is only a 50 percent possibility of contracting an incurable debilitating disease? What if the disease is not necessarily life-threatening, like cerebral palsy or multiple sclerosis? What if genetic screening shows that the baby will be blind or deaf? What if it shows the baby will be a boy and not the girl the couple wants? Under which of these situations would abortion be moral? Where does a responsible society draw the line?

The questions these changes raise are all but overwhelming in their import. Who would decide what is "normal," what is preferable? Could it be decided that all genes that controlled certain "antisocial" qualities would be destroyed? Upon whom would such genetic engineering be implemented? What is the morality of experimentation in genetics when it may directly affect the nature of unborn human beings? Should the government control the use of such techniques? Or, would government control make it much easier to create a totalitarian society? What are the implications of the new techniques—artificial insemination, genetic restructuring, possibly even cloning—for the concept of parenthood? Does it make sense to speak any longer of natural parents? Finally, is there a point beyond which we should not go in the tampering with and the creation of human life, or are all advances in the science of genetics necessarily good?

A Radical Proposal: Ethical Impact Statements

A generation ago, public consensus about protecting the environment led the government to require environmental impact statements before any new projects that might negatively affect the environment could be undertaken. The result of these requirements was to reshape the kind of development America would undertake. It provided policy makers with sufficient time to assess the environmental implications of new undertakings and required that they be provided with the facts necessary to make an informed decision. Finally, it sent a message to everyone in America that the environmental integrity of our nation was a priority concern for America.

Perhaps it is time to demand similar "ethical impact statements" for new technological developments. Before any new major technological developments could be implemented, a study would have to be done by scientists, ethicists, politicians, economists, etc., on what the ethical (including the economic, environmental, privacy, social) impact of that development would be. The beneficial results would be the same: providing time and information necessary to assess the ethical implications of new technologies and their applications, and sending a powerful message to the nation that America cares about its ethical integrity. Could such a system work—and perhaps save us from a catastrophic development—or would it simply impede the advancement of science? These questions will haunt us into the twenty-first century.

≡ 15 ≡

AN ETHICAL LEGACY
FOR THE FUTURE

There's a remarkable Jewish tradition that many of our ancestors practiced and preserved. They would write and pass on to their children an "ethical will." Such wills did not deal with the conveyance of things (land, property, jewelry, or animals) to one's heir. In this ethical will, Jews would take measure of their lives and sum up the values that had been tried and tested through the years, distilling on to paper those eternal truths that they wished, above and beyond all wordly posessions, to transmit to their children and to their children's children. And they knew that, if their children and their children's children would hearken to their words, the claim of Jewish continuity would remain unbroken.

Trust in God, fealty to the faith of our ancestors, justice to one's fellows, charity to the poor and the hopeless, commitment to the community, learning, truth, confidence that the seed of a world of peace and justice is being nurtured beyond the horizon despite the agonies and heartbreak of the day, invincible belief that God's people will be an instrument for the redemption of humanity—these were among the incandescent beliefs that, beyond all else, Jews sought to implant in the hearts of their children.

Each ethical will spelled out, with individual particularities and nuances, the glories and the burdens of Jewish survival. And now it is our turn and our time.

The twentieth century is waning. A new century of the Jewish experiment hovers just ahead. Our duty is not merely to await it patiently or to endure it stoically or even to welcome it actively. Our duty is, with renewed vigor, to enter it wisely, having plumbed the meaning of our own experience—the experience of people who have endured the depths and witnessed the peaks of the twentieth century—and then to produce our own ethical will, a testament to what we seek to preserve and what we believe wants change, a testament we can then pass on to the new generations that follow ours, a testament to be read not as a mandate but as a guide, not as the fossilized end product of Jewish history but as a shaping vision that gives hope and strength and spirit to those who come after us.

For this is the only true immortality: to keep alive for all generations to come a way of life that has endured in grandeur through all the traumas that history has hurled at this people, the Jews, whose unique tale winds through all the recorded history of humankind. To fail in this—to embrace our Jewish destiny but fail to hand it on to generations yet unborn—would be to bequeath a gross posthumous victory to our enemies, to commit an act of moral negligence. No, our task—our privilege—is instead to seize the future and to shape it according to the best traditions of the past, including those keenest insights we ourselves have added. That is our title deed, our ethical will, our immortality.

Dreams, words, hopes—but how? How can the Jews and all that they—we—have learned be vouchsafed? There can be no guarantees in such an explosive and volatile world, but there are some truths we do know: we know that Judaism—the religious civilization of the Jew—provides the most powerful answer to the mystery of Jewish survival—the answer to why we Jews survive. The faith of the Jew—God, Torah, Israel—has preserved a people, a God-intoxicated people, whose moral vision has graced the world—a people that has sought relentlessly to keep humanity human. So we know that Judaism is both the reason and the purpose of the Jews.

And, if we endure, what is it that will distinguish us from the legions of other ethnic, communal, civic, and cultural groups on this planet? The marvels of Jewish intellect and culture, of social justice and civic creativity, of benevolence and charity, of Jewish peoplehood—all these qualities radiate outward from the magnetic core of a historic Judaism. This is what has linked the generations as a distinctive people. Sever the Jewish people from its spinal cord, and it will shrivel into paralysis and be rendered trivial.

The American Judaism of the twenty-first century cannot be a mere carbon copy of the Judaism of antiquity—animal sacrifice, Temple and Sanhedrin, castes and superstitions. Judaism lives because it evolves and changes to meet the needs of new eras. And, today, on the threshold of a new century, Judaism faces challenges of a magnitude undreamt of by the patriarchs and matriarchs: biomedical revolutions and bioethical challenges, the threat of nuclear holocaust and the reality of war, the danger of pollution of the environment, the wrenching changes in the traditional family, the rising curve of intermarriage, the spread of personal anomie, the hunger for new approaches to Jewish learning, our profound connections with a beleaguered and often problematic Israel, the inchoate yearning for spiritual sustenance, the erosion of politics— all these must be faced by a clear-eyed Jewish community that reveres the past but is not trapped by it, that has instead the courage and capacity to take charge of the challenge and rise to the imperatives of change that an uncertain future demands.

This volume is neither a Jewish catechism nor a Reform *halachah*. It is a wide-ranging summary of the fundamental social justice issues that test our Jewish values. These issues will dominate the headlines of the twenty-first century. There is no specific Jewish "right" answer to most of these dilemmas. But there is a Jewish mandate to care, to study the issues, to be engaged in the work of the community, and to undertake the social action that will help to heal this battered and weary world. There is a recognition that it is a sin—not less than that—to do nothing when moral decisions must be made.

Long ago, we stood at the foot of Sinai. From our encounter with the Divine, we brought forth a message of justice and hope that transformed human history. From that time on, the need for such a transforming vision has never been more urgent than it is now. Today.